Labour Economics and Public Policy

Managing the Labour Markets for Competitiveness

Labour Economics and Public Policy

Managing the Labour Markets for Competitiveness

Chew Soon Beng

NTU, Singapore

World Scientific

NEW JERSEY · LONDON · SINGAPORE · BEIJING · SHANGHAI · HONG KONG · TAIPEI · CHENNAI · TOKYO

Published by

World Scientific Publishing Co. Pte. Ltd.

5 Toh Tuck Link, Singapore 596224

USA office: 27 Warren Street, Suite 401-402, Hackensack, NJ 07601

UK office: 57 Shelton Street, Covent Garden, London WC2H 9HE

Library of Congress Cataloging-in-Publication Data
Names: Chew, Soon Beng, 1948–   author.
Title: Labour economics and public policy : managing the labour markets for competitiveness /
    by Soon Beng Chew (NTU, Singapore).
Description: New Jersey : World Scientific, [2017]
Identifiers: LCCN 2016048235 | ISBN 9789813149809 (hc : alk. paper)
Subjects: LCSH: Labor market. | Manpower policy. | Wages.
Classification: LCC HD5706 .C4843 2017 | DDC 331.12/042--dc23
LC record available at https://lccn.loc.gov/2016048235

British Library Cataloguing-in-Publication Data
A catalogue record for this book is available from the British Library.

Desk Editors: Herbert Moses/Lum Pui Yee

Typeset by Stallion Press
Email: enquiries@stallionpress.com

Printed in Singapore

This book is dedicated to my wife Rosalind Goh Seow Lung

Contents

Preface

The book is written for two purposes. Firstly, it is an undergraduate text book in Labour Economics. Secondly, it examines public policy in labour markets using Singapore as the benchmark for illustration. The book consists of 16 chapters.

Chapter 1 examines the uniqueness of labour markets. As labour demand is a derived demand, labour market analysis is shown to be dependent on public policy in trade, the labour markets as well as market structure of product market. This chapter shows the importance of using labour market to attract foreign investment. This strategy is extensively used by Singapore, among other countries.

Chapter 2 uses income–leisure model to derive the labour supply curve on the basis of utility maximization. The slope of the labour supply curve is dependent upon whether income effect is stronger than the substitution effect. Based on the income–leisure model, we can also derive the reservation wage. An increase in non-labour income will raise the reservation wage. When the labour supply curve is not horizontal, there is labour surplus in competitive labour markets.

Chapter 3 uses income–leisure model to examine relationship between labour supply and business cycle. But labour supply is critically dependent on whether there is pension in the society. Income–leisure model is extended to examine how labour supply is affected when pension or wages are indexed to inflation.

Chapter 4 examines the impact of public policy on labour supply based on income–leisure model. Public policy can take the form of cash grant, wage subsidy and Earned Income Tax Credit (EITC). Wage subsidy will produce income and substitution effects and the impact on labour supply depends upon which effect is stronger. But for EITC, over a certain range, both income effect and substitution reduce labour supply.

Chapter 5 uses isoquant curves to show the demand for capital and labour based on cost minimization which takes place when the slope of isoquant is tangent upon the isocost line. We also examine a situation where labour can be an inferior input. Chapter 5 also derives labour demand curves based on value of marginal product (VMP) when the VMP is below the value of average product (VAP). Marshallian rules of labour demand are also examined in this chapter.

This chapter also shows that workers are exploited when they work for firms under non-competitive product market. But most workers would still want to work for firms with monopoly power in the product market because firms under competitive product markets do not pay workers well although the workers are not exploited.

Chapter 6 examines impact of public policy such as minimum wage, wage subsidy and mandated benefits on wages and employment. This chapter also examines how Singapore's foreign worker levy is calibrated.

Chapter 7 argues that, without government intervention and labour unions, there is labour exploitation in the labour market and if the product market is monopolistic, there is also labour exploitation in the product market. However, this chapter also shows that labour market tools such as minimum wage can remove labour exploitation in the labour market but not in the product market.

In Chapters 1 and 2, we present the income–leisure model which assumes that workers will not shirk work duties. In Chapter 8, because of asymmetric information and principal-agent problem, we show how employers choose the right wage system to reward workers. This chapter also discusses wage reform in Singapore.

Chapter 9 examines the impact of labour union in labour market. We show that the ability of traditional unions which want to raise wages to protect workers at the expense of employment is impaired by globalization. Consequently, the strengths of traditional unions have declined worldwide.

Chapter 10 shows that Singapore's style of labour unions which are regarded as macro-focused works better than traditional labour unions.

However, macro-focused unions face free ridership problem and this chapter also shows how this free ridership can be overcome.

Chapter 11 examines impact of human capital in the labour market. This chapter shows how human capital is determined based on present value approach. It also discusses job signal model and on-the-job training. Singapore's Skills Development Fund is analyzed in this chapter.

Chapter 12 examines impact of various types of discrimination in the labour markets. This chapter also discusses gender wage gap and explains why not all of the gender wage gap is due to gender discrimination.

Chapter 13 first discusses various types of unemployment and argues that actual unemployment should be as close to natural unemployment rate as possible. This chapter next uses job search theory to explain frictional unemployment and efficiency wage theory to explain involuntary unemployment.

Chapter 14 discusses income inequality using Gini coefficient. The chapter next examines income inequity across generations. We also look at some data on income inequity in USA and Singapore.

Chapter 15 extensively examines public policy in Singapore with regard to savings and purchasing power of wages. In essence, a person who works for about 30 years or more should be able to afford to buy a public housing flat, able to give his children good education, able to pay for cost of healthcare and also has a stream of income at his old age. In other words, the purchasing power of wages is examined in the context of Singapore economy. To achieve this objective, this chapter shows that both the citizens and the government need to work together.

Chapter 16, which is the last chapter, discusses how Singaporean workers can earn more and, at the same time, be competitive in the world market. This chapter shows that when firms have a high surplus ratio, these firms can afford to pay workers more and still be competitive. In other words, Singapore has to move up the value chain at all times.

CHEW Soon Beng
28 February, 2017

About the Author

Professor Chew Soon Beng is Professor of Economics and Industrial Relations at Nanyang Technological University (NTU), Singapore. He received his PhD from the University of Western Ontario, Canada. He is author of *Small Firms in Singapore* (Oxford University Press), *Trade Unionism in Singapore* (McGraw Hill), *Employment-Driven Industrial Relations Regimes* (Avebury), *Values and Lifestyles of Young Singaporeans* (Prentice-Hall), and *Foreign Enterprises in China: Operation and Management* (in Chinese). He has also published in journals such as the *Singapore Economic Review* and the *China Economic Review*. His recent publications include *Union Social Responsibility* in *International Journal of Comparative Labour Law and Industrial Relations*, and *Strategic Collective Bargaining* in *Bulletin of Comparative Labour Relations*. His current research interests include labour markets, trade unions, fiscal prudence and competitiveness. The awards Prof Chew receives include Certificate of Honour from NTU in Student Monitoring (2016), Best Teacher Award for Masters of Science in Managerial Economics at NTU for 2010, 2012 and 2013 and NTU Alumni Service Award, 2011. Academic recognitions received include National Book Prize, 1996; Honorary Professorship, Institute of Legislation "Khalkh Juram", Mongolia 2001; Honorary Professorship, Moscow External University of the Humanities, 1997; Honorary Professorship at Liaoning Administrative College, China, 1997; Visiting Professorship at North East University of Finance and Economics, China, 1997 and Program Professorship at China University of Science and Technology, 2011.

Acknowledgements

I would like to thank NTU for giving me the opportunity to exploit my potential as a teacher, as a researcher and as an academic entrepreneur of academic programmes. I would also like to thank Ms Zhu Jiahua, Ms Eng Qiao En and Mr Herbert Moses for their research and editorial assistance. The proceeds of this book will be contributed to Professor Lim Chong Yah Bursary Fund at NTU.

Chapter 1

Labour Markets and Competitiveness

The purpose of this chapter is to discuss various issues relating to the labour markets. These issues which will dictate how firms, workers and governments react in the labour markets will be examined with explicit theoretical models in the book. But first, let us look at the nature of labour markets.

Is It Important to Study Labour Markets?

Labour economics is the study of labour markets, how economic agents value between leisure and work, and how firms engage employees against the backdrop of more efficient use of technology, how labour unions choose to either work with the management/government or bargain with the management/government, and how public policy affects labour markets.

Human society now regards work as essential. Without work, there is no income and there is no life for most people. Work defines our identity. So we cannot be happy without work. Substantial amount of our time is spent on work.

Work is the outcome of decisions of the people looking for work, of the firms employing workers and of the government regulating the labour markets. Economic agents will do the utility maximization exercise to find work. Firms will employ workers on profit maximization motive. And public policy can affect creation of work and how work is remunerated. There are too many examples of how poor public policy destroys

1

investment leading to high unemployment rate. Too many governments reward their public sector employees with a generous pension scheme that bleeds the government coffers. With a sustained wrong set of public policy in the labour markets, ordinary citizens are the losers.

To complicate the matter, there is principal-agent problem and asymmetric information in the labour markets. This is why it is important to analyze how firms deal with these issues, how workers shirk work duties if they can avoid detection, and how public policy can influence labour market outcomes.

Are Labour Markets Unique?

Labour markets are the same as other markets in the sense that they are determined by the buyers and sellers. But labour demand and supply of labour are very different from product demand and product supply, although they are related.

Labour demand is a derived demand. When the demand for product falls, the labour demand in producing that product will fall. This is why trade negotiations are important. When there is less trade, there will be less demand for the products and hence less labour demand and unemployment rate will be high.

Labour demand is demand for labour services. Labour demand is not the same as demand for slaves. As labour services are performed by workers, workers have to deliver the labour services personally. This means working conditions are important. However, valuation of working conditions varies from person to person. For instance, some people like jobs which involve more risk. Others like to work in an enclosed room e.g., air-conditioned work places. Jobseekers would ask for wage compensation if working conditions are not conducive. This implies that wage demand may vary although the nature of work is the same.

Labour services cannot be hoarded. If you do not work on a day, you cannot work the next day to recover the lost labour markets services for the previous day. Of course, if you do not work on a day, you can enjoy leisure. But utility is higher if the outcome is a choice rather than lack of choice. Hence, there is more urgency in the labour markets compared to most markets.

At the macro level, the wage share out of GDP is generally in excess of 50% in advanced economies although this percentage declines due to changing technology. Technology makes work more efficient and reduces the number of workers per unit of output. Although one would argue there is a scale effect, meaning we produce more and hence demand for labour is not much affected, many researchers have found evidence that middle income jobs have disappeared.[1]

If there is less work, where can people find income to sustain life? If technology can make the society rich, and if technology can aid the government to tax the rich effectively without chasing them away, then there is an upside to using technology in a big way. With rich coffers, the government can implement a social safety scheme to allow the workforce to work only, say, four hours a day for a four-day week per person and at the same time, the workers can have enough purchasing power to pursue leisure and other utility yielding activities including learning, we all will embrace technology. There will be a win–win outcome for inventors, entrepreneurs, general public and the government. And no one would complain about the extent to which technology makes people redundant. At this point in time, we do not see this happy outcome coming. Indeed, the evidence consistently shows that technology widens income distribution. The role of government is even more important. But we need smart government and not big government.

If a country is on fixed exchange rate regime, the government can hide bad economic management by artificially selling foreign assets to support the home currency. But when the country does not do well, the government cannot hide bad economic indicators as labour markets indicators will reveal the bad economic outcome and most citizens would know as they would feel the impact of bad economic management in the labour markets. Voters increasingly do not tolerate high unemployment rate. At the same time, in a parliamentary system, the political candidates would propose populist policy in the labour markets. The country may end up with high unemployment, high labour cost, low GDP growth and a big budget deficit. All these would cause the home currency to fall. A vicious cycle will develop.

In sum, when a country has not performed well, the labour markets cannot perform well as unemployment rate will be high. At the same time, bad labour market policy is generally the reason why the country has not performed well economically. In other words, labour markets' developments are both symptoms and causes of economic development.

---

[1]For detail, see Maarten Goos *et al.* (2009).

Table 1.1 shows the unemployment rate for selected countries.[2] Among high income countries, Singapore's unemployment rate is the

Table 1.1:   Unemployment Rates of Selected Countries

Country	Unemployment rate in 2014 (%)
United States	6.20
United Kingdom	6.10
Germany	5.00
Greece	26.5
Japan	3.60
Hong Kong SAR, China	3.30
Taiwan	3.96
Singapore	2.00
Malaysia	3.20
China	4.10
Korea, Rep.	3.50

Sources: Greece, Germany, Japan, US, UK: Eurostat (2015). *Unemployment rate by sex and age groups — annual average, %.* Retrieved from http://appsso.eurostat.ec.europa.eu/nui/show.do

Hong Kong: Census and Statistics Department (2015). *Labour Force, Unemployment and Underemployment.* Retrieved from http://www.censtatd.gov.hk/hkstat/sub/sp200.jsp?tableID=006&ID=0&productType=8

Taiwan: The Straits Times (2015). *Taiwan's 2014 unemployment at seven-year low: Govt.* Retrieved from http://www.straitstimes.com/asia/east-asia/taiwans-2014-unemployment-at-seven-year-low-govt

Singapore: Ministry of Manpower (2015). *Summary table: Unemployment.* Retrieved from http://stats.mom.gov.sg/Pages/Unemployment-Summary-Table.aspx

Malaysia: The World Bank. *Unemployment, total (% of total labor force) (modeled ILO estimate).* Retrieved from http://data.worldbank.org/indicator/SL.UEM.TOTL.ZS

China: Business Insider (2015). *China's urban unemployment rate fell.* Retrieved from http://www.businessinsider.com/r-china-says-unemployment-rate-eased-to-405-percent-at-end-first-quarter-2015-4?IR=T&

Korea: OECD (2015). *Short-Term Labour Market Statistics.* Retrieved from http://stats.oecd.org/index.aspx?queryid=36324#

---

[2]Although the table reports the unemployment rate for 2014, the figure for unemployment rate is quite stable from year to year for these selected countries during the normal period.

lowest. The low unemployment in Singapore is by design and not by chance. The latter chapters of this book are devoted to examine the costs and benefits of Singapore's strategy in developing a world-class labour market.

Labour Cost, Business and Profitability

There is news, very often, in popular media that report some firms have done well because they can employ cheap labour. On the other hand, we also hear of reports that other firms have done well because they pay their workers well.

Both can be right. But looking at the wages is like looking at one side of the coin. We need to examine the other side of the same coin. We all know that firms want to make a profit as expected. Firms can make a profit provided the wages can bring revenue to the firms in sufficient quantity. Hence, I propose that we look at unit labour cost (ULC) which is total wage cost over output (value added). Firms can be competitive if ULC is not high. When firms use cheap labour, the wage cost is low and ULC is not high if quality of the workers is acceptable. But cheap labour can hurt the firms if the workforce cannot produce sufficient output or in some cases, there may be a fall in output due to poor quality of the workforce, causing ULC to rise. On the other hand, when firms pay high wages and they are able to get good value from these high wage workers, then ULC is not high.

Similarly, we can analyze competitiveness in terms of unit business cost (UBC). Singapore is an expensive place to do business because total business cost is very high. The fact that many firms find Singapore still a good place to do business is because of the competitive UBC.

Table 1.2 shows ULC for selected countries. Singapore is not competitive as its ULC is higher than that of USA and it is almost on par with that of Japan. As Singapore is both a country and a city, we should compare Singapore with big cities in the USA. But plants in the USA are not all located in the cities. This table does indicate that Singapore ought to be careful not to price itself out of competition. On the other hand, as we will examine economic restructuring later in the book, capital intensive firms have lower ULC and those figures in Table 1.2 are also influenced by the composition of the industrial structure in the country concerned.

Table 1.2:   ULC of Selected Countries in the Manufacturing Sector, US (Dollar Basis)

Country	ULC in 2011 (US$)
United States	85.69
United Kingdom	112.00
Germany	143.65
Japan	109.68
Taiwan	84.09
Singapore	107.84
Korea, Rep.	114.94

Source: US Bureau of Labor Statistics (2012). *International Comparisons of Manufacturing Productivity and Unit Labor Cost Trends, 2011 Data Tables*. Retrieved from http://www.bls.gov/web/prod4.supp.toc.htm

MNCs set up offices across many countries for profit seeking. Table 1.3 shows the cost of employing an employee in key cities in 2008 and 2015. In 2008, Hong Kong is the most expensive city but its business cost has increased marginally in 2015. The business cost in San Francisco has increased the most among the cities listed here, followed by New York City, LA and London. Mumbai and Shanghai, the respective business cost is very low in US$. Although the business cost is low in these two giant cities, the increase in the respective business cost has been small, implying that low business cost does not necessarily promote business. Only in three cities namely Tokyo, Dubai and Singapore, the cost of business decreased in 2015. The decrease in cost of operation could be due to recession which is the case for Dubai or a deliberate attempt to bring down cost which is the case for Singapore. As mentioned earlier, cost is half the story. Ability to generate business volume is the other half of the story. The ease of doing business in a city is being measured by per capita GDP of that city. We will examine UBC for across cities in Chapter 16.

Table 1.3:   Business Costs for Selected Countries, 2008 and 2015

| City | Average per head live/work accommodation costs | | |
	Dec 2008 (US$)	June 2015 (US$)	Change since 2008 (%)
San Francisco	55,184	88,177	▲59.8
New York	88,913	114,208	▲28.4
Los Angeles	43,838	53,192	▲21.9
London	98,093	118,425	▲20.7
Sydney	44,915	52,994	▲18.0
Shanghai	38,089	44,043	▲15.6
Paris	81,723	84,344	▲3.2
Mumbai	28,394	29,088	▲2.4
Hong Kong	116,202	116,661	▲0.4
Tokyo	77,500	71,296	▼8.0
Dubai	69,012	59,426	▼13.9
Singapore	**80,936**	**67,491**	**▼16.6**

Source: http://www.worldsrichestcountries.com/worlds-richest-cities.html

Knowledge Economy

In the old economy, the law of scarcity prevails in the sense that if you can produce goods that others do not and cannot, you enjoy a profit in production because you have a comparative advantage. The same law of scarcity still prevails in the new economy or the knowledge economy in which you still must have a comparative advantage to profit in business, whether in the production of goods or in services.

One of the main differences between the old economy and the knowledge economy is that there is increasing importance of knowledge, creativity and skills in changing the way firms compete and the sources of comparative advantage between nations.[3] In the old economy, natural resources were the main factors determining comparative advantage. Next in importance was capital, followed by process technology.

Perhaps the most critical difference between the old economy and the knowledge economy is that knowledge is a global public good.[4] Hence, any competitive advantage will not last long. So, it is a race between creating knowledge and keeping it as a private good for as long as you can possibly maintain.

Knowledge economy implies that competition is keen and there is no home court advantage. Having a huge domestic market has certain advantages but it can be compensated for through the formation of trade blocs. Both knowledge economy and globalization imply there is no room for inefficient firms, an unproductive workforce, militant trade unions, or for inefficient government.

In the knowledge economy, how is ULC played out? Entrepreneurs are well rewarded. Top executives may be paid beyond their respective value of marginal products (VMPs). Hence, their ULCs may be high at the expense of other executives and workers. Later in the book, we will explore the tournament theory to explain the differences of ULCs among executives.

At the same time, executives and workers are worried about jobs being replaced by technology. Frey and Osborne (2013) report that occupations such as telemarketers, technical writers, etc will disappear within two decades. In the chapter on human capital, we will examine the importance of lifelong learning on employability.

Development through Competitive Advantage

Growth of a country needs investment, especially from foreign countries. With the inflow of foreign capital and the accompanying management and technical expertise, a country can slowly develop and hence GDP and employment level will increase.

---

[3]For detail, see Coates and Warwick (1999).
[4]See Stiglitz (1999).

Figure 1.1 shows that foreign capital is normally attracted to a new country by low wages.[5] This type of labour intensive investment, labelled as *M* here, implies that providing employment is the pressing objective of the government. When *M* reaches a critical level relative to the productive capacity of the country, wages will rise and the cost of business will also rise. To the government, this is a mixed blessing. Aiming for high wages and bigger government revenue is the objective of attracting foreign investment but it also implies that a higher level of ULC and UBC can reduce attractiveness of attracting foreign investment and hurt the existing foreign firms.

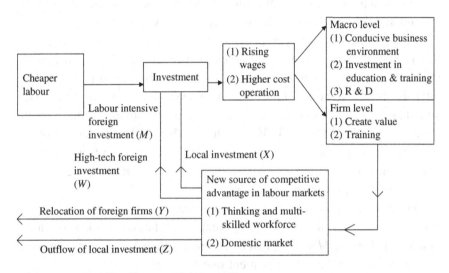

Low wages attract *M* and human capital attracts *W*

Figure 1.1:   Development Cycle

Source: This slide is modified from Verma *et al.* (1995).

At this stage of rising wage costs and business costs, the government can continue to attract foreign investment and help the existing foreign firms by improving business environment and by implementing conducive Employment Acts such that ULC and UBC will not rise.

---

[5]The figure is modified from a chart in Verma *et al.* (1995).

At the earliest, the government has to improve the quality of the workforce by providing education and training and by employing skilled labour, apart from improving the business environment and infrastructure. This emphasis on quality of the workforce will produce new competitive advantage which is a multi-skilled and disciplined workforce. As the chart shows, this new competitive advantage will attract *W*, skill intensive foreign investment. When *W* comes on board, the wages and the cost of doing business will rise at a faster pace. So, the race is on-going between wanting higher wages and higher government revenue and at the same time maintaining ULC and UBC competitive.

As local people learn from economic development the local GDP will expand and the new breed of local entrepreneurs will emerge as shown in Figure 1.1. The local entrepreneurs will invest, labelled as *X*. Hence, at this moment, there will be three types of investments, *M*, *W* (*M* and *W* can co-exist if the country is big) and *X*. *W* by definition is more skill intensive than *M*. The *W* which came in this year will be more skill intensive than those *W* who came in a decade ago. Eventually, some foreign firms will find ULC and UBC too high. They will relocate to other countries, labelled as *Y*. *Y* will first come from *M* and then from those *W* which came a decade ago. Also, the local firms will start investing abroad, labelled as *Z*, for a variety of reasons.

For sustainable development, total investment must exceed outflow of funds by the amount required to keep new labour market entrants employed. That is, *M* + *W* + *X* must be greater than *Y* + *Z* by the amount necessary to keep the unemployment rate constant.

But if we want higher standard of living for our people, we have to aim for higher wages and at the same time keep ULC and UBC competitive. The only way is to allow *W* to create *Y* via higher wages and cost of doing business. This is industry upgrading. By using *W* to chase labour intensive firms away, we move up the value chain. With a large amount of *W*, our state enterprises can invest overseas and not to worry about keeping unemployment rate low locally.

Are labour markets important to Singapore?

When people invent products successfully, they enjoy the monopoly profits like the top American entrepreneurs have been enjoying.

America has done very well in the sense that X is big. High profitability will motivate people to innovate and invest. If domestic markets are big and there is critical mass in engineers, scientists, etc., the government can promote product innovation. Based on the government policies in the past few decades, there was no solid evidence that the Singapore government wanted to promote product innovation in a fundamental way. However, there has been a deliberate strategy to develop Singapore into a world-class labour market where firms and businesses can invest and do business in Singapore and make money. A world-class labour market means firms are interested to do business here, there are plenty of job vacancies, wages have good purchasing power, the government can collect good revenue and ULC and UBC can remain competitive.

Common Sense Solution

Emerging countries should focus on developing their workforce in terms of quality and competitiveness, and at the same time meeting the aspirations of the young. But this is easier said than done. Workers want good wages but they may not want to put in maximum work effort. Firms have to compete to survive based on competitive ULC and UBC. Citizens want housing, world-class education, world-class healthcare to be the wage goods. At the same time, the retirees want to have financial freedom. At another level, all these aspirations will help the country to compete well. A happy workforce is a competitive workforce. But government cannot possibly pay for all these aspirations without incurring persistent budget deficit because there is moral hazard, among other issues. Without an effective government, there is likely to be extensive poverty. The common sense solution calls for citizen–government partnership in meeting these challenges. But the common sense solution is in short supply in the real world.

The labour markets in Singapore is one of the most competitive labour markets in the world. We have an individually funded pension scheme that does not require government to cross subsidy. The purchasing power of wages is good. We have schemes that train the workforce effectively and we have a national body to influence workers' wage expectations in line with the fundamentals of the macro economy. The labour unions in

Singapore are macro-focused in the sense that the unions work with the government and the management. All these labour markets measures and more will be examined in the following chapters. The common sense solution is neither easily enforced nor implemented.

Review Questions

1. A firm sells shoes in a competitive market. This means that the demand for shoes is very price elastic. Use this firm to explain the concept of labour demand for this firm as a derived demand.
2. A big firm in Singapore has a subsidiary in South Africa. The firm needs a Singaporean to manage this firm. Both John and Bob are top executives with this firm in Singapore. Both of them have been asked to consider this post in South Africa. John is single and loves outdoor activities. Bob is married. His wife has a good career and his only daughter goes to primary school in Singapore. Discuss how John and Bob would negotiate a wage package with this firm for the post in South Africa.
3. Discuss what determines ULC. Can public policy affect ULC?

The above review questions would help to emphasize the message that labour markets are complex and the functioning of the markets is the key to competitiveness. In the subsequent chapters, more analytical tools will be presented.

Bibliography

Coates, D. and Warwick, K. (1999). "The Knowledge Driven Economy: Analysis and Background", Paper presented at the conference entitled "*The Economics of The Knowledge Driven Economy*", London, 27 January 1999.

Frey, C. and Osborne, M. (2013). The Future of Employment: How Susceptible are Jobs to Computerisation? Working paper, University of Oxford.

Maarten, G., Manning, A. and Salomons, A. (2009). "Job Polarization in Europe", *The American Economic Review*, Vol. 99, No. 2, Papers and *Proceedings of the One Hundred Twenty-First Meeting of the American Economic Association* (May 2009), pp. 58–63.

Stiglitz, J. E. (1999). "Knowledge in the Modern Economy", Paper presented at the conference entitled *"The Economics of the Knowledge Driven Economy"*, London, 27 January 1999.

Verma, A., Kochan, T. and Lansbury, R., eds. (1995). *Employment Relations in the Growing Asian Economies*. Routledge: London.

Chapter 2

The Basic Model of Labour Supply

The purpose of this chapter is to present the basic model of income–leisure model. This basic model will be used to analyze decisions concerning whether a person is to enjoy leisure or work subject to the wage rate and wealth.

Income–Leisure Model (Y–L Model) for a Jobseeker

We will use Y–L model to analyze the decision making process of a jobseeker. Y represents income and L represents number of leisure hours. This kind of analysis is known as neoclassical model of labour–leisure choice. The Y–L model is presented on a daily framework with 24 hours available to the jobseeker.[1] This is of course a simplifying assumption as it can be a monthly or yearly model. Given his endowment (wealth), his human capital upon which he can command a market wage rate (W) and his preference towards work, the jobseeker will decide whether to work or not. If he does decide to work, he will decide how many hours to work. Factors such as endowment, market wage rate and his preference toward work are known as external factors to the model. The model will determine number of hours of work (H), hours of leisure (L), his labour income (Y) and level of satisfaction (U) for the jobseeker.

The Y–L model is built on three premises. Firstly, we have to take into account the jobseeker's preferences with regard to leisure and work.

---

[1]This is of course a simplifying assumption as it can be a monthly or yearly model.

Secondly, we have to factor his market wage rate. Finally, we have to assume that he is rational and wants to maximize his welfare.

The Jobseeker's Preferences

The jobseeker in the Y–L model derives satisfaction both from the purchasing power of income (Y) and from the consumption of leisure (L).

In Economics, we use utility to measure satisfaction in the following manner:

$$U = F\,(Y, L). \tag{2.1}$$

Equation (2.1) transforms purchasing power of income and consumption of leisure into an index which is called utility. The higher the level of utility, U, the happier the jobseeker is. Given the amount of Y, an increase in L will produce higher utility. Similarly, given the same number of leisure hours, the greater the amount of Y, the higher the utility. In other words, Y and L are good goods as compared to pollution which is a bad good. As implied in Equation (2.1), a combination of Y and L will produce a given level of utility. This combination is known as a bundle consisting of a given level of Y and of L.

In Figure 2.1, suppose based on the utility function, Bundle A which represents a combination of $Y = 110$ and $L = 13$ can produce, say, 1,000 utils of utility. In the same figure, besides Bundle A, Bundle B and Bundle C, can also produce 1,000 utils each. If we connect Bundles A, B and C on a single curve, then this curve would represent the same level of utility which is 1,000 utils. This curve is known as an indifferent curve which is labelled as U_1. There is another way to think about the indifference curve. If the jobseeker is to move from Bundle A to Bundle B, he enjoys one more hour of leisure ($\Delta L = 1$) but he has to give up $20 in Y ($\Delta Y = -20$) in order to remain on the same indifference curve. Hence, he is indifferent between Bundles A and B, and he is also indifferent between Bundles B and C. And of course, by the same reasoning, one can get U_2, U_3 and so on. This will represent a map of indifference curves of the jobseeker.

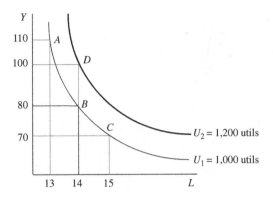

Figure 2.1:   A Map of Indifference Curves

Bundle D in Figure 2.1 rests on U_2 which contains a higher level of utility than U_1. Though both Bundles B and D have the same number of leisure hours, Bundle D is superior to Bundle B as it has more income, Y.

Being on a higher indifference curve also has another meaning. In Equation (2.1), Y represents nominal income. In this neoclassical model, real income (y) can be connected to the indifference curve. Hence, we can say that Bundles A, B and C have the same real income y (in terms of level of satisfaction), and Bundle D has a higher real income as it rests on a higher indifference curve. Later on, we will show that, if the jobseeker is able to move from Bundles A to D, the jobseeker is said to have a higher real income, he would want to consume more leisure. In this analysis, we assume that leisure is a normal good.

When indifference curves intersect with each other as shown in Figure 2.2, the relationship between various Bundles of Y and L and respective utility level is inconclusive. For instance, Bundles K and V rest on U_2, indicating both have the same level of utility level. But Bundle K also rests on U_1 together with Bundle J, implying that Bundles V and J should have the same level of utility. But this is not the case as Bundle V is superior to Bundle J as it is on a higher indifference curve. Hence, we will get inconsistent results if a jobseeker's indifference curves can cut across with each other. However, different individuals can have different maps of indifference curves. Interpersonal comparison of utility is meaningless.

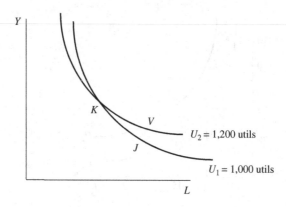

Figure 2.2:   Inconsistency of Indifference Curves

If we move from Bundles A to B on U_1 in Figure 2.1, we can see that one leisure hour is worth \$20. If we move from Bundles B to C, then one leisure hour is worth only \$10 now. So this emotional trade-off is not constant. The emotional trade-off between Y and L and there-fore between Y and H is not the same as the wage rate (W), which is determined in the market place. This emotional substitution between Y and L changes as we move down the indifference curve. This is because when a jobseeker has more leisure, leisure is less valuable to the jobseeker.

As we move from Bundle A to B, we substitute leisure for income. This marginal rate of substitution (MRS) can be expressed as $\Delta Y/\Delta L$ which is the slope of an indifference curve. If we move down on the same indifference curve, for every hour increase in L, ΔY decreases and hence MRS decreases because the indifference curve is convex to the point of origin.

Another example of estimating MRS is given in Figure 2.3. At J, the jobseeker is willing to give up \$110 to enjoy 15 leisure hours. His MRS at J is 7.33. His MRS at K is 3.33.

We want to derive an expression for the slope of the indifference curve ($\Delta Y/\Delta L$). When we move from Bundles A to B on U_1, the gain in utility from enjoying ΔL must be the same as the loss of utility from losing some

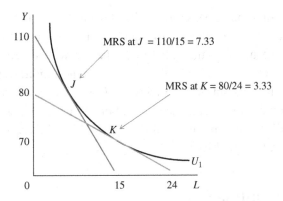

Figure 2.3:   Using Slope to Calculate MRS

income (ΔY) such that there is no change in utility ($\Delta U = 0$) as shown below:

$$\Delta L \text{ times } MU_L + \Delta Y \text{ times } MU_Y = \Delta U = 0.$$

After rearranging, we get,

$$\Delta Y/\Delta L = - MU_L/MU_Y. \qquad (2.2)$$

Hence, the absolute value of the slope of an indifference curve which is also MRS is equal to the ratio of marginal utilities.

Now, we use an explicit utility function to represent the jobseeker's preferences as shown below:

$$U = (Y)(L), \qquad (2.3)$$

where U represents his level of utility, Y is labour income he earns and L is number of leisure hours he enjoys.

Suppose his hourly wage is $10, indicating $W = \$10$ per hour. In a daily model, $L = 24$ hours. If $L = 16$, number of hours of work represented by H is 8. Then $Y = 8$ times $\$10 = \$80$. If $L = 13$, then $H = 11$. Then $Y = \$110$.

Based on Equation (2.3), suppose $Y = \$80$ and L is 16 hours of leisure, we can estimate that U is equal to 80 times $16 = 1,280$ utils. Holding L constant, if we increase the value of Y, then U will increase in value, indicating that this jobseeker will be on a higher indifference curve. Similarly, if Y is constant and we increase L, the jobseeker will be on a higher indifference curve. This means that both Y and L are goods that will increase his utility. The marginal utility of Y (MU_Y) and marginal utility of L (MU_L) is therefore positive.

The Budget Constraint

The jobseeker needs to work to get labour income. His market hourly wage is W. In the later chapters, we will discuss how to increase human capital to raise W. For the moment, W is given. His labour income, Y, is equal to W times H where H is hours of work per day in the daily model. We can allow non-labour income, V.

Hence, his total income, TY is equal to

$$TY = V + (W \cdot H) \text{ where } Y = W \cdot H.$$

We also have to bring in the time constraint. In this daily model, the total number of hours (T) is 24.

Hence, $T = L + H$.

Rearranging, we get,

$$TY = V + W (T - L).$$

Hence, the budget constraint is

$$TY = V + WT - WL. \qquad (2.4)$$

We want to draw the budget constraint. We put TY on the vertical axis and L on the horizontal axis.

Figure 2.4 shows the budget constraint line without V. The slope of the budget constraint, TA, is W. If the jobseeker is at T, it means he enjoys 24 hours of leisure and he is not working. If he chose to be at K, he enjoys 16 hours of leisure and works 8 hours. His labour income is Y. His maximum labour income in this model is WT. This model is simple and useful to analyze whether a jobseeker decides to work or not. If he wants to work, he can decide how many hours to work (we will introduce institutional constraint later in this chapter). Hence, for this model, we measure number of leisure hours (L) from the point of origin to the right. We measure number of hours of work (H) from T to the left.

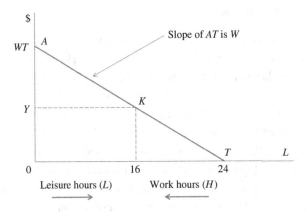

Figure 2.4:   The Budget Constraint without Non-labour Income, V

We allow non-labour income (V) into the model as shown in Figure 2.5. The maximum income is now equal to $V + WL$. If the jobseeker chose K on AT, it means that he chose to work 8 hours and his labour income is $Y - V$ and his non-labour income is V.

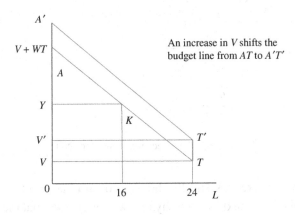

Figure 2.5:   The Budget Line with V

When there is an increase in V, the new budget line is $A'T'$, indicating that his hourly wage remains the same as both budget lines are parallel. As we will show later, the non-labour income or wealth can affect the jobseeker's decision to work.

To work or not to work

The jobseeker has a utility function which is summarized into a map of three indifference curves as shown in Figure 2.6. He has a skill set that commands a market wage rate at W. His ability to improve his well-being is dictated by the budget constraint, AT. Given his preferences and the budget constraint, he will choose a point on his budget line such that his utility is maximized. In other words, he is rational.

In Figure 2.6, the jobseeker can choose Bundle B which rests on the indifference curve, U_0. But he can do better than U_0. If he chose Bundle J, he can move to a higher indifference curve which is U. He cannot choose Bundle D as Bundle D is beyond his budget constraint.

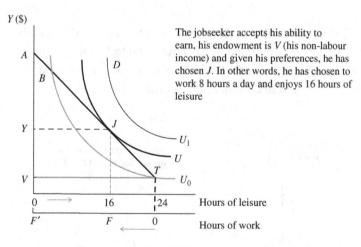

Figure 2.6: The Decision to Work or Not

Given his preferences and the budget constraint, his utility is maximized at J. In this context, we can say that we can predict that the jobseeker will choose J because he is rational. It is also likely that the jobseeker chooses T as his equilibrium point. In this case, he has chosen not to work. In this case, T is the chosen equilibrium point which is regarded as a corner solution. An interior solution shows that the jobseeker has chosen to work and to consume leisure as a bundle which is represented by J.

J is a point of tangency between the budget line and the chosen indifference curve. In other words, at J, the slope of the budget line is equal to the slope of the indifference curve.

As mentioned earlier, the slope of the budget line is the hourly wage, W. The slope of the indifference curve is MRS which is also equal to the ratio of marginal utilities. Hence, utility maximization gives us:

$$W = \text{MRS} = MU_L / MU_Y. \tag{2.5}$$

The following exercise makes use of the above equilibrium condition and budget condition.

Given the utility function is $U = Y \cdot L$, there is no non-labour income.

Then marginal utility of income (MU_Y) is $dU/dY = L$.

And marginal utility of leisure (MU_L) is $dU/dL = Y$.

Based on utility maximization, the equilibrium condition is

$$W = \text{MRS} = MU_L / MU_Y = Y/L. \tag{2.6}$$

Based on budget constraint, $Y = W \cdot H = W(24 - L)$. $\qquad$ (2.7)

If $W = \$10$ per hour, in both Equations (2.6) and (2.7), we have only two common variables, namely Y and L.

From Equation (2.6), we get $10\,L = Y$ and from Equation (2.7), we get $Y = 10(24 - L)$. Rearranging, we get

$$10\,L = 10(24 - L)$$

$$L = 24 - L$$

$$2\,L = 24.$$

Hence, $L = 12$, $H = 12$, $Y = \$120$, $U = 120 \cdot 12 = 1{,}440$ utils.

The outcome of this exercise is summarized in Figure 2.7.

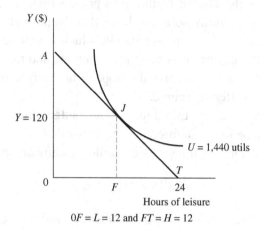

Figure 2.7:   He Chose to Work 12 Hours

Exogenous and endogenous variables

In a model, there are independent (or external) and dependent variables. Independent variables such as the wage rate, the total number of hours and the utility function are regarded as exogenous variables. These are the facts that the model accepts. Given the exogenous variables, the model then determines the values of dependent variables which are known as endogenous variables. Examples of endogenous variables are L, H, Y and U as shown in Figure 2.7. In other words, given AT and the map of indifference curves, the jobseeker has chosen J as the equilibrium point. Hence, if there is a change in the exogenous variables, the values of endogenous variables will change accordingly.

Comparative Statics Analysis

When the value of an exogenous variable changes, the values of all endogenous variables will change. We will move from one equilibrium point to another. For instance, an increase in wage rate is a change in an exogenous variable. The original wage is *W*, which is the slope of *AT*. The original equilibrium point is *J*, indicating that the jobseeker has chosen to work 8 hours as shown in Figure 2.8. Now, the new wage rate is W′ which is greater than *W*. The new budget line is now *A′T*. Based on another round of utility maximization, the new equilibrium point is *J′* and the jobseeker has increased his hours of work from 8 to 10. This representative worker now is happier as he rests on a higher indifference curve, which indicates a higher real income. The labour supply curve has a positive slope. Comparing the new equilibrium point to the original equilibrium point is known as comparative statistics analysis which is adopted throughout this book.

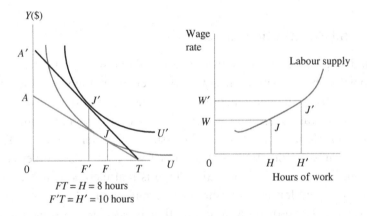

Figure 2.8: Higher Wage Rate, More Labour Supply

The outcome of a higher wage rate can lead to fewer hours of work as shown in Figure 2.9. With a higher wage rate, the worker is happier but in this case, the number of hours worked has reduced from 8 to 6. The labour supply curve has a negative slope.

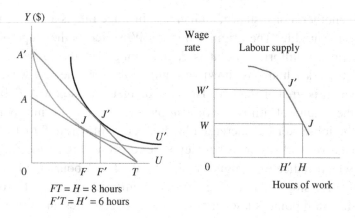

$FT = H = 8$ hours
$F'T = H' = 6$ hours

Figure 2.9:   Higher Wage Rate, Less Labour Supply

Income and Substitution Effects

We would like to explain why the slope of labour supply curve can be mostly positive but sometimes negative. An increase in the wage rate produces two effects, namely income effect and substitution effect. An increase in the wage rate indicates that the price of enjoying leisure per hour is higher. Hence, the worker will consume fewer leisure hours. This is known as substitution effect. With a higher wage rate, the worker is on a higher indifference curve, indicating that his real income is higher. He will consume more leisure as leisure is a normal good. This is known as income effect. Both effects have conflicting impact on consumption of leisure and therefore on the hours of work.

   If substitution effect of a rising wage is stronger than the income effect, the labour supply curve has a positive slope. If income effect is stronger than the substitution effect, then the labour supply curve has a negative slope.

   When people are poor, any increase in wage rate would produce strong substitution effect. But when wages have reached a threshold level, income effect will dominate.

   In Figure 2.10, the supply curve has a positive slope when wages start to rise from low level. But once the wage rate reaches a critical level, the labour supply curve starts to bend backwards.

   When there is an increase in the wage rate, the budget line will shift from AT to $A'T$. The equilibrium point will move from J to J' as shown in

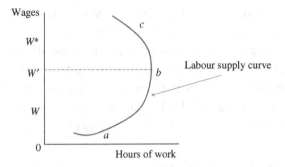

Figure 2.10: Backward Bending Supply Curve

Figure 2.11. This is regarded as the total effect of wage increase. This total effect can be decomposed into the substitution and income effects with the aid of an imaginary budget line, *BB'*. The *BB'* is drawn with two conditions. Firstly, *BB'* has to find a point of tangency with the initial indifference curve which is *U*. The second condition is that the slope of *BB'* is the same as the slope of *A'T*. The substitution effect is measured from *J* to *K* because both *J* and *K* rest on the same indifference curve and therefore have the same real income but at *K*, the wage rate is higher. From *J* to *K*, as the wage rate is higher, the cost of enjoying one hour of leisure is higher, which leads to less consumption of leisure and therefore more

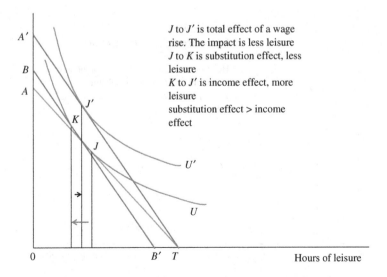

Figure 2.11: Substitution and Income Effects of Wage

working hours. Both K and J' have the same wage rate and J' has a higher real income as J' rests on a higher indifference curve. From K to J' is income effect because higher real income will cause the worker to consume more leisure and therefore less work (note that leisure is a normal good). The situation depicted in Figure 2.11 refers to the ab segment of the labour supply in Figure 2.10. For the bc segment of the labour supply curve, income effect is greater than the substitution effect.

Income Tax and Labour Supply

Consider a proportional income tax rate of 50%. A tax on labour income is the same as a wage decrease. The AT line will change to $A'T$ with the slope being smaller as shown in Figure 2.12. It goes without saying that the tax makes the worker worse off as he now rests on a lower indifference curve, having smaller real income. As usual, we draw the imaginary budget line, BB'. The total effect is from J to J', indicating less consumption of leisure. From J to K is substitution effect, meaning as the wage is lower, the cost of consuming leisure is lower and hence more consumption of leisure and less work. From K to J' is income effect, meaning with smaller real income, the worker will consume less leisure and hence works more hours. In this case, income effect is smaller than the substitution effect as the tax rate is very high.

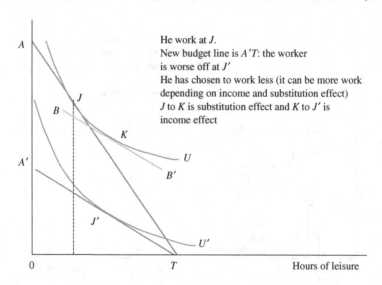

Figure 2.12:   Substitution and Income Effects of Proportional Tax

Impact of Non-labour Income on Labour Supply

Figure 2.13 starts with a given level of non-labour income, V. The equilibrium point is J. With an increase in non-labour income to V', the budget line will change from AT to $A'T'$, implying no change in the wage rate. According to the figure, the worker chose J' as the new equilibrium point, indicating more consumption of leisure. There is only income effect here and no substitution effect. It is possible that, especially with a big increase in non-labour income, the worker may choose T', not to work at all, a corner solution. In the next section, we will show how the indifference curve passes through T or T'.

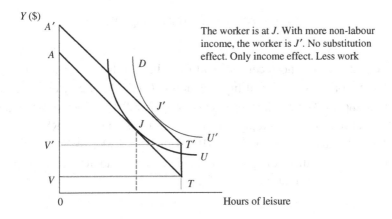

Figure 2.13: Impact of Non-labour Income on Labour Supply

Reservation Wage Rate

When a jobseeker looks for a job, he does have a minimum wage below which, he rather not work. In Figure 2.14, the jobseeker has a given level of non-labour income, V. According to his ability, his market wage rate is W'. If he accepts that job, he will rest on the indifference curve, U'. However, he will choose T' as his equilibrium point because T' rests on U, which is a higher indifference curve. At T', he chose not to work. It is a corner solution. The slope of the indifference curve at T' is known as the reservation wage, W_R. For him to work, he will have to find a job that pays better than W_R. Each individual has the respective W_R. For poor people, the reservation wage is slightly lower than subsistence wage rate.

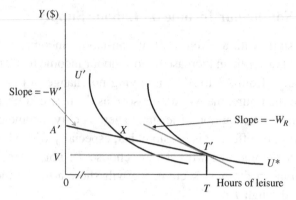

At W_R, the jobseeker prefers to enjoy leisure at T'

Figure 2.14:   The Reservation Wage, W_R

Consider Jane who receives $100 from her mother regardless of how much she works a day. Her utility function is $U(Y, L) = Y \cdot L$. Her $T = 24$ in the daily model. What is her reservation wage, W_R? The slope of her indifference curve at T' which represents not working is equal to MRS which is equal to Y/L. At T', $L = 24$ and $Y = \$100$. Her $W_R = 100/24 = \$4.2$ per hour. It is obvious from this example to conclude that non-labour income is positively related to reservation wage, W_R.

Supply Curve of Labour and Worker Surplus

The supply curve is the locus of the individual minimum wage (W_{IM}) of each worker for each hour of work. W_{IM}, by definition, will exceed the reservation wage for each hour of work of the respective worker. Figure 2.15 shows that John's minimum wage for the fifth hour is $10 and $15 for the tenth hour. If an employer wants to employ John for 10 hours, John would demand area $0AJF$ in wages. If John is not paid this amount, he will not work for 10 hours. He has a choice of working somewhere else or enjoys his leisure. Area $0AJF$ is known as transfer earnings (TE). In a way, TE is the value of leisure to John. TE is not a cost to society.

Suppose the market wage for John is $15 per hour. John would choose to work for 10 hours. His total labour earnings is area $0BJF$ which exceeds area $0AJF$. Thus, John's worker surplus is area ABJ. If John's labour supply is horizontal, he has no worker surplus. He is likely to be an unskilled

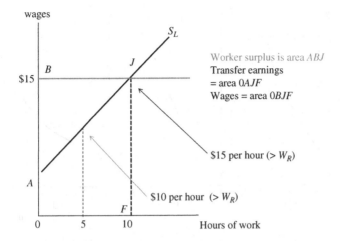

Figure 2.15: Supply Curve of Labour, Transfer Earnings and Worker Surplus

person. The purpose of investment in human capital is to be able to earn more and make the supply curve steeper.[2]

Market Supply Curve of Labour and Individual Labour Supply Curves

In this chapter, we use the basic model to derive the individual labour supply curve. In this book, like in other books as well, the labour supply curve is drawn with a positive slope. We also show that the jobseeker's choice in choosing a bundle with regard to income and leisure is dictated by income and substitution effect and change in non-labour income.

In this chapter, the wage rate is an exogenous variable. In the later chapters, we will need labour market supply curve and labour market demand curve to determine the market wage rate which will be endogenous. In Figure 2.16, we show John's and Mary's labour supply curves, with John's W_R lower than Mary's W_R. At the wage rate, W', John plans to work "a" hours and Mary "b" hours. Assume that we only have these two workers, then the number of hours available at the labour market is "$a + b$" at the wage rate, W'. Hence, the labour market supply curve is a horizontal summation of these two workers' labour supply curves.

---

[2]The chapter on human capital will examine the rate of return on investment in human capital.

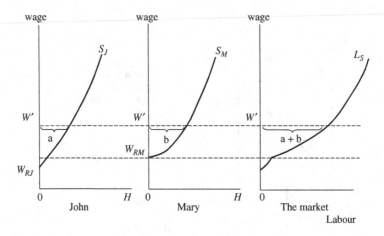

Figure 2.16: Market Supply Curve of Labour (L_s) — A Horizontal Summation of Individual Labour Supply Curves

Discussion Questions

1. Use a figure to show income effect is greater than substitution effect of a wage increase.
2. Use a figure to show income effect is greater than substitution effect of an imposition of proportional income tax.
3. Use a figure to show an increase in non-labour income has no impact on consumption of leisure.
4. Use a figure to show that an increase in non-labour income can increase reservation wage.

Bibliography

Borjas, G. J. (2013). *Labor Economics*, Seventh edition. New York: McGraw-Hill.

Ehrenberg, R. G. and Smith, R. S (2003). *Modern Labor Economics*. Boston: Addison Wesley.

McConnell, C. R., Brue, S. L. and MacPherson, D. A. (2006). *Contemporary Labor Economics*, Seventh edition. New York: McGraw-Hill.

Chapter 3

The Life Cycle, the Family and Labour Supply

In Chapter 2, we use the Y–L model to determine number of hours of work per day. We show that a change in wage rate will produce substitution effect and income effect. In conducting the analysis, we assume that workers have a choice to work more hours or fewer hours. There seems to be no restrictions on working hours. And the workers do not seem to worry about lifetime expenses. Does the worker's decision to work depend on his household's condition? At the same time, how do we take into account self-employment? In this chapter, we will consider all these situations.

The Socialist Model

In many countries ranging from developed to developing countries, the public sector employers and university professors receive pension when they reach the official retirement age. Singapore is an exception where public sector employees and university professors are not under a pension scheme. Almost all employees in Singapore are under the Central Provident Fund scheme which will be analyzed in Chapter 15.

Figure 3.1 shows the financial situation of an employee under government-funded pension scheme. XY represents lifetime expenses of a typical person. CD represents the earning of this person before retirement age. After retirement age, this person's earning is his pension till death. If life expectancy is longer, the government will face a bigger fiscal deficit. Area B is net savings. Area A is required expenses when the person is under the care of his parents while Area K is the excess of the expenses over the earnings.

33

From an employee's perspective, Area B should be equal to the sum of areas $A + K$. If B is expected to be smaller than $A + K$, in some countries, the public sector employees can negotiate with the government on the condition of bad health so that they can retire at age 55 and be able to receive pension starting from 55 to death.[1] This arrangement would then allow them to work in the private sector to get more labour income. This model works beautifully for the citizens but the government will face budget deficits ultimately.

Area under the XY curve is lifetime expenditure. Area under the $CDD'Z$ curve is lifetime earnings. $D'Z$ is pension from the government

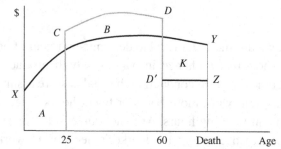

If $B < A + K$, move D' at 55, and work in private sector

Figure 3.1:   The Socialist Model

Note: Area under the XY curve is lifetime expenditure. Area under the $CDD'Z$ curve is lifetime earnings. $D'Z$ is pension from the government.

Thailand, a low per capita income country in Southeast Asia, has a universal health scheme and a universal pension scheme in which every elderly citizen reaching 65 years in age gets S\$20 per month.[2] In Singapore, the social security scheme is employment based. Chapter 15 will discuss social security in Singapore.

The Life Cycle Hypothesis

Here, we want to introduce the life cycle perspective of a typical worker with regard to wages and hours of work. Figure 3.2 shows that the lifetime

---

[1] Public sector employees generally are against raising the official retirement age.
[2] A specialist at the Asia-Pacific office of the United Nations Population Fund in Bangkok made this point. See S.T. 16/01/2016 on page A33, "17M in Thailand will be above 65 by 2040: Report".

expenditure of a typical worker is the area under *XY*. The area under *CD* represents the lifetime earnings of the worker.[3] The Life Cycle Hypothesis assumes that all workers and households will be able to earn sufficiently to pay all the bills. This is a bold assumption.

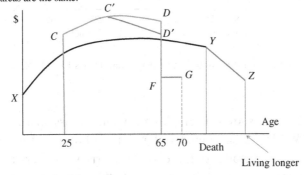

Area under the *XY* curve is lifetime expenditure. Area under the *CD* curve is lifetime earnings. The life cycle model assumes that both areas are the same.

Figure 3.2: The Life Cycle Model (Without Pension)

Note: Area under the *XY* curve is lifetime expenditure. Area under the *CD* curve is lifetime earnings. The life cycle model assumes that both areas are the same.

In Figure 3.3(a), *cd* represents the wage level over the life cycle of the worker. When a worker starts working, the wage level is low. So we expect his wages to rise as he approaches the 30s and start to fall in early 50s. Figure 3.3(b) also shows his life cycle of hours of work (labour supply), represented by *ab*, which shows that this person would choose to work fewer hours when young and the number of working hours increases as he approaches the middle age. His working hours start to fall when he is in his 50s. Making use of low wages to consume more leisure and working more hours when wages are high is known as Inter-temporal Substitution Hypothesis. The Inter-temporal Substitution Hypothesis which implies that *cd* and *ab* curves move in tandem with each other, also assumes that the worker would have no problem financing his lifetime expenses.

---

[3]We assume retirement age is 65. The current retirement age in Singapore is 62.

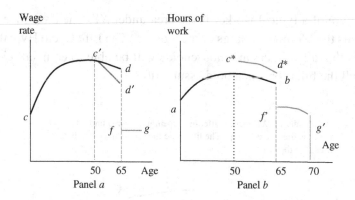

Figure 3.3:   The Life Cycle Path of Wages and Hours for a Typical Worker

As Chapter 1 shows, unemployment rate across many countries is very high. While the basic model of Y–L is still useful, it is complicated by the following factors. As life expectancy rises, workers need to earn more to pay for extra expenditures. Next, both globalization and advanced technology have been making many jobs redundant, eliminating especially middle income jobs. Wages therefore fluctuate over the life cycle of a typical worker. When wages fall, the young workers may want to enjoy more leisure or invest in human capital. But for workers past 50 in age, when their wages fall, they may have to work longer hours to earn more but can they work more hours?

In the following discussion, we allow unanticipated increase in life expectancy which results in an increase in expenses, represented by YZ in Figure 3.2. We also allow reduced earnings, represented by $C'D'$ in Figure 3.2 and $c'd'$ in Figure 3.3. This means that the worker has to earn more to meet the unexpected increase in lifetime expenses.

In terms of working hours, these low wage workers may get second job and hence the extra hours are represented by c^*d^* in Figure 3.3. After the official age of retirement, low wage workers' labour supply is $f'g'$ and the earnings are represented by fg. Thus, we see all over the world, especially in Singapore, many workers in their late 60s and early 70s still work full time as labourers.

The Family, the Business Cycle and Labour Supply

Labour supply is sum of employment and unemployment. During a recession, some workers lost their jobs and many more workers saw their take home pay reduced. Do we have more labour supply during a recession? In a typical household, some main bread winners earn less during a recession. Consequently, the secondary workforce such as the wife and adult children may join the labour market to look for a job to supplement family income. As they enter the labour market as jobseekers, the labour supply increases. This is known as added worker effect. On the other hand, during a recession, some jobseekers get so discouraged of not being able to get a job that they quit the labour market. They are therefore not counted as part of the labour force, although they still want to work. This is known as discouraged worker effect, which reduces labour supply. Hence, whether labour supply would increase depends on the strength of these two opposing forces.

During an economic recovery, the workers' earnings have increased. The secondary workforce may opt to quit the labour market either to look after the household or back to school. This is known as withdrawal effect, which reduces labour supply. On the other hand, many people who quit the labour markets on the account of discouraged worker effect now want to enter the labour market because of economic recovery. This is known as encouraged worker effect. During the first year of economic recovery, where encouraged worker effect is strong, we may see the situation where both employment level and unemployment level increase.

Retirement and Pension

In the Y–L model, the utility function of a jobseeker consists of income and leisure. The focus is on leisure. When the price of leisure is high, the worker will consume less leisure. When there is an increase in real income, the worker will consume more leisure. In this section, we use the same model but the focus is on retirement. When the cost of retirement is high, the worker consumes less retirement. When there is an increase in real income, the worker consumes more retirement.

We can modify the *Y–L* model to analyze the trade-off between continued employment and retirement with pension for 20 years. This is a theoretical situation with the following simplifying assumptions. In Figure 3.4(a), the annual salary of a public sector employee is represented by ab line. If he retires at age 60, he can collect pension benefits (*B*) each year till death. His pension line is *cd*. He has two options: The first option is to retire at 60 and his stream of income is *cd* from age 60 to death. His second option is to continue to work beyond 60. The most he can continue to work in the public sector is 20 years. His wage line is *bb'*. After *b'*, he receives pension from *f* till death.

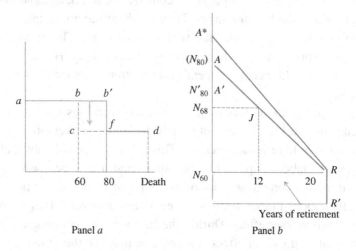

Figure 3.4:   Retirement Model with Pension Scheme

Hence, he faces two decisions: to retire at 60 from the civil service or continue to work. If he wants to continue to work, he can choose to work for 1 year or 5 years or 20 years. If he chooses to work for 5 years, he enjoys his active retirement for 15 years and he, of course, still receives his pension at the dotted line, five years later at age 65. After age 80, both options have the same payouts, he will enjoy his "golden" retirement till death.

As the annual salary (*W*) is greater than the annual pension benefits (*B*), the public sector employee's net worth (*N*) will be greater if he works after age 60 as is shown in Figure 3.4(b). If he decides to stop working at age 60, his net worth is N_{60}, enjoying 20 years of active retirement. In other words, he has chosen *R* in Figure 3.4(b). If he wants to work for another 20 years after age 60, he will be at *A* with the greater net worth at N_{80}, with zero active retirement year. The slope of AR is equal to $(W-B)$. Assume that, based on utility maximization (indifference curve is not drawn), the public sector employee has chosen J, which indicates that he has chosen to enjoy 12 years of active retirement. This implies that he has chosen to work 8 more years after official retirement at age 60. His net worth will be N_{68}.

Perhaps, it will be easy to understand the retirement model if we define the equation for the budget line, AR, as follows:

$$N_H = N_{60} + (20 - R)(W - B),$$

where W is the wage rate, B represents retirement benefits, number of years of employment is $(20 - R)$ which is equal to H.

Let ΔW represent $(W - B)$, we have

$$N_H = N_{60} + H \Delta W,$$

when H is zero, $N_H = N_{60}$;
when H is 20, $N_H = N_{80}$;
when H is 12, $N_H = N_{72}$.

Figure 3.5 shows that John has to decide whether to work or not after reaching 60 in age. AR is the budget line. J is his equilibrium point. He has chosen to work for 8 years and thereby enjoy 12 years of retirement.

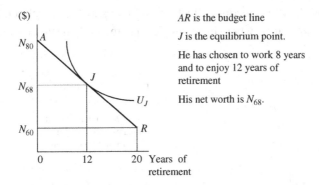

Figure 3.5: The Basic Retirement Model

If there is an increase in annual wages but the pension benefits remain the same, the cost of retirement is higher. The budget line will shift from

AR to *A*R* in Figure 3.4(b), with a steeper slope showing continued employment is more attractive. This will produce substitution effect and income effect. For substitution effect, as cost of active retirement is higher, consume less retirement. There is income effect as the worker is on a higher indifference curve. The worker will consume more retirement as retirement is a normal good.

We can also consider a case where inflation rate is high and wages are not indexed to inflation but the pension benefits are. In this case, *R* remains the same but N_{80} will become N'_{80}, smaller in value. The new budget line connecting *A'* to *R* (See Figure 3.4(b)), is flatter, indicating continued employment is less attractive.

If pension benefits are not indexed to inflation but the wages are and inflation rate is high, *R* will become *R'*, indicating a lower net worth. The new budget line is *R'A* (not drawn in Figure 3.4(b)). The budget line is steeper, implying continued employment is more attractive.

We use Figure 3.6 to show substitution and income effects. Suppose there is an increase in wages but retirement benefits remain the same. This will cause the budget line to change from *RA* to *RA**. The starting point is *J*. From *J* to *K* is substitution effect, indicating that retirement is more expensive and the worker should consume less retirement and work more. The new equilibrium point has to be the point of tangency between *RA** and the higher indifference curve (not shown in figure). J_1 and J_2 are two possible equilibrium points and therefore two possible income effects. Income effect is from *K* to J_1 where income effect is less than substitution effect. Income effect 2 is from *K* to J_2 where income effect is greater than substitution effect.

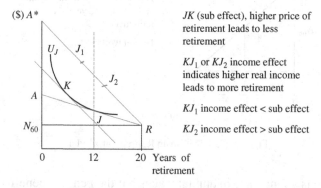

($) *A**

U_J J_1

A

N_{60}

0   12   20 Years of
retirement

J_2

K

J

R

JK (sub effect), higher price of retirement leads to less retirement

KJ_1 or KJ_2 income effect indicates higher real income leads to more retirement

KJ_1 income effect < sub effect

KJ_2 income effect > sub effect

Figure 3.6:   Increase in the Wage But Retirement Benefits Remain

The Household and Family Size

It is commonly observed that the relation between household income and family size is inversely related. Based on Economics 101, one is tempted to draw the conclusion that children are an inferior good. But rich families adore their children. They spend more time with their children and the expenditure on children has been increasing. Hence, it is counter-intuitive to argue that children are an inferior good.

In this context, we will introduce the new fertility model to explain the negative relation between household income and family size without relying on children being an inferior good.

Brook (2015) argues that a child has a head start if his parents are more educated in the USA. He has cited evidence in support of the assertion. Roughly 10% of the children in the USA born to college grads grow up in single parent households. The corresponding figure for children born to high school grads is 70%. High school educated parents dine with their children less, talk to them less, take them to church less, encourage them less and spend less time engaging in development activity.

For a typical household, the utility function consists of consumption of goods and services and children. We use G to represent all goods and services. The price of G is P_G. The cost of raising children is C_C. The budget constraint can be stated as follows:

$$I = P_G \cdot Q_G + C_C \cdot Q_C, \tag{3.1}$$

where I = nominal income, Q_G = quantity of goods and services consumed and Q_C = number of children.

Equation (3.1) is a basic budget constraint in theory of consumer behaviour. But the new fertility model departs from standard theory by incorporating two conditions. Firstly, the new theory argues that

$$C_C = t \text{ times } (P_t),$$

where t = time spent on children and P_t is price of time of parents.

Next, it is further argued that t is positively related to P_t. When the parents earn more especially on the account of more human capital, the time of parents is more expensive, and they would want to spend more time, causing t to increase in value. The child will receive more and better parental care and has a better learning environment. It is possible that the increase in C_C is greater than the increase in household income, especially if the mother is more educated.

In Figure 3.7, *AB* is the budget line and the utility maximising household has chosen *J* to be the equilibrium point. The household has three children. But for future households, we want to analyze the decision making process when there is a significant increase in household income. Assume that there is a 20% increase in the household income and for the time being holding cost of children constant, the budget line is *A'B'*. But we know from the new fertility model that the cost of raising children will rise. Assume that there is also 20% increase in the cost of raising children.[4] Then, the budget line becomes *A'B*. In this case, the budget line has shifted from *AB* to *A'B*. There will be substitution effect as the slope of the budget line has changed. There will be income effect as the household will rest on a higher indifference curve. These two effects are not drawn in Figure 3.6.

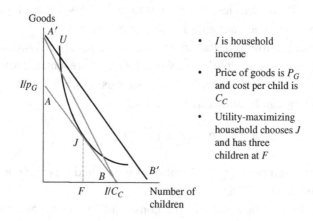

Figure 3.7:   The Fertility Model

In Singapore and in many societies, mothers who are more educated tend to have fewer children which is the focus of new fertility model. Consider two households with the same nominal income but for Household *G*, the mother is a graduate and for Household *N*, the mother is not a graduate. As the fertility model implies, the cost of children is

---

[4]It can be less than 20% or more than 20%.

higher for Household *G* than for Household *N*. Figure 3.8 shows that Household *G* has fewer children than Household *N*. The two households' indifference curves are not comparable.

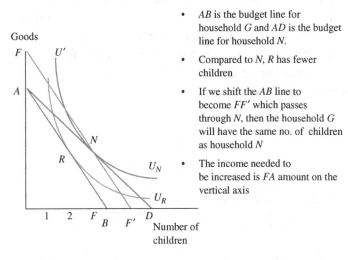

Goods

- *AB* is the budget line for household *G* and *AD* is the budget line for household *N*.

- Compared to *N*, *R* has fewer children

- If we shift the *AB* line to become *FF'* which passes through *N*, then the household *G* will have the same no. of children as household *N*

- The income needed to be increased is *FA* amount on the vertical axis

Figure 3.8: Graduate Mother has Fewer Children than Non-grad Mothers

Some governments, such as Singapore government, want to encourage Household *G* to have more children. In this case, we can give one time subsidy to encourage Household *G* to have more children. One time subsidy will not increase the cost of raising children. With the subsidy, the new budget line is *FF'*, which passes through *N* for Household *G*. It will not be a point of tangency between the *FF'* line and the indifference curve of Household *G* as *N* is not a free choice for Household *G*. Please note that U_N is not the indifference curve of Household *G*. The cost of the subsidy is *FA* amount on the vertical axis.

Overtime and Overtime Pay

The Employment Act in most countries puts a restriction on the number of working hours per day and per week. For instance, in many countries, for a five day week, the number of working hours is 9, which means it is 45 hours a week. When firms want to increase output, the firm can increase the number of workers. Alternatively, the firm can ask existing workers to do extra hours. This is known as overtime. And there is a limit on number of overtime hours too. We shall now examine the economics of overtime.

In Figure 3.9, AT is the budget line in the Y–L model. The worker has chosen J as his equilibrium point. The worker is satisfied with the existing wage rate and rests on the indifference curve, U. He is in his comfort zone. If his employer asks him to do extra hours, he will say no (in real life, he cannot say no). The employer can increase the wage rate but only for the extra hours. Hence, the overtime budget line is $A'J$. The worker has chosen J' to be his new equilibrium point. The worker now is on a higher indifference curve.

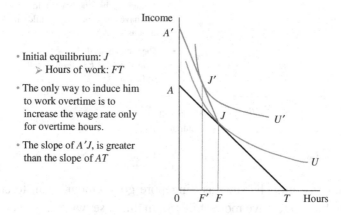

- Initial equilibrium: J
  - ➢ Hours of work: FT
- The only way to induce him to work overtime is to increase the wage rate only for overtime hours.
- The slope of $A'J$, is greater than the slope of AT

Figure 3.9:   Overtime and Overtime Pay

Moonlighting

It is common to observe that many workers take on a second job on a daily or weekly basis. We can use the Y–L model to analyze the economics of moonlighting. In Figure 3.10, the worker would want to choose J_D as his equilibrium. However, due to institutional constraint which is represented by the thick line, FF^*, he is forced to choose J. Hence, J is not a point of tangency between the budget line and his chosen indifference curve. This worker can move to a higher indifference curve by taking on a second job. If the wage rate of the second job is slightly lower than the wage rate of the regular job, he will still accept as he can move beyond U, the existing indifference curve.

- The worker wants to work more hours but is unable to due to institutional constraint.
  - J is not the point of tangency.
  - His dream point is J_D
  - He is forced to work fewer hours, FT hours.
- Worker may moonlight.
  - He may take on a second job in the evening at the same wage or even at a lower wage

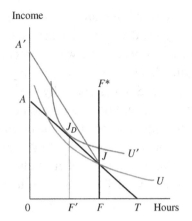

Figure 3.10:   Moonlighting

Self-Employment

The number of self-employed in Singapore has been increasing. In 2014, the number has exceeded more than 200,000 and the educational level of self-employed has also increased. The self-employed, as the term implies, employs himself and can decide to divide his business surplus between his profits and his annual labour earnings. This is why in most countries, the company income tax rates do not differ much in time compared with personal income tax rates.

We still can use the Y–L model to analyze the situation facing a self-employed. If we know his reported annual labour earnings and his reported number of working hours. We can work out his wage per hour on a daily basis. In this case, we can still draw the budget line for a self-employed and this self-employed will choose an equilibrium point. In general, most of the self-employed work long hours and wage rate per hour is not high.

Discussion Questions

1. The Life Cycle Hypothesis assumes perfect information and there will not be any involuntary unemployment. Discuss the consequences if these assumptions are wrong.

2. If you are a civil servant approaching age 60, given Figure 3.4(a), what will be your decision on whether to continue to work or not. What other factors would you want to include in making this decision?

3. In Figure 3.4, suppose AR is the original budget line and $A'R$ is the new budget line. Show graphically the substitution effect and the income effect with regard to consumption of retirement.

4. In Figure 3.5, suppose AB is the original budget line and $A'B$ is the new budget line. Show graphically the substitution effect and the income effect with regard to number of children.

5. Use the Y–L model to show an equilibrium point for a self-employed.

Bibliography

Borjas, G. J. (2013). *Labor Economics*, Seventh edition. New York: McGraw-Hill.

Brooks, D. (2015). "Parents Count in Children's Development", *Straits Time*, Vol. 13, March, page A37.

Goos, M., Manning, A. and Salomons, A. (2009). "Job Polarization in Europe", *The American Economic Review*, Vol. 99, No. 2, Papers and *Proceedings of the One Hundred Twenty-First Meeting of the American Economic Association* (May 2009), pp. 58–63.

Chapter 4

Wage Subsidy and Labour Supply

Capitalism is relentlessly efficient but it is capable of producing a market economy where income inequity is high. Hence, in most countries, many governments do spend a significant fraction of the GDP in helping the poor. But the cost of a big government is inefficiency, wastage and moral hazard dynamics. In this chapter, we will analyze the impact of two government policies in the labour markets. The first policy is cash grant for poor families and the second policy is wage subsidy to encourage people to work.

Cash Grant

In Figure 4.1, John who is unemployed is at T where he rests on his indifference curve, U_0. He has no labour income (how can he and his family survive is beyond the scope here). He is unemployed because his reservation wage (the slope of ab line) is higher than his market wage rate (the slope of AT line). Suppose he is given $500 in cash grant without conditions. His new budget line will move from AT to $A'T'$. His market wage rate remains unchanged, of course. His reservation wage is slightly to be higher[1] (the slope of $a'b'$ line is higher than the slope of ab line). We can conclude that, with the aid of the cash grant, he will not find work. If this public policy aims to encourage people to work, then this public

---

[1]Cash grant is the same as an increase in non-labour income. An increase in non-labour income can increase reservation wage.

policy has failed to achieve the objective. If the public policy aims to help needy families, then this public policy has achieved its objective but how much is enough? Is there any other better way to help the poor? We will examine this issue in other chapters using Singapore as a case study.

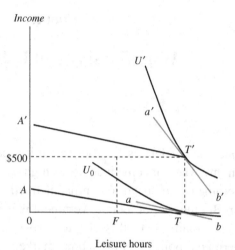

- Cash grant puts the unemployed from T to T'

- Original reservation wage = slope of indifference curve at T, which is greater than the slope of AT, his market wage

- New reservation wage = slope of indifference curve at T'.

- The gap between the new reservation wage and his market wage is bigger.

- The unemployed remains unemployed despite the cash grant

Figure 4.1:   Cash Grant Increases W_R

In Figure 4.2, the worker is at J. He is poor as his labour income is not high. Hence, the government gave him $500 in cash grant. His new budget line is now $A'T'$. The new reservation wage is now higher than his market wage rate. He, of course, would want to move to a higher indifference curve. So, he has chosen T'. In sum, the cash grant has transformed him from a worker to an unemployed. It is obvious that if the cash grant is much less than his original labour income, then, he may be still in the labour market as part of the workforce as we will present this case soon. But, how low is low such that we can motivate this worker to work and at the same time, help his family?

In Figure 4.3, the worker is at J, resting on U. With the cash grant, his budget line is now $A'T'$. He has chosen to be at J'. He is still employed but at J', he chose to work fewer hours.

The conclusion of the above three cases is that cash grant should aim to help single parent families and those with aged parents.

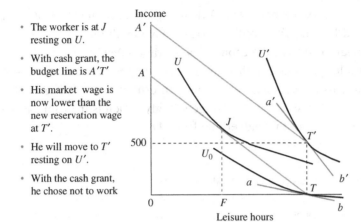

- The worker is at *J* resting on *U*.

- With cash grant, the budget line is *A'T'*

- His market wage is now lower than the new reservation wage at *T'*.

- He will move to *T'* resting on *U'*.

- With the cash grant, he chose not to work

Figure 4.2:   Cash Grant Can Cause a Worker to Choose Unemployment

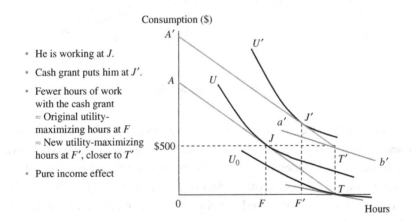

- He is working at *J*.

- Cash grant puts him at *J'*.

- Fewer hours of work with the cash grant
  ≈ Original utility-maximizing hours at *F*
  ≈ New utility-maximizing hours at *F'*, closer to *T'*

- Pure income effect

Figure 4.3:   Cash Grant Reduces Hours of Work for those Who Continue Working

Wage Subsidy

The purpose of wage subsidy is to encourage employment and continued employment. Many governments have implemented wage subsidy programme but they are called by different names. In Singapore, wage subsidy is called Workfare (or Work Income Supplement, WIS). In UK, it is known as in-work benefits (IWB) programme. In the USA, it is known as Earned Income Tax Credit (EITC). They are all the same. We will use $Y–L$ model to analyze the economics of wage subsidy.

First let us consider the simple case of proportional wage subsidy applicable to workers earning below a threshold level. In Figure 4.4, the worker is at J, resting on U. A wage subsidy which is the same as a wage increase will move the budget line from AT to $A'T$.

- Wage subsidy is for workers with low wages

- A wage subsidy of 10% is the same as increase in wages by 10%

- Budget line changes from AT to $A'T$. The worker is on a higher indifference curve.

- The worker moves from J to J', working more hours.

- The worker remains employed

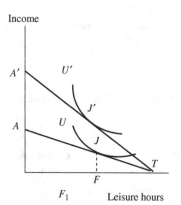

Figure 4.4:   Wage Subsidy

The worker has chosen J' on new budget line, resting on U'. He has chosen to work more hours. In principle, whether he chooses to work more hours or few depends on his substitution effect and income effect. For low income workers, income effect is not strong on wage subsidy. The kind of jobs that they are forced to get onto due to poor human capital, do not have much employment flexibility.

Earned Income Tax Credit

EITC is a form of wage subsidy. It is the same as WIS of Singapore or IWE of the UK in principle. We will use the $Y–L$ model to analyze the economics of EITC.

EITC aims to subsidize poor families, the amount of subsidy depends on the labour income level. In Figure 4.5, the budget line is AT without

EITC. For those who earn between Y_1 and Y_2 monthly, the wage subsidy is 40%. The budget line for these recipients is *TK*. There is substitution effect and income effect for workers earning between Y_1 and Y_2. For those who earn between Y_2 and Y_3, the wage subsidy is a fixed amount. Hence, the budget line for this group of workers is *KH*. There is only income effect for this group of workers. For those who earn between Y_3 and Y_4, for every dollar they earn extra, they will get less from the wage subsidy. There is substitution effect as the wage rate is lower now as the new budget line, *HG*, is flatter than *AT* line. There is income effect as the recipients are on higher indifference. Those who earn more than Y_4 are not entitled to EITC. It is not shown in Figure 4.5 that those who earn more than Y_4 are expected to pay income tax.

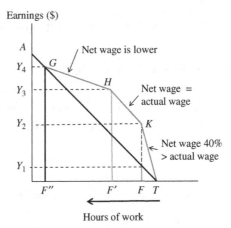

- *AT*: Budget line without EITC
- *TKHGA*: Budget line with EITC
- If a worker works less than *FT* hours, he gets wage subsidy of 40%.
- If he works between *F* and *F'* hours, he gets a fixed amount in wage subsidy.
- If he works between *F'* and *F''* hours, the amount received decreases with each extra working hour.

Figure 4.5:   Earned Income Tax Credit (EITC)

It is not intuitively clear why the *HG* line is flatter than the *AT* line. Figure 4.6 gives an example to explain. At *H'*, the labour markets earnings are $2,000 a month. EITC will give $2,000. Hence, the total earnings are at *H* with $4,000. Now, if earnings are at *X'* with $3,000 a month, EITC now only gives $1,500. The total earnings at *X* are only $4,500. Although this person earns more than $1,000, his net earnings only increase by $500, indicating that the *HG* line is flatter than the *AT* line.

- At H', labour earning is $2,000. EITC is also $2,000 ($H'H$). Total earning at H is $4,000.

- At X', labour earning is $3,000 >$2,000 by $1,000. But XX' is only $1,500 from EITC. Total earning at X is $4,500 which is greater than $4,000 by $500.

- Hence, although earnings increase by $1,000, total earnings only increase by $500.

- Hence, the GH line is flatter than the AT line, producing substitution effect. There is income effect as GH is above AT line.

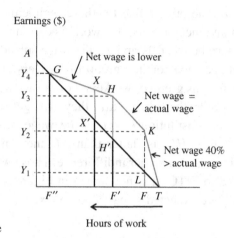

Figure 4.6:   How to Explain HG Segment of EITC

We shall now examine the impact of EITC in the labour market. In Figure 4.7, the person has chosen T, not to work. With EITC, he will move to J', resting on a higher indifference curve, U'. He has chosen to work. EITC at this level is very effective in drawing inactive people to the labour markets.

- This person is at T, not working
  - Reservation wage higher than market wage
  - EITC puts him at J' as his effective net wage is above his reservation wage

- ⇒ EITC targeted at low income group will be effective in increase labour market participation rate

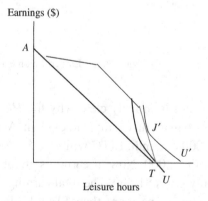

Figure 4.7:   EITC Draws Worker into the Labour Market

Consider a worker who is at *J* in Figure 4.8. With EITC, he will move to *J'*, resting on *U'*. EITC will not be too happy with this labour market outcome.

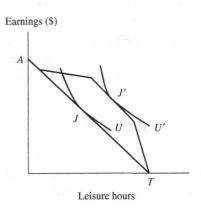

The worker is at *J*.
EITC effectively increases this worker's net earnings

- ⇒ income effect

- No impact on effective wage
  – net wage unchanged
  ⇒ no substitution effect

- Worker maximizes utility by working fewer hours –
  moves from *J* to *J'*

Figure 4.8: EITC Reduces Hours of Work

Now consider those workers who earn between Y_3 and Y_4. In Figure 4.9, suppose that *J* is between Y_3 and Y_4. The worker is at *J*. With EITC, he has chosen to be at *J'*, resting on a higher indifference curve. *BB'*

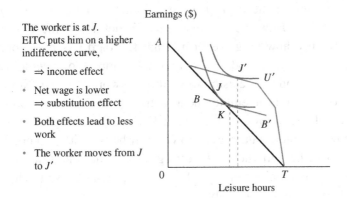

The worker is at *J*.
EITC puts him on a higher indifference curve,

- ⇒ income effect

- Net wage is lower
  ⇒ substitution effect

- Both effects lead to less work

- The worker moves from *J* to *J'*

Figure 4.9: EITC: Both Substitution and Income Effects Lead to Less Work is the imaginary budget line. The substitution effect is from J to K. As the effective wage is lower, the worker will consume more leisure and work less. From K to J', there is income effect. Higher real income will cause the worker to consume more leisure and work less. Hence, the impact is conclusively less work.

The impact of EITC on the employed is not very favourable. But the negative impact may be limited because those who qualify EITC work in certain occupations where working hours may not be flexible.

Unemployment Benefits

Unemployment benefits scheme is common in many countries. After working for a period of time, when a worker is unemployed, he is entitled to receive unemployment benefits weekly for a period of time. The financing of unemployment scheme varies from country to country. For instance, everyone in the UK pays National Insurance (NI) contributions to build up their social security benefits, including a State Pension. If a UK citizen is unemployed and if he has paid NI contributions, he will get the jobseekers allowance for six months. After that, he can only claim financial assistance, if he has few savings and little income from other sources.[2]

Later in the chapter on unemployment, we will consider the unemployment benefits scheme in the US where a firm has to contribute a fixed percentage of the payroll to be a member of the unemployment benefits scheme. How the unemployment benefits scheme is financed would influence how long the firms want to hoard unused labour. But now we use the $Y–L$ model to analyze the impact of unemployment benefits scheme on the decision to work. The worker is at J. Now, he is retrenched. Without unemployment benefits, he chose to work for another employer at lower wage rate at F_0 as is shown in Figure 4.10 (it may not be a point of tangency). However, if he is entitled to unemployment benefits, he will choose T' resting on a higher indifference curve, U'. When the unemployment benefits run out, he will have to choose F_0 provided the job is still available.

---

[2]See http://www.internations.org/great-britain-expats/guide/16133-social-security-taxation/social-security-in-the-uk-16128/unemployment-benefits-in-the-uk-4 .

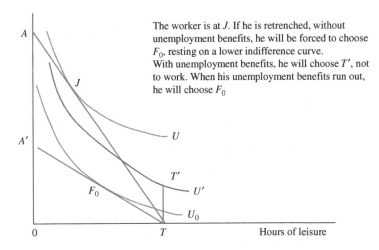

The worker is at *J*. If he is retrenched, without unemployment benefits, he will be forced to choose F_0, resting on a lower indifference curve.
With unemployment benefits, he will choose *T'*, not to work. When his unemployment benefits run out, he will choose F_0

Figure 4.10: Unemployment Benefits and Labour Supply

Discussion Questions

1. The budget line under ETIC has a few segments, *TK*, *KH* and *HG*. Each segment restricts certain amount of earnings to qualify for tax credit. Discuss whether the length of each segment should be widened or narrowed?

2. If you have to design an unemployment benefits scheme, how do you decide on the level of unemployment benefits?

3. Countries which implement unemployment benefits scheme have higher unemployment rate. Singapore does not have unemployment benefits scheme but unemployment rate is low in Singapore. Are you surprised?

Bibliography

Borjas, G. J. (2013). *Labor Economics*, Seventh edition. New York: McGraw-Hill.

Chapter 5

Demand Curve for Labour

Firms employ workers to produce goods and services for the product markets. If firms are not profitable, the firms will shut down and there will not be any demand for labour. Hence, labour demand is closely linked to the product demand. Of course, product demand is also subject to business cost. High labour cost, high cost of funds and lack of modern technology can make a good business project look bad. But first let us examine a typical firm as a producer of output.

Profit Maximizing Level of Output

Firms sell products in the products markets. The product markets are either competitive or monopolistic. We will consider monopolistic product market later. If product market is competitive, the firm is a price taker. The firm accepts the price (P) which is determined in the product market. Hence, price is constant and marginal revenue (MR) of product is also constant. In Figure 5.1, we show the MR curve at P and the conventional marginal cost (MC_0) curve. The equilibrium condition for profit maximization point is J_0, where $MC_0 = MR$. The profit (π) maximizing level of output is thus $Q\pi_0$. If MC curve shifts down to become MC_1 curve, the profit maximizing level of output is higher at $Q\pi_1$.

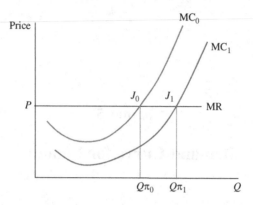

Figure 5.1:   Profit Maximising Level of Output

Theory of Production

Firms need to use capital (K) and number of workers (E) to produce an output using a production function. A production function specifies a technical relation between monthly output (Q) and two inputs, capital (K) and number of workers (E) as stated below:

$$Q = f(K, E). \tag{5.1}$$

We need to make simplifying assumptions that each worker works the same number of hours and all workers are homogeneous and capital is measured in units with each unit having the same efficiency. In Figure 5.2, we show that the firm at X can use 10 units of capital and 30 workers to produce Q_0. Technology can also allow the firm at Y to produce Q_0 using 8 units of capital and 35 workers. If we connect X and Y (of course other points using the same reasoning) we can draw an iso-quant curve for Q_0. Similarly, we can derive another indifference curve for higher output level, Q_1. Note that those quantities (Q_0, Q_1) are without the symbol π. This indicates that these are just quantities and not profit maximizing level of output. At a given technology, the firm will have a map of isoquant curves. A change in technology will create another map of isoquant curves.

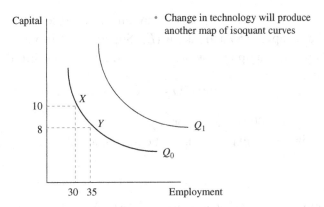

Figure 5.2: Map of Isoquant Curves

The slope of an isoquant is the negative of the ratio of marginal product of labour (MP_E) over marginal product of capital (MP_K), i.e., $\Delta K/\Delta L = - MP_E/MP_K$. The absolute value of this slope is called the marginal rate of technical substitution (MRTS).

As we move from X to Y, we substitute 2 units of capital with 5 workers. MRTS is $\Delta K/\Delta E = 2/5$. MRTS will decrease as we move down the isoquant curve because the isoquant curve is convex to the original point.

The MRTS can be derived along an isoquant curve where output level is constant, ΔQ is 0. When we move from X to Y, the gain in output ($\Delta L \cdot MP_E$) must be the same as the loss in output ($\Delta K \cdot MP_K$). This presents the following equation:

$$\Delta L \cdot MP_E + \Delta K \cdot MP_K = 0.$$

By rearranging we get,

$$\Delta K/\Delta L = - MP_E/MP_K. \qquad (5.2)$$

Isoquant curves alone will not help the firm to minimize cost of production. We need to bring in the price of labour (w) and the price of capital (r). It is not easy to compute price of capital because of depreciation of capital stock. Economists argue that if we can rent a machine and the rental per month is r, then r is the price of capital.

Given the value of w and r, a given amount of expenditure, the firm can purchase capital (K) and labour (E). Suppose the firm has $100,000, the firm's purchasing power with regard to K and E is as follows:

$$\$100,000 = r \cdot K + w \cdot E.$$

Hence, $100,000 is the cost outlay (C).
Accordingly, we express this cost equation as follows:

$$C_0 = r \cdot K + w \cdot E. \tag{5.3}$$

Equation (5.3) implies that with a cost outlay of C_0, the firm can purchase different combination of K and E.
Rearranging Equation (5.3), we get

$$K = C_0/r - w/r\, E. \tag{5.4}$$

In Figure 5.3, we drew Equation (5.4). This line is known as an isocost line with C_0 as cost of production. The slope of the isocost line is w/r. With varying levels of costs, we can get a map of isocost lines as shown in Figure 5.3. Suppose wage rate is lower from w to w' as labour is cheaper. Each isocost line is flatter as shown in Figure 5.3. We will get another map of isocost lines.

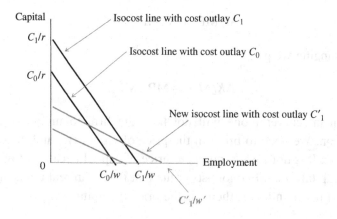

Figure 5.3:   Map of Isocost Lines

Cost Minimization and Profit Maximization

Suppose the firm wants to produce profit maximizing level of output, $Q\pi_0$. As shown in Figure 5.4, the firm can produce at A or at B, costing the firm C_1. Under cost minimization, the firm will find the cheapest way to produce $Q\pi_0$. The cost minimization point is J_0 where an isocost line is tangent to the isoquant curve. The lowest cost outlay of producing $Q\pi_0$ is C_0. In other words, Isocost$_0$ is the chosen isocost line. Note that $Q\pi_0$, w and r are exogenous variables of cost minimization and J_0, K_0, E_0, C_0 and Isocost$_0$ are endogenous variables (answers).

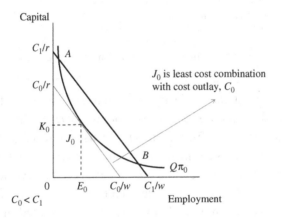

Figure 5.4:   Cost Minimization Point

In Figure 5.5, we start with the original cost minimization point at J_0. J_0 is also the profit maximization point as we aim to produce $Q\pi_0$. Y_0X_0 is the initial equilibrium isocost line with cost outlay, C_0. Suppose w is lower, the new isocost line will be flatter and we get another map of isocost lines (refer to Figure 5.3). As w is part of MC, the MC curve will shift down and we get a new profit maximizing level of output, $Q\pi_1$ (refer to Figure 5.1). Hence, with labour coming cheaper, the new profit maximization is now J_1. J_1 is a point of tangency of a new isocost line with the isoquant curve, $Q\pi_1$. Thus, $Y'_1X'_1$ is the new equilibrium isocost line with cost outlay, C'_1 with a different slope from Y_0X_0. The total effect of cheaper labour is from J_0 to J_1, indicating that the firm employs more capital and more labour using J_0 as a reference point.

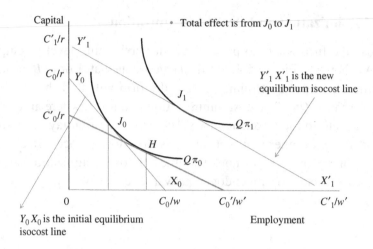

Figure 5.5:   Impact on Production of Cheaper Labour

The total effect can be decomposed into substitution effect and scale effect. The substitution effect starts from J_0 to H on the same isoquant curve. When we move from J_0 to H, we use more labour as labour is cheaper. Note that H is an imaginary point. The scale effect which implies that the firm has to produce more output based on the new slope of isocost line, starts from H to J_1. The scale effect, using H as a reference point, shows that both capital and labour usage have increased in order to produce more output. In Economics, when a firm needs to produce more, the firm uses more capital, then capital is a normal input. Thus, based on Figure 5.5, both inputs are normal inputs based on scale effect.

Consider a businessman starting a car washing business. Each day, his output is 50 cars. So, he employs four workers. If his business becomes very good and the output is 300 cars a day, he would buy a car washing machine and employ only 2 workers. In this context, labour is an inferior good. Capital is not likely to be an inferior good.

Figure 5.6 is similar to Figure 5.5 except we remove the isoquant curve producing $Q\pi_1$. The substitution effect is still the same. But we draw a vertical and a horizontal line at H. The new equilibrium point of having cheaper labour can be J_1, J_2 or J_3, depending on the nature of technology. Using H as a reference, at J_1 both capital and labour are normal inputs. If at J_2, then labour is inferior input and if at J_3, then capital is an inferior input.

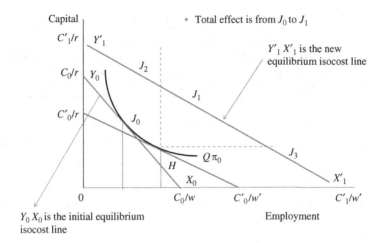

Figure 5.6: Normal and Inferior Inputs

Labour Demand is Derived Demand

Labour demand is linked to output demand. How firms behave in the product markets has an impact on labour demand. How firms use technology for product output also has an impact on labour demand. We shall now consider competitive product market where price is constant. Monopolistic product market will be considered later in the chapter.

To derive labour demand curve, we need to know MP_E, implying that capital is held constant (K_F) as shown below:

$$Q = f(K_F, E). \qquad (5.5)$$

We assume that each worker works the same number of hours and all workers are homogeneous. Given Equation (5.5), we can derive MP_E and MP_K. Let us consider a firm in competitive product market where price is constant at \$10 per unit of output. In the short run, we hold capital constant, we can increase output by increasing one worker at a time. When there is no labour, output is zero (see Table 5.1). When one worker is brought in, total output (TQ_E) is 100 units. Total revenue (TR) is equal to $P \cdot Q = \$1,000$. Average product of labour (AP_E) is equal to $Q/E = 100$ units. Average value of product (AVP_E) is $Q/E = \$100$. $MP_E = 100$ units and value of marginal product $(VMP_E) = P \cdot MP_E = \$1,000$.

Table 5.1: $Q = f(K_F, E)$ Per Month; Price of Product $(P) = \$10$

K_F	E	Q (TP$_E$)	Total revenue (TR = $P \cdot Q$)	Average product per worker (AP$_E$)	Value of average product per worker (VAP$_E$)	Marginal product of labour (MP$_E$)	Value of marginal product of labour (VMP$_E$)	Marginal cost (MC = $W = \$500$)
10	0	0	0			0	0	
10	1	100	1,000	100	1,000	100	1,000	500
10	2	290	2,900	145	1,450	190	1,900	500
10	3	370	3,700	123	1,230	80	800	500
10	4	440	4,400	110	1,100	70	700	500
10	5	500	5,000	100	1,000	60	600	500
10	6	550	5,500	92	920	50	500	500
10	7	590	5,900	84	840	40	400	500
10	8	620	6,200	76	760	30	300	500

Note: Factor proportion (K/E); MP$_E$ falls as K/E deteriorates.

If we increase the number of workers from one to two workers, then the output increases by more than 100% i.e., from 100 units to 290 units. This implies that the capital–labour ratio improves from 10/1 to10/2. As expected, among other output indicators, MP$_E$ has continued to increase from 100 units to190 units. When the number of workers is increased from 2 to 3 workers, MP$_E$ starts to fall from 190 units to 80 units. This indicates that the best factor proportion is a firm size of 5 workers for this firm.

We want to explain the significance of value of marginal product of labour (VMP$_E$). When the first worker is employed, his contribution (VMP$_E$) to the firm is $1,000. The VMP$_E$ of the second worker is $1,900. The third is $80 and thus we know VMP$_E$ has been falling beyond the second worker. All workers are homogeneous. VMP$_E$ varies due to changes in factor proportion.

How many workers will the firm want to employ? Labour demand of course is also dependent on wages per worker. To a competitive firm in the labour market, the firm accepts the market wage. In Table 5.1, the monthly market wage (W) is $500 a month. Hence W is equal to MC of employing an additional worker. The firm would want to employ the second worker because VMP ($1,900) > W = ($500). The firm would want to employ the third worker because VMP of third worker exceeds W. Using this principle of profit maximization, the firm will employ the sixth worker where

VMP ($500) = *W* ($500). The firm breaks even with the sixth worker but it enjoys a surplus for each of the first five workers. The firm will not employ the seventh worker as its VMP < *W*. In other words, the firm will lose money in employing the seventh worker.

Now, we know that the firm's demand for labour is six workers. This is known as profit maximizing level of employment. But can the firm make a profit at this level of output? With the six workers, the TR is $5,500 (from Table 5.1) and the wage bill is $W \cdot E$ = $3,000. It is possible for the firm to survive as TR exceeds the wage bill at the profit maximizing level of employment. The firm does survive and the firm will employ six workers. There is therefore labour demand for six workers given the production function, *P* and *W*.

In economics, we want to use graphs for analysis. Based on Table 5.1, if we put TP_E on the vertical axis and *E* on the horizontal axis, we can plot TP_E curve. In Figure 5.7, we show the TP_E curve in the top part of the figure. We can draw AP and MP using the figures from Table 5.1. But we can also derive AP and MP from the TP_E curve (any introductory textbook on economics will provide the proof). In the lower part of Figure 5.7, we show the relations between AP and MP. We can see that MP curve cuts AP curve from the above at AP curve's highest point.

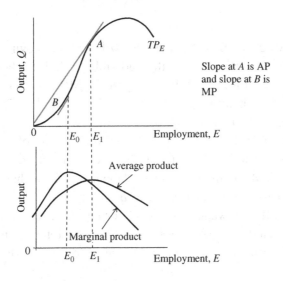

Figure 5.7:   Total Product, Average Product and Marginal Product Curves

The firm is interested in making a profit. We need to express those curves in dollars and cents. Hence, as price is constant in this example, the shape of VTP, VAP and VMP are all the same as is shown in Figure 5.8.

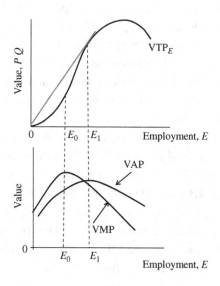

Figure 5.8:   VTP, VAP and VMP

Earlier, we concluded that the firm will stop employing additional workers when $W = \text{VMP}_E$. It is thus possible to derive labour demand curve from VMP_E. Figure 5.9 shows a typical VMP_E curve. If the market wage is W_0, MC is therefore equal to W_0. At C, $W_0 = \text{VMP}_E$. Then the firm will employ E_0. If there is an increase in market wage to W_1, then B is the new equilibrium point and E_1 is profit maximizing level of employment. Hence, wages and labour demand are inversely related. In order to conclude that the VMP is the demand for labour curve, we have to ensure that the firm can earn a profit at C, at B and at A, respectively as each point faces a different wage level. At C, for instance, we know the wage bill which is area $0\,W_0 C_{E0}$ but we need to know the total revenue in order to know if the firm can survive at C. We need to bring VAP_E curve into the analysis.

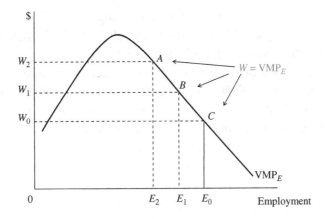

Figure 5.9: VMP_E Can Determine Profit Maximising Level of Employment

We can obtain TR from Table 5.1. But if we are given E and VAP_E, we can also obtain TR as TR is equal to E times VAP_E. Figure 5.10 presents a typical VAP_E curve. We cannot determine profit maximizing level of employment from VAP_E but only from VMP_E. Let us assume that employment level is E_0, then TR at F on VAP_E curve is equal to area $0\,G_0 F_{E0}$. At each employment level, we can get the respective TR.

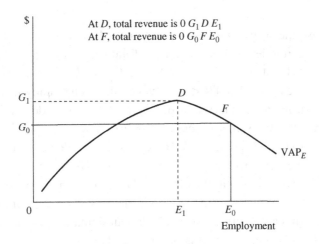

Figure 5.10: We Can Get Total Revenue from VAP Curve

We now want to put VAP_E and VMP_E together as it is shown in Figure 5.11. Note that VMP cuts VAP from above at the highest point of VAP curve. When the wage level is W_0, the equilibrium point is C on VMP curve. The profit maximizing level of employment is E_0. The total wage bill at C is area $0\ W_0\ C\ E_0$. To get TR, at E_0, VAP is at D. The total revenue is area $0\ G\ D\ E_0$. As TR > total wage bill, it is possible for the firm to survive. Hence, C is a point on labour demand curve.

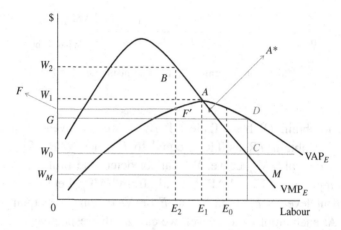

Figure 5.11:   Labour Demand with Competitive Product Market

Suppose the wage rate is W_2. At B on VMP curve, $W = VMP$. E_2 is profit maximizing level of employment. Total wage bill is area $0\ W_2\ B\ E_2$. When employment level is E_2, VAP is at F' on VAP curve. TR is area $0\ FF'\ E_2$. We can see that TR < total wage bill when employment level is at E_2. The firm cannot survive at B. There is no labour demand at B on VMP curve. For the same reasoning, the firm barely can survive at A as TR is equal to total wage bill at A. Hence, the labour demand curve is part of VMP curve provided the segment is below VAP curve. For ease of presentation, we depict that the effective labour demand curve is $A*M$, as W_M is the lowest wage level in the labour markets. $A*$ is an arbitrary point where the firm can barely survive. The labour demand curve in this book refers to the $A*M$ curve which is part of VMP curve.

Given $A*M$ is the labour demand curve, is unit labour cost (ULC) on the labour demand curve high? In Chapter 1, we have discussed the concept of ULC which is total wage bill divided by TR for the firm. But for the firm to employ an additional worker, the firm will look at ULC which is the ratio of wages over VMP. If VMP > W, the ULC is below one and the firm will continue to employ more workers till $W = $ VMP, where ULC is equal to one. According to Figure 5.12, the government has imposed a minimum wage, W_M. At this wage rate, M is the equilibrium point and the profit maximizing level of employment is 50 workers as an example. Note that it can be any wage level as long as the wage level is between W_{A*} and W_M. For the 50th worker, it is $W = $ VMP$_E$ at M. The firm breaks even at the 50th worker. Thus, at M, ULC which is W over VMP is equal to one for the 50th worker. But for each of the first 49 workers, it is VMP > W. The average surplus per worker is MD. The total surplus is MD times 50 workers.

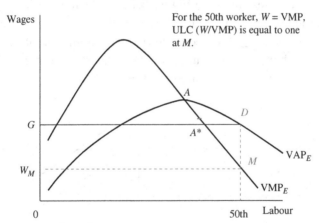

From 1st to 49th worker, $W < $ VMP. This is how the firm makes money. At M, the firm's surplus is area W_M GDM

Figure 5.12: VMP and ULC

Many countries face intense competition in the product markets and rising wage costs in the domestic markets. This presents a serious problem to many governments. Note that VAP$_E = P \cdot AP_E$ and VMP$_E = P \cdot MP_E$. When product markets are very competitive, the price is not high and no firms dare to raise the price. Unless marginal product of labour can be raised in the short run which is difficult, both firms and the government cannot shift the VAP$_E$

curve and VMP$_E$ curve upward. If the wage level starts to rise, the labour demand curve ($A*M$) will shrink, indicating that the M will approach $A*$. If the labour demand curve shrinks in length, the range of wages for which employment is demanded is shorter. No government would like that.

In the long run, all governments want to increase the length of the labour demand curve and at the same time to raise the wage level for economic development. Moving up the value chain can raise product prices. Effective training scheme and better capital stock can increase marginal product of labour. Hence, in the later chapters, we will discuss how to raise VAP$_E$ curve and VMP$_E$ curve.

Labour Demand Curve for the Industry

Suppose we have 100 firms in an industry, each has the same labour demand curve, dL, as shown in Figure 5.13. At each wage level, we will know the quantity of labour demand from each firm. Thus, labour market demand curve, $D_{LM} = \Sigma D_L$ based on horizontal summation of all D_L. This derivation of labour demand curve for the industry is correct only when the product price remains the same as $D_L = P \cdot M_{PL}$.

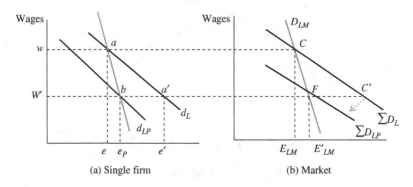

(a) Single firm   (b) Market

Figure 5.13:   Labour Demand Curve for the Industry is the CF Line

When the wage level falls from W to W', the typical firm will move from a to a', indicating that the number of workers will increase from e to e' for each firm as shown in the left panel of Figure 5.13. At the market level, the industry will move from C to C'. When each firm employs more workers and therefore produces more output, the supply of output for the industry will increase and the product price will fall. ΣD_L will fall at each wage level as the price falls. Ultimately, ΣD_L will become ΣD_{LP}, due to the product price effect. With this price effect, each firm will move from *a* to *b*, the increase in number of workers is smaller only from *e* to e_p. The industry will move from *C* to *F*. Connecting *C* and *F* is the labour demand curve for the industry (D_{LM}) which is less elastic than the individual labour demand curves (d_L without price effect). Hence, due to the product price effect, the elasticity of labour demand at the firm level is greater than the elasticity of labour demand for the industry.

Short Run and Long Run Labour Demand Curve

The labour demand curve derived from Table 5.1 under the condition of fixed capital stock is a short run labour demand curve. When capital and labour are both variable inputs, then we can derive the long run demand curve for labour. Figure 5.14 presents two labour demand curves. D_{SR} is short run labour demand curve. An increase in the wage level from *W* to *W'* will lead to a fall in labour demand from *E* to E_{SR}. But in the long run, firms will have time to use capital to substitute labour. Hence, the fall in labour demand is greater from *E* to E_{SR}, indicating that the long run labour demand curve (D_{LR}) is more elastic than the short run labour demand curve (D_{SR}).

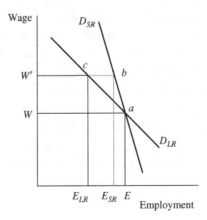

Figure 5.14: Short Run and Long Run Demand Curves for Labour

Elasticity of Labour Demand and Marshall's Rules of Derived Demand

The elasticity of labour demand is defined as percentage change in quantity demanded over percentage change in wages. As labour demand curve is downward sloping, the elasticity of labour demand is always negative. When wages rise, firms will use capital to substitute labour. The size of the substitution effect depends on the curvature of the isoquant. Elasticity of substitution is the greatest if the isoquant is a straight line.

Hence, according to Marshall's rules, if labour demand is more elastic, then greater will be the elasticity of substitution for labour. Furthermore, if capital can easily replace labour, and if supply of capital is more elastic, then labour demand is more elastic. If foreign labour can substitute local labour, then the local labour demand will be extremely elastic as the supply curve of foreign workers is unlimited (of course, the government would not open the flood gate).

Marshall's rules also state that labour demand is more elastic if product demand is more elastic, and if wage bill accounts for a bigger proportion of total cost of production, then labour demand is more elastic. We will use figures to explain these two Marshall's rules of labour demand.

In Figure 5.15, we have two product demand curves and the respective labour demand curves for Sectors 1 and 2. Labour demand curve for Sector 1 is more elastic because its product demand curve is more elastic. For the same wage level at F, the labour demand E is the same in both sectors. If the price rises from P to P' (due to reason rather than wage increase), then the fall in quantity demand is bigger for Sector 1 than for Sector 2. To produce less, we need less labour. Hence, D_{L1} will shift downward to cut g_1 while D_{L2} will shift downward to cut g_2. This explains why the labour demand curve for Sector 1 is more sensitive to price increase than that for Sector 2, and by the same argument, labour demand curve for Sector 1 is more sensitive to wage change. Suppose the wage has increased from W to W' in Figure 5.15(a), the fall in labour demand is bigger in Sector 1 than in Sector 2 (not shown in the figure). This is because, a wage increase will increase product price and reduce product demand more in Sector 1 than in Sector 2.

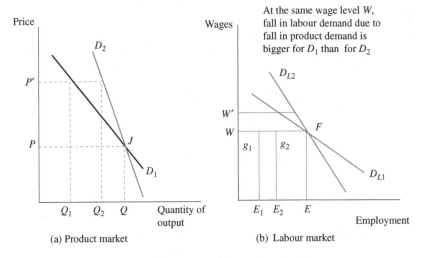

Figure 5.15:   Product Demand Curves and Labour Demand

Suppose in Figure 5.15, D_{L1} is the labour demand curve for a textile firm while D_{L2} is the labour demand curve for a government ministry. Suppose there is a wage increase in both the textile firm and the ministry. The textile firm will retrench workers because it has to raise the price of product from P to P'. For the ministry, there is little retrenchment because it might not have to raise the price of the services.

In Figure 5.16, we have two product demand curves, one for labour intensive industry and one for capital intensive industry and two respective labour demand curves. For the moment, we assume that the labour intensive industry will have more elastic labour demand curve. Suppose there is a wage increase from W to W'. For labour intensive firm, this will translate into bigger increase in price from P to P_{Lab} than from P to P_{Cap} because wage bill is a big proportion of total cost of production for the labour intensive industry. Hence, reduction in product demand is bigger for labour intensive industry than for capital intensive industry. This explains Marshall's rule 4 that if wage bill accounts for bigger proportion of total cost, the labour demand is more wage elastic, which support our assumption that the labour intensive industry will have more elastic labour demand curve.

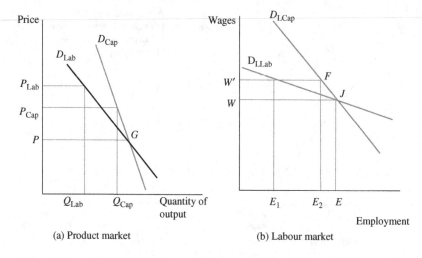

Figure 5.16:   Product Demand Curves and Labour Demand Curves

Labour Demand, Product Markets Structure and Product Output

Firms sell products in the products markets. The product markets are either competitive or monopolistic. Figure 5.17 shows that the demand curve for products facing a competitive firm is horizontal line at P, where $P = MR = AR$. A typical firm's labour demand curve is based on the VMP.

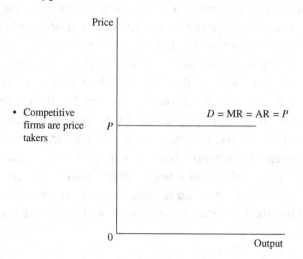

Figure 5.17:   Competitive Firms Face Horizontal Demand Curve for its Products

However, when product markets are monopolistic, firm faces a downward sloping demand curve for its product, as is shown in Figure 5.18. The firm sets the price, P. Hence, P is not constant. As the firm has to lower the price in order to sell more, its MR falls and at a given output level, $P > MR$. The firm's demand curve for labour is marginal revenue product (MRP) which is equal to MR. MP_E.

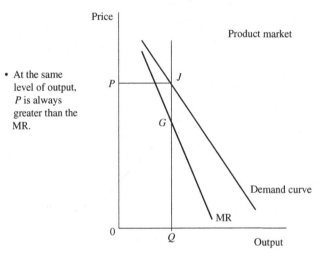

Figure 5.18: Downward Sloping Product Demand Curve

As is shown in Figure 5.19, VMP curve is always above MRP curve as P is always greater than MR in monopolistic product markets.

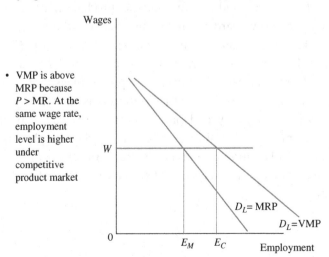

Figure 5.19: Two Labour Demand Curves Under Different Product Markets

If the labour demand curve in Figure 5.20 is for a country and the employment level is E, then the GDP of this country is area $0BAE$. The wage bill is area $0WJE$. The labour share of the GDP is $0WJE/0AJE$. If this is a labour demand curve for a firm, then output is area $0BAE$ and the firm's wage bill is $0WJE$. The firm uses VMP to pay its workers.

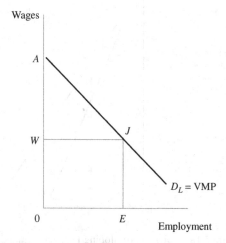

Figure 5.20:   Using Labour Demand Curve (VMP) to Measure Product Output

Consider a firm under monopolistic product market. This firm sells product on downward sloping demand curve where price is greater than MR. The firm's labour demand curve is based on MRP. For each point on MRP, there is a corresponding point on VMP as shown in Figure 5.21. In this case, the firm's output is measured using VMP. If employment level is E, the firm's output is area $0FG_E$. The firm will use MRP to employ and pay workers. The wage bill is $0WJE$. The firm surplus is area $WFGJ$. There is worker surplus as long as the labour supply curve is not horizontal. But the workers are still short-changed as the firm uses the MRP curve instead of VMP curve to pay them.

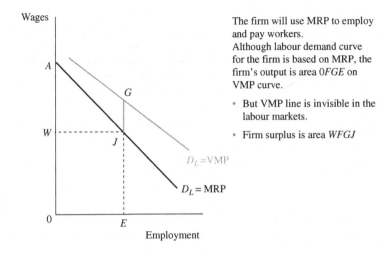

Figure 5.21: Labour Demand Curve for a Firm with Monopolistic Product Market

In other words, workers are short-changed when they work for monopolistic employers. This assertion seems to be counter intuitive because most jobseekers would like to work for monopolistic firms and not competitive firms as the former pays better. The fact of the matter is most jobseekers would like to work for firms with high VAP and firms with high VAP often sell products at high prices in monopolistic product markets. In Figure 5.22, the labour demand curve for a big firm is based on MRP. Hence, the wage rate of its workers is W_{BF} and the workers are short-changed by BG amount. The labour demand curve for a small firm is based on VMP and the wage rate of its workers is W_{SF}. This explains why people prefer to work for monopolistic firms because W_{BF} is greater than W_{SF}. However, as Figure 5.19 shows, employment effect of a monopolistic firm is smaller. Hence, most governments want to prevent creation of monopoly. In Singapore, we have Competition Law to encourage more competition in the product markets.

Most governments also want to promote small firms because as a group, they employ more workers than large firms.

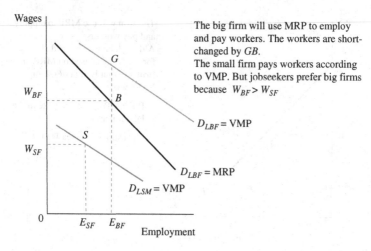

Figure 5.22:   Big Firm vs Small Firm

Labour Demand Curve, ULC and Income–Leisure Model

Given the labour demand curve, at each wage level, the firm will determine the number of workers based on $W = VMP$. Hence, at each point of the labour demand curve, ULC is equal to one. In Figure 5.23, we reproduce the income–leisure model. The firm offers the wage rate which is the slope of AT and John has chosen J as his equilibrium point. At J, to the firm, the ULC is equal to one. If John chose G due to institutional constraint, to the firm, the ULC is still equal to one at G. At any point on the AT budget line except T, the ULC is equal to one.

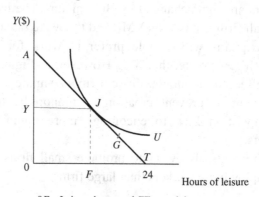

OF = Leisure hours and FT = work hours

Figure 5.23:   John's Equilibrium is J.

In this book, for a group of workers, ULC is measured as the ratio of total wage bill over total revenue. For the last worker employed where $W = \text{VMP}$, the ULC is of course measured as W/VMP.

Discussion Questions

1. If technology allows firms to substitute capital for labour at the fixed proportion, what is the shape of the isoquant curves?
2. If technology dictates that firms use capital and labour in fixed proportion, what is the shape of the isoquant curves?
3. When labour becomes more expensive, do isocost lines shift? How is cost outlay affected?
4. Is the demand for labour for textile industry elastic with regard to wages?

Bibliography

Borjas, G. J. (2013). *Labor Economics*, Seventh edition. New York: McGraw-Hill.
McConnell, C. R., Brue, S. L. and MacPherson, D. A. (2014). *Contemporary Labor Economics*, Nineth edition. New York: McGraw Hill/Irwin.

Chapter 6

Labour Markets and Public Policy

In Chapter 2, we derive market supply curve of labour and in Chapter 5, we derive market demand curve for labour. In this chapter, we show how the market wage rate is determined by market forces. We will also examine how public policy can affect market wages.

Competitive Labour Markets

As shown in Figure 6.1, the market demand curve for labour is D_L and the market supply curve for labour is S_L. This is a competitive labour market

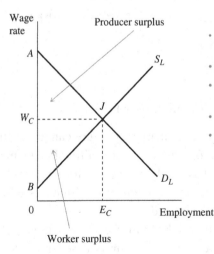

- Labour market in equilibrium at J when $S_L = D_L$
- Employment level is E_C
- All workers are paid the same wage rate, W_C
- Wage bill $= E_C$ times W_C
- Transfer earning is area OBJ E_C
  Competitive labour market is efficient because economic surpluses are maximized at J.

Figure 6.1:   Equilibrium in Competitive Labour Market

81

because there are many jobseekers, many employers and there is neither government intervention nor labour unions. J is the equilibrium point where labour demand curve meets labour supply curve. The market equilibrium wage is W_C and employment level is E_C. At J, there is no unemployment because those who want to seek work at W_C are able to find employment. Competitive labour market is efficient because economic surpluses which are the sum of firm surplus and worker surplus are maximized at J. The firm surplus is area AJW_C and the worker surplus is area $W_C JB$. Transfer earning is area $OBJE_C$.

If, for one reason or another, the employment level is E', then there is a decrease in both firm surplus and worker surplus as is shown in Figure 6.2. The total output would decrease by area $E'GJE_C$. But $E'FJE_C$ is transfer earning which is not a cost to society. The dead weight loss of having employment level at E' is area GJF.

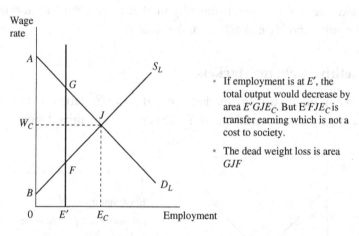

Figure 6.2:   Less than Optimal Level of Employment

As explained in Chapter 5, product market structure can affect firm's demand curve for labour. Figure 6.3 shows a competitive labour market with a competitive product market as the demand curve for labour is based on VMP. The competitive equilibrium point which is still at J is efficient as total economic surpluses are maximized.

Figure 6.4 shows a competitive labour market with a monopolistic product market as the demand curve for labour is based on MRP. As explained in Chapter 5, there is a VMP curve above the MRP curve but

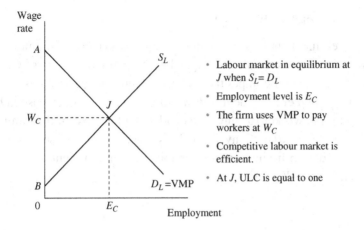

Figure 6.3: Equilibrium in Competitive Labour Market with Competitive Product Market

this curve is not visible in the labour market. It is obvious from Figure 6.4 that if we have started from a competitive product market, the competitive equilibrium point would be at F and the total output would be $0AFG$. But now, when we move to a monopolistic market, although the labour market is still competitive at J, the output will be reduced by area E_CKFG. Area E_CJFG is transfer earnings which is not the cost to society. The dead weight loss from the product market is thus area KFJ, although the labour market is competitive.

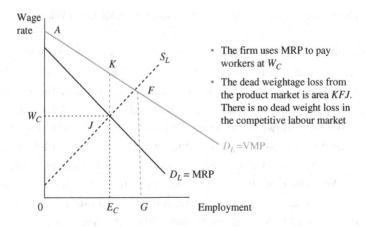

Figure 6.4: Equilibrium in Competitive Labour Market with Monopolistic Product Market

Minimum Wage Law (W_{min})

When government intervenes in the labour market via minimum wage rate, the labour market will no longer be competitive. In Figure 6.5, the labour market is non-competitive. The minimum wage law has pushed wages to W_{min} and employment is down to E_{min}. There is a decrease in both firm surplus and worker surplus. The dead weightage loss of the minimum wage law is area *FJG*. Many jobseekers spend resources searching for jobs at W_{min} due to limited number of jobs available. Potential loss from job search is area W_{min} *FGK*.

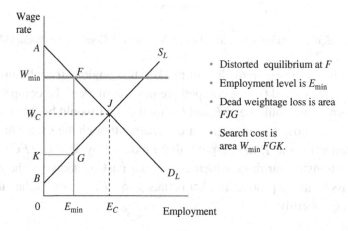

Figure 6.5:   Non-competitive Labour Market with Minimum Wage Law

Economists still debate about the effectiveness of minimum wage law. Opponents of minimum wage law argue that there is a strong trade-off between minimum wages and employment. Supporters of the minimum wage law argue that minimum wage law will shift the labour demand curve up for the following two reasons: Firstly, it will lead to higher productivity as it would work like efficiency wage, which we will examine in the chapter on incentive pay, and secondly, it will increase consumer spending. We will examine the second reasoning now. Table 6.1 shows that using US data, with each subsequent increase in minimum wage rate, the number of families benefited from the minimum wage rate has increased and the reported increase in consuming spending is greater too.

Table 6.1: Minimum Wage on Consumer Spending

Minimum wage in US$	Time of increase in min wage	Number of families benefited from min wage	Increase in consumer spending ($M)
5.85	2007	719,111	1,750
6.55	2008	1,284,191	3,125
7.25	2009	2,282,205	5,553
8.25	2010	5,114,280	17,777
9.50	2011	9,655,640	41,954

Source: Kai Filion (2009, p. 2).

Although the causality test was not performed to determine if the increase in consumer spending is due to the rise in minimum wages, the data did support the argument that minimum wages can lead to increase in consumer spending and therefore shifting the labour demand curve for labour. The trade-off between higher wage and employment may not be there.[1] Figure 6.6 shows that when minimum wage rate (W_{min1}) is imposed, the labour demand curve shifts upward to D_{L1} with a time lag of course. If this upward shift happens, then the negative impact of

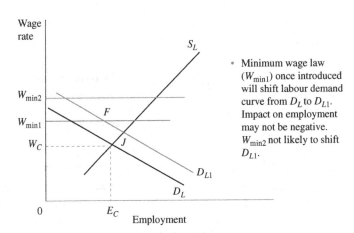

Figure 6.6: Minimum Wage Law Increases Consumer Spending and Shifts Labour Demand Curve Upward

---

[1]For more discussion, see Card and Krueger (1995).

minimum wage law is not big. However, it is reasonable to argue that further increase in min wage rate such as W_{min2} might not shift the labour demand curve. Minimum wage law is not a silver bullet as the unemployment rate is high in countries that rely on minimum wage law to protect the poor.

Payroll Taxes and Subsidies in the Labour Markets

Figure 6.7 shows that employers have to pay payroll tax. The original wage is W_0 and employment level is E_0. Now, firms have to pay payroll tax of t amount. The labour demand curve will shift down by the t amount to D_{L1}. The new labour market equilibrium point is C and workers' wage is now W_1. The wage cost to the firms is $W_1 + t$. Hence, workers' wage is reduced from W_0 to W_1 and firms' wage cost is increased from W_0 to $W_1 + t$. The message is clear. Although firms have to pay payroll tax, both the firms and the workers bear the cost of payroll tax. The distribution of the tax burden depends on the relative slopes of labour demand curve and labour supply curve. The tax revenue is area $ABCW_1$. The new employment level is E_1 which is lower than the competitive employment level, E_0. The dead weight loss is area BJC.

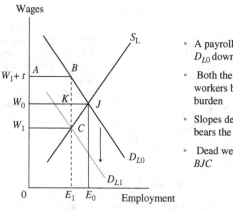

* A payroll tax of \$ t shifts D_{L0} down to D_{L1}

* Both the firms and workers bear the tax burden

* Slopes determine who bears the bigger burden

* Dead weight cost is area BJC

Figure 6.7:   Payroll Tax Assessed on Firms

Figure 6.8 considers a case where workers have to pay the payroll tax. Workers now are paid W_1 but after tax, their net wage is $W_1 - \$t$. Firms pay more and workers get less. It is the same result regardless of whether the payroll tax is assessed on firms or workers. This is because in both cases, we use the same labour demand and labour supply curves.

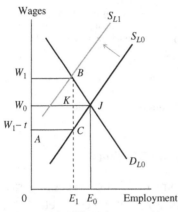

- A payroll tax of $\$t$ shifts S_{L0} up to S_{L1}
- Both the firms and workers bear the tax burden
- Slopes determine who bears the bigger burden
- Dead weight cost is area BJC

Labour supply shifts up because workers expect higher wages

Figure 6.8: Payroll Tax Assessed on Workers

Apart from payroll taxes, many countries also provide payroll subsidies to help low income workers and families. Payroll subsidy is wage subsidy. In Figure 6.9, payroll subsidy shifts the labour demand curve from D_{L0} to D_{L1}, as it is now cheaper to employ workers. Employers now pay W_1 but effective wage for the firms is $W_1 - S$. Employment level is higher with payroll subsidy. As the labour supply curve is not totally inelastic, the increase in wage from W_0 to W_1 is less than $\$S$ due to increase in employment. Economists frequently debate between minimum wage law and wage subsidy as an effective way to help low income workers. For minimum wage law, the government spending is nil but wage subsidy is costly. But if we take a longer perspective, those who are unemployed due to minimum wage law may cause spending on social welfare to increase in near future.

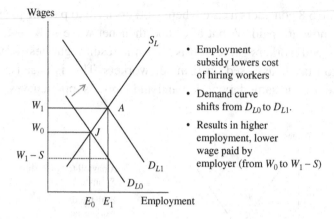

Figure 6.9:   Payroll Subsidies of $$S$ Amount

Mandated Benefits in the Labour Markets

Without government intervention, some firms offer wages to attract workers but workers are not protected against accident, illnesses, etc. If the government requires firms to legally provide healthcare and work safety insurance, this will increase the cost of employing workers. This kind of provision is known as mandated benefits. Mandated benefits will increase employment cost by $$m$ in the same way as payroll tax as is shown in Figure 6.10.

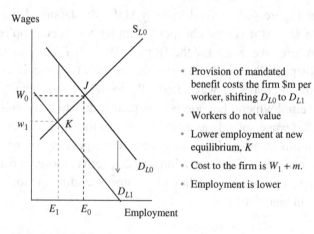

Figure 6.10:   Mandated Benefits but Workers Do Not Value

The impact on employment is the same as the payroll tax. The new equilibrium point is K. Firms pay W_1 in wages plus $m in mandated benefits. But there is a big difference between the two government actions. A main reason for imposing payroll tax is to raise government revenue. But mandated benefits are meant to correct a bad externality in the labour markets.

Workers who work on short term basis may not care about mandated benefits but workers who plan to work for 30 or more years do value mandated benefits. Figure 6.11 shows the situation where workers fully value mandated benefits which causes labour supply curve to shift down to the same extent as mandated benefits. Hence, both the labour demand curve and labour supply curve shift to the same extent. The employment level is the same. The composition of remuneration has changed. Earlier, without mandated benefits, total employment cost was W_0. With mandated benefits, total employment cost is still the same except it is the sum of $W_F + $m per worker.

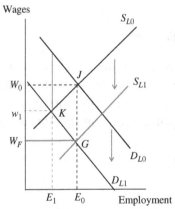

- Provision of mandated benefit costs the firm $m per worker, shifting D_{L0} to D_{L1}
- Labour supply curve will shift from S_{L0} to S_{L1} as workers fully value
- Same employment at new equilibrium, G
- Composition of remuneration has changed but total cost remains the same

Labour supply curve shifts down because workers substitute benefits for wages

Figure 6.11:   Mandated Benefits and Workers Fully Value

However, when workers value partially, then the labour supply curve will shift down but not as much as the labour demand curve shifted down. This outcome is illustrated in Figure 6.12. Hence, V is the new equilibrium point. The result is lower employment level compared to G. The policy implication is that when governments want to introduce any changes in

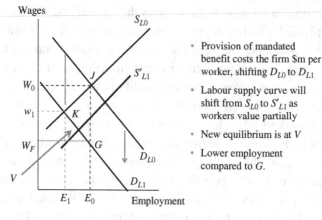

Figure 6.12:   Mandated Benefits but Workers Value Partially

the labour laws to benefit workers, it does pay to educate both workers and general public about the merit of government actions.

Regulated and Non-regulated Sectors

Suppose there are two sectors in an economy, the formal sector and informal sector. The formal sector is regulated and the informal sector is not regulated. Suppose again that the wages in the two sectors are the same as W^* as is shown in Figure 6.13. When government introduces minimum

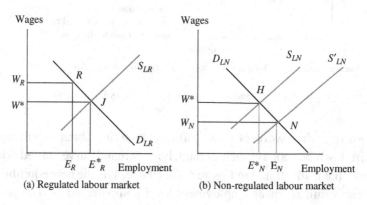

Figure 6.13:   Regulated and Non-regulated Sectors

wage law (and mandated benefits, etc.), in the regulated sector, we will move from J to R, reducing the level of employment to E_R. The unemployed will have to move to unregulated sector, causing the labour supply curve to shift to S'_{LN}. The equilibrium point in the unregulated sector will move from H to N. Now, there is a big wage gap between the two sectors. The new wage in the regulated sector is W_R and the new wage in the non-regulated sector is W_N.

Labour Mobility across the Labour Markets

Labour mobility can equalize wages across labour markets. In Figure 6.14, the wage (W_N) in Northern labour markets is higher than the wage (W_S) in Southern labour markets. Suppose the workers in the Southern labour markets can move to seek jobs in the Northern labour market freely without friction, then, the wages in the two labour markets will be equalized at W^*. In terms of GDP, Southern output would decrease by area *HKSV* but this is more than compensated by the increase in Northern output of area *GNJF* by area *NJM*. The increase in *NJM* can hardly please the workers in the northern labour markets. But if this process takes place gradually, it may not be a political issue.

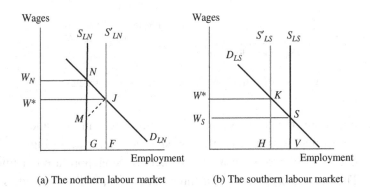

(a) The northern labour market   (b) The southern labour market

Figure 6.14: Competitive Equilibrium in Two Labour Markets Linked by Migration

However, if the above two labour markets are not regional markets but two national markets in the respective country, then the workers in the North country would not welcome the workers from the South country.

This is why capital mobility is a goal so easily achieved but it is not so with labour mobility across countries. The fact that workers in the UK resent migrants from Poland working in the UK in the early 2000s is a good example of resistance toward any degree of labour mobility in the European Union (EU). EU was not happy that Swiss voted to limited immigration in 2014 (S.T. 2014).

Figure 6.15 presents a simplistic case where natives and immigrants are perfect substitutes. In this case, the result is obvious. The labour supply curve of the country will shift down and wage for natives will fall to W_1. Hence, the natives suffer and immigrants benefit (or else the immigrants would not come). In this simplistic situation, no national government would dare to allow immigrants to live and work at the expense of local population.

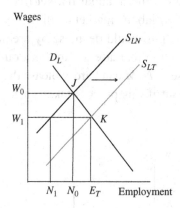

Assume: Immigrants and natives are perfect substitutes in production

• Immigrants enter labour market, shifts supply curve right
 – Total employment increases
 – Equilibrium wage decreases

• N_1 E_T immigrants

• Employment of native-born workers falls to N_1

Figure 6.15:   Immigrants and Natives are Substitutes

In Singapore, the local workforce is about two million and foreign workforce is about 1.4 million. But the situation depicted in Figure 6.15 did not occur in Singapore. Foreign workers in Singapore are not immigrants. They are guest workers in three categories, highly skilled, semi skilled and low skilled. For semi-skilled and low-skilled foreign workers, their employers have to pay foreign worker levy per month. Hence, the levy increases the cost of employing guest workers. Figure 6.16 shows that without guest workers, the equilibrium point is J for Singapore.

Allowing guest workers, the total labour supply curve is now S_{LT}. But guest workers are brought in to attract foreign investment, shifting the labour demand curve to D_{L1}. The new wage for Singaporean workers is W_1. The unskilled guest workers are paid according to their horizontal labour supply curve at W_F. The foreign worker levy is equal to KG. There is no worker surplus for guest workers. One may argue that the supply curve of guest workers in their home country may not be horizontal. If their supply curve has a positive slope, the worker surplus would be captured by employment agents.

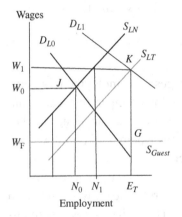

- More investment due to guest workers; labour demand curve will shift right to D_{L1}

- Market wage is W_1
- $N_1 E_1$ = No of guest workers in Singapore

- Employment of singaporeans rises to N_1

- Supply curve of guest workers from home country is S_{Guest}

- Levy = $KG = W_1$-W_F

Figure 6.16:   Foreign Workers in Singapore

The Cobweb Model

Figure 6.17 shows a typical labour market for engineers. The initial equilibrium point is A with the equilibrium wage and employment level being W_0 and E_0, respectively. Suppose the demand for engineers has increased, shifting the labour demand curve to D_{L1}. The new equilibrium point is J. Comparing J to A, we conclude that the wage and employment levels of engineers have both increased. This is Comparative Statics Analysis. We compare the results of two equilibrium points. We do not analyze how the labour market would move from A to J. In other words, we are not interested in the interim path from A to J.

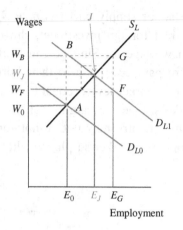

- With new labour demand curve at D_{L1}, we move from A to B, causing wage to rise to W_B.

- Next, we move from B to G, causing increase in labour supply to E_G which brings down wages via F to W_F

- Wage and employment levels fluctuate around W_J and E_J interactively and respectively

- Finally back to J

- Comparative statics analysis is still useful.

Figure 6.17:   The Cobweb Model

However, we do observe that wages and employment of certain occupations such as engineers fluctuate a lot. Comparative statics analysis of course would not be able to explain this phenomenon, but the cobweb model can, e.g., for certain occupations where it takes a few years to train a specialist, in this case, an engineer.

The Cobweb model implies that we cannot move from A to J immediately as it takes time to train engineers. Instead, we move from A to B, holding supply of engineers constant. This will cause wages to raise to W_B. With higher wages, the supply of engineers has increased to E_G via G. With higher labour supply, the wage will fall from W_B to W_F via F. With lower wages, employment will decrease from E_C to E_1 (not shown in the figure). During this interim process, we observe that wages and employment fluctuate around W_J and E_J, respectively in an interactive manner. In the final analysis, from start to finish, we move from A to J which is the conclusion of comparative static analysis.

The Cobweb model does produce some interesting inferences. This model assumes that people in general are misinformed about labour market changes in the near future. In other words, economic agents do not form rational expectations. Rational expectations are formed if economic agents correctly perceive the future and understand the market forces at work.

Discussion Questions

1. Use Figure 6.2 to show the area of dead weight loss if employment level exceeds *E*.
2. A monopolistic firm has the incentive and resources to shift the demand curve upward for its product. Use a figure similar to Figure 6.4 to show that the new monopolistic VMP curve can be higher than the old VMP curve in the labour market.
3. Use a figure to show whether firms or workers pay more payroll taxes if labour demand curve is totally inelastic.
4. Use a figure to show that wages and employment levels may not converge if the absolute value of the slope of demand curve is one and the slope of the supply of labour is also equal to one.

Bibliography

Borjas, G. J. (2013). *Labor Economics*, Seventh edition. New York: McGraw-Hill.

Card, D. and Krueger, A. B. (1995). *The New Economics of the Minimum Wage*. New Jersey: Princeton University Press.

Filion, K. (2009). Increases in minimum wage boost consumer spending, Economic Snapshot, May 27, 2009. Available at http://www.epi.org/publication/snapshot_20090527/.

McConnell, C. R., Brue, S. L. and Macpherson, D. A. (2014). *Contemporary Labor Economics*, Nineth edition. New York: McGraw Hill/Irwin.

Parkin, M. (2014). *Economics*, Eleventh edition. Boston: Pearson.

Straits Times (2014). "EU is furious at Swiss vote on immigration quotas", Page A4, 20/02/2014.

Chapter 7

Monopsony in the Labour Markets

In Chapter 6, we examine government actions in situations where there are many buyers and sellers of labour services in the labour markets. In this chapter, we discuss how market forces work when there is only one buyer of labour services (monopsony) in the labour market. We examine two cases, one when the monopsonist has discriminating power and another case without discriminating power. In order to appreciate the economics of monopsony, we will first examine the notion of consumer surplus.

Consumer Surplus

Figure 7.1 presents a demand curve for pizza for a typical consumer, John. He is prepared to pay $4 for a slice of pizza and he is prepared to pay $3.5 for a second slice of pizza, etc. Suppose we have a monopolist in selling pizza and suppose he knows John's preferences for pizza. He could sell $4 to John for the first slice, then $3.5 for second slice and so on. If John bought six slices, his total expense which is the sum of $4, $3.5, $3, $2.5, $2, $1.5 and $1 is the area under the demand curve. The last price he paid is $1 per slice. He is known as a perfectly discriminating monopolist in this situation, which seldom happens in the real life. In a normal situation, the monopolist can only charge one price, say $1 per slice. Then, John would pay $6 for the six slices. In this case, John's consumer surplus is the sum of $3, $2.5, $2, $1.5, $1 and $0.5. In other words, when there is only one price for the product, the area between the demand curve and the price line is consumer surplus (similar to firm's surplus in Chapter 5).

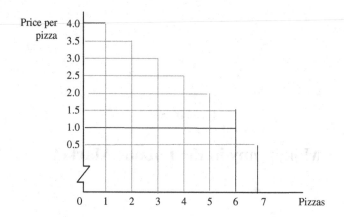

Figure 7.1:   Demand Curve for Pizzas

Competitive Labour Market with Competitive Product Market Revisited

Before we discuss the situation involving monopsony in the labour market, let us consider a competitive labour market. In Figure 7.2, given the labour supply curve (S_L) and labour demand curve (VMP = D_L), the equilibrium point is J. The equilibrium wage is W_{20} and there are 20 workers employed (E_{20}). The worker surplus is $W_{20}JW_R$. Note that the product market is competitive and there is a single wage in the labour markets.

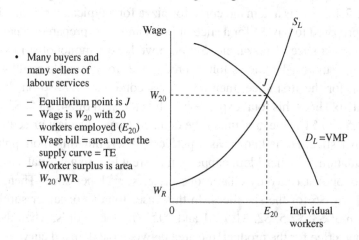

Figure 7.2:   Competitive Labour Market

Perfectly Discriminating Monopsony with Competitive Product Market

In Chapter 2, we defined the meaning of a labour supply curve in terms of minimum wage that each individual worker would demand (see Figure 2.15). Suppose we have a monopsonist in the labour market and he knows the minimum wage that each worker is willing to work for. In other words, he knows the labour supply curve as is shown in Figure 7.3. Hence, he would pay W_{IM1} for the first person (Per$_1$), W_{IM2} for the second person and W_{IM3} for the third person. If he has hired one more worker, he has to pay higher wage. Each new wage is his marginal cost of employing (MC$_E$) an extra worker. In other words, the labour supply (S_L) becomes his marginal labour cost curve MC$_E$. Given the labour demand curve which is based on VMP (we will consider monopolistic product market later), the equilibrium point is J based on equality of MC$_E$ and VMP. The last worker employed is the 20th person. The last wage is W_{IM20}. Hence, using the last wage, the wage level and the employment level are the same as in competitive labour market but there is no worker surplus in perfectly discriminating monopsony.

- Hires different workers at different wage rates

  - Each worker is paid his individual min wage, (W_{IM})
  - Labour supply curve is also MC$_E$ curve
  - Note: MC$_E$ here refers to MC of employment, not MC of production
  - Wage bill = area under the supply curve = TE
  - No worker surplus

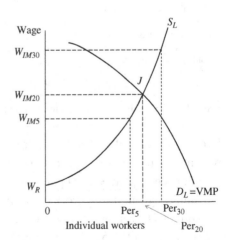

Figure 7.3: The Perfectly Discriminating Monopsonist with Competitive Product Market

Non-discriminating Monopsony with Competitive Product Market

A non-discriminating monopsonist is expected to pay all workers the same wage rate. Consider the Ministry of Defence as a non-discriminating monopsony. As is shown in Figure 7.4, the Ministry first employs 20 soldiers. Each of the soldiers is paid the same wage W_0 at G. Suppose the Ministry wants to employ 10 more soldiers. The Ministry needs to pay W_1 to each of the 10 new soldiers at J. The Ministry, however, cannot stay on the labour supply curve at J. As the Ministry is a monopsony, it also has to raise the pay of the first 20 soldiers. Hence, the marginal cost of employing an extra soldier is not W_1 but $W_1 + (W_1 - W_0)$ which is MC_E. Hence, the Ministry is now not at J but K on the MC_E curve.

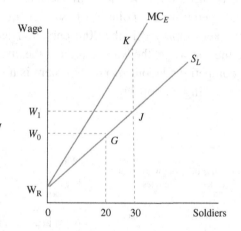

- Ministry of defence is a non-discriminating monopsony.
- To employ 20 soldiers, the Ministry needs to pay W_0 at G.
- To increase no of soldiers to 30, it needs to pay W_1 at J The ministry needs to pay not only W_1 for extra 10 soldiers but also needs to pay W_1 for the first 20 soldiers; hence, the $MC_E= W_1 + (W_1-W_0)$; $MC_E >W_1$

Figure 7.4:   A Non-discriminating Monopsony Pays Same Wages to all Workers

We can use the following example to show why marginal cost of employment is greater than the prevailing wage. Suppose we have 15 workers and each is paid $1,000 per month. The wage bill is $15,000 per month. To employ one more worker, we need to pay $1,300 per month. The wage bill of 16 workers is $15,000 + $1,300 + ($300 x 15) = $20,800. Hence, $MC_E = 20,800 - 15,000 = $5,800 which is greater than $1,300.

Figure 7.5 shows the decision making process of a non-discriminating monopsony with competitive product market. The market labour supply is S_L with the corresponding MC_E curve. The labour demand curve is based on VMP. The monopsonist will maximize profit at F where VMP = MC_E. At F, the monopsonist will employ E_M workers. The monopsonist will pay workers according to the labour supply curve at Z. Accordingly, all workers are paid a wage of W_M. Compared to competitive labour market outcome, the monopsonist employs fewer workers and pays workers below their VMP. The gap (FZ) between VMP and wages is known as labour exploitation in the labour market.

- The monopsonist maximizes profit at F and uses VMP_E to pay workers at Z on labour supply curve. Workers' VMP is FE_m. But workers are paid . Hence, workers are exploited by FZ.

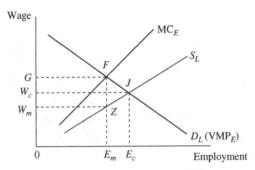

Figure 7.5: The Non-discriminating Monopsony with Competitive Product Market

Figure 7.6 shows almost similar outcome of a non-discriminating monopsony but with monopolistic product market. Note that the labour demand curve is based on MRP. Similarly, the monopsonist will maximize profit at F where MRP = MC_E. At F, the monopsonist will employ E_M workers. The monopsonist will pay workers according to the labour supply curve at Z. Accordingly, all workers are paid a wage of W_M. Again, this wage is lower than MRP. This gap (FZ) is known as labour exploitation in the labour market. As mentioned in the earlier chapters, there is one to one correspondence between VMP and MRP curves. Although VMP curve is not visible in the labour market, we can still conclude that workers' effort should be assessed based on VMP. Hence, VF represents labour exploitation in the product market. Due to monopsony, output has decreased by $E_M VQE_Q$. TR is equal to area $E_M ZQE_Q$ and hence the dead weight loss is area ZVQ.

- The monopsonist maximizes profit at F and uses MRP_E to pay workers at Z on labour supply curve. Workers' VMP = VE_m. As workers are paid W_m, workers are short-changed by VZ. VF is labour exploitation in the product market. FZ is labour exploitation in labour market. Q is the equilibrium point if product market were to be competitive. Dead weight loss to society is area ZVQ.

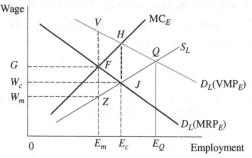

Figure 7.6:   The Non-discriminating Monopsony with Monopolistic Product Market

Under monopsony, workers suffer in terms of lower wages and employment. But we can remedy this distortion by imposing minimum wage law. Figure 7.7 shows how minimum wage law can change labour supply curve and therefore E_M curve. The minimum wage law in the form of W_{Min}, does not allow wages to fall below this level. Hence the wage is constant till J on the labour supply curve. When the wage is constant, MC_E is also constant. Hence, the new labour supply curve is $W_{Min}\, GS_L$. The new MC_E curve is W_{Min} $GKMC_E$. Note that we have a competitive product market in Figure 7.7.

- To introduce a min wage law (W_{Min}) and therefore alter the labour supply curve to $W_{Min}\, GS_L$; new MC_E curve is now the dotted line, W_{Min} GK MC_E

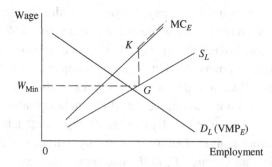

Figure 7.7:   Government Minimum Wage Law on Labour Supply Under Monopsony

Figure 7.8 shows how monopsony works within the constraint of W_{Min}. The monopsonist will maximize profit at F where VMP = MC_E. The employment level is at E_{Min}. The wage which is W_{Min}, is the same as VMP via F. Hence, there is no labour exploitation in the labour market.

- Monopsonist maximizes profit at F where VMP = MC_E.
- Employment level is E_{Min}.
- There is no labour exploitation in the labour market

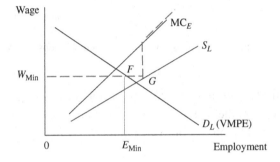

Figure 7.8: Government Minimum Wage Law and Monopsony with Competitive Product Market

It is counter intuitive to think that monopsonist sells in competitive market. Hence, Figure 7.9 shows that the labour demand curve is based on MRP. The profit maximizing equilibrium point is still F. There is no labour exploitation in the labour market but there is still labour exploitation (VF) in product market. The policy implication is intuitive as minimum wage law is a labour market instrument and it can be effective only in the labour market and not in the product market. If one wants to remove labour exploitation in the product market, we need instruments in the product markets. We need laws to ban formation of big monopolies.

- Monopsonist maximizes profit at F where MRP $=$ MC$_E$.
- Employment level is E_{Min}. There is no labour exploitation in labour market
- There is still labour exploitation (VF) in the product market

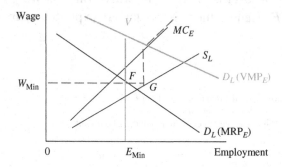

Figure 7.9: Government Minimum Wage Law and Monopsony with Monopolistic Product Market

Government minimum wage law is not the only factor that affects labour market. Another active factor in the labour market is labour unions. We will examine labour unions in Chapter 9.

Discussion Questions

1. Given an upward-sloped labour supply curve of $E = 20w - 120$ where E is the number of workers hired each hour and w is the hourly wage rate, find total wage bill and marginal cost of employment curve.
2. The daily inverse demand curve for toy is: $P = 20 - 0.1Q$ where P is the price per toy and Q is the number of toys each day. Find the equation for marginal revenue.
3. If a worker produces 5 units of output per hour, what is the marginal product of labour?
4. Discuss in what context you need to know marginal cost of employment, marginal product of labour and marginal revenue?

Bibliography

Borjas, G. J. (2013). *Labor Economics*, Seventh edition. New York: McGraw-Hill.

Ehrenberg, R. G. and Smith, R. S. (2003). *Modern Labor Economics*. Boston: Addison Wesley.

McConnell, C. R., Brue, S. L. and Macpherson, D. A. (2006). *Contemporary Labor Economics*, Seventh edition. New York: McGraw-Hill.

Chapter 8

Wages and Incentive Pay

Throughout much of this book, we assume that every agreement in the labour market will be honoured. For instance, in the competitive labour market, the equilibrium wage and employment are W_C and E_C respectively as shown in Figure 6.3 of Chapter 6. Workers will get paid W_C and each worker will produce VMP according to the figure. In other words, no one shirks the work duties. This means that the unit labour cost (ULC) is always equal to one at J. However, some employees do put in less effort than they are supposed to if they know they would not be caught. This problem of shirking will lead to a rise in value of ULC.

This uncertainty about whether an employee will give his best effort is caused by three factors, namely, asymmetric information, principal-agent problem and the cost of monitoring workers. We can use asymmetric information to explain recruitment dynamics in the sense that employers do not know with certainty whether a particular jobseeker will be a good employee until he is employed. Principal-agent problem on the other hand describes a situation where a firm employs a CEO but the interest of the CEO may not be aligned with the interest of the firm and if they are not aligned, the firm would only know when the damage emerges months or years later. Both asymmetric information and principal-agent problem are not a problem in the labour market if employer has zero cost in monitoring the performance of his workers.

For instance, a house owner wants to engage a painter to paint his house. He faces two options: Option 1 is to pay the painter X per hour for painting the house and watch him work or use CCTV to monitor his performance. The cost of monitoring is high and few painters would like this arrangement. Option 2 is to pay him an agreed amount when the painting is done subject to quality assurance. Option 1 is time rate while option 2 is piece rate. The choice in this case is, of course, piece rate. In this chapter, we will examine the rationale for time rate, piece rate, bonus and stock options, etc.

A Variety of Payments System

In time rate, as the term implies, employees are paid per week or per month. Most full time employees if not all, are paid time rate. All full time rate employees will be appraised by the respective superiors or supervisors. If they exceed the thresholds of key performance indicators (KPI), the monthly wages will be increased by an increment or two increments. Many firms also give bonus based on individual performance or team performance or firm performance. A two months' bonus means the employee will be given two extra months of pay, in addition to the monthly salary.

Piece rate means workers are paid based on output produced. In Singapore, it is common to engage tutors for private tuition for students in the primary and secondary schools. Tutors are paid piece rate. Many self-employed people are paid on piece rate too in the sense that, when their projects are successfully accepted, they are paid by the firm who contracted them to do the work.

Insurance agents are paid a combination of time rate and piece rate. Normally, insurance agents are paid a low time rate and they have to work hard to get sales so that they can earn commissions based on the sales value or volume. University professors in research intensive universities are also paid a combination of time rate and piece rate. All of them receive monthly salary. If they teach well based on teaching evaluation from students and especially publish in top journals, they get promoted and are placed on higher monthly salary. The cost of monitoring performance in these two occupations is almost zero.

Many listed firms use stock options to align the interest of the top executives to the interest of the firm. Stock options mean that a top executive is given a number of shares of the listed firm. The top executive is not allowed to sell the shares until a few years later. The CEO therefore is fully aware that his current decisions can affect his future earnings as the future share price of the listed firm would depend on his current performance. Hence, the stock options can induce good behaviour on the part of the top executives of the listed firms.

Stock option is a form of profit sharing. Most firms have informal profit sharing in the sense that if the firm does well, the employees will get a bonus ranging from one month of salary to a few months.

Work Effort and Payments Systems

When a worker is paid by piece rate, his earning is $Y = r$ times q where r is rate per unit of q and q is quantity of output. Hence, when a worker completes one unit of output, he will be paid $\$r$ per unit. Marginal revenue of his effort is MR = $\$r$. From Chapter 2, we know that leisure will generate utility and work will generate disutility. Marginal cost of effort, labelled as MC, is assumed to be upward sloping. In Figure 8.1, John's equilibrium is represented by J. Hence, John will produce five units per period. Mike's MC line is lower and hence, Mike will produce more than John.

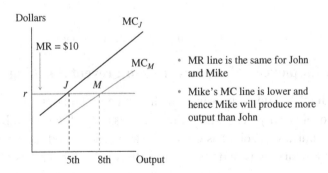

Figure 8.1: Allocation of Effort by Piece-Rate Workers

In Figure 8.2, we show two firms, Firm A pays workers on time rate while Firm B pays workers on piece rate. Workers of Firm A have a wage profile of W while workers of Firm B have an earning profile of Y. Y is equal to $\$r$ times Q. Time rate workers will allocate acceptable effort as long as they can maintain the jobs. Piece rate workers will give maximum effort to earn more money (how much more is already explained in Figure 8.1). Hence, there is incentive to work harder under piece rate. Workers who turn out to be more productive are more likely to choose to work for Firm *B* while workers who turn out to be less productive will choose to work for Firm *A*. The distribution of workers between the two firms is not random but based on utility maximization. This is sorting effect as workers vote with their feet. If Firm *B* decides to raise $r to a higher level, the *Y* line will shift upward and Firm *B* will get more good workers at the expense of Firm *A*.

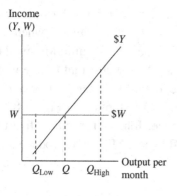

- Firm *A* pays workers on fixed wages per month. The wage profile is *W*

- Firm *B* pays workers on piece rate. The earning profile is *Y* which is equal to $r times *Q*. Workers who can produce more than *Q* per month will choose Firm *B*

- Less productive workers will choose Firm *A*

- Self-selection of workers between time-rate jobs and piece-rate jobs is known as sorting effect

Figure 8.2:   The Sorting of Workers Across Firms

Why an Employee Shirks and How to Prevent Shirking

Suppose John is paid daily wages (it should be monthly but our income–leisure model is daily). His equilibrium point is at *J* in Figure 8.3. Based on utility maximization, John has chosen *J*. He is paid Y_1 and rests on U_1. He will work 8 hours a day and put his best effort in each hour. His employer is happy as the ULC is equal to one. However, John has an incentive to shirk as he can move from U_1 to U_2. So, his VMP will fall and it is a matter of time that his employer will find out. Most employers want a trouble free arrangement. John's employer can promise to pay John an income of Y_2. If John is caught at *K*, his employer will not lose as his ULC is still equal to one. If John is at *J* as he promised, John's earnings will be Y_2 + bonus. The bonus is $Y_1 - Y_2$. John's ULC to his employer is still equal to one.

- John chose J and works 8 hours, $TF_1 = 8$
- His daily income is Y_1 with utility U_1
- Given Y_1, if John puts in less effort in his work, he can move from J to K and move to a higher indifference curve.
- Hence, there is incentive for John to shirk
- Overcome incentive problem by paying John Y_2 in the first instance. If John is at J in terms of full effort, his earning will be $Y_2 +$ bonus. The bonus is $Y_1 - Y_2$

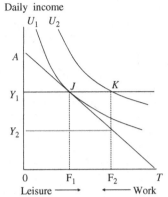

Figure 8.3: Salary Plus Bonus

In this chapter, we will examine various ways whereby employers can ensure that ULC is equal to one.

Efficiency Wage

In some poor countries, workers are dirt cheap. The competitive market wage level is the subsistence wage. Workers paid at this wage can barely support themselves. It is a wage that can barely buy food on the daily basis. To the firms, the ULC of employing these cheap workers is equal to one individually. This is because, although wages are low, VMP is low due to poor nutritious diet which affects ability to focus, learn, etc. This is a low wage trap.

It has been observed that some firms (not all the firms) pay workers at the wage of W_E, which is above the competitive market wage (see Figure 8.4). W_E is known as efficiency wage. There is excess labour supply at the efficiency wage level. What is the rationale of these firms paying workers at the efficiency wage as this would lead to ULC being above the value of one? According to efficiency wage theory, the VMP of the workers will increase, shifting the labour demand curve upward from D_L to D'_L. The employment level is E_E which is likely to be less than E_C. The ULC of these workers getting paid at the efficiency wage will therefore be still equal to one because $W = $ VMP on the new demand curve.

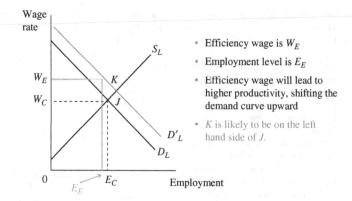

Figure 8.4:   Efficiency Wage

The upward shift of the labour demand curve is explained in terms of the following reasoning:

(i)   The increase in wages will improve the diet and hence their ability to learn and focus will improve.

(ii) These workers realize that at the efficiency wage, there is excess labour supply. These workers, if they do not work hard, can be replaced immediately and the pay of the alternative job is the market wage. This argument is valid if the cost of monitoring workers is very high. As we will examine other methods later in this chapter, paying efficiency wage may not be the cheapest method of inducing workers to work hard.

(iii) The firms which pay efficiency wage can select better quality workers from the pool of jobseekers.

(iv) The firms are likely to experience lower labour turnover and hence reduce disruption in operation and save in training cost.

These rationales for paying efficiency wage apply to developed countries too except perhaps the diet argument. We shall now examine how to determine efficiency wage level. The basic idea of efficiency wage is that the relation between output and wage is not only positive but non-linear. Suppose a firm pays its workers at $10 an hour and each worker produces 10 units of output. If the firm raises the wages from $10 to $13 per hour and the output of each worker is now 15 units of output per hour the firms'

ULC will decrease because the pay increase is only 30% but output increase is 50%. Hence, the firm should keep increasing wages till percentage increase in wages is equal to percentage increase in output. Figure 8.5 shows that the product curve (TP) between output and wage level is non-linear. At low wage level, output increase is responsive to rising wage level. Beyond G, large output growth can only be motivated by high wage growth. Beyond F, high wage growth can only lead to small growth in output increase. The slope on each point on the TP curve is the marginal product of wages (MP). MP will increase till G and beyond G, MP will decrease and is equal to zero at K. The slope of OH line represents average product of wages. If we move from O to G to F, the average product of wages (AP) rises and beyond G, AP of wages decreases. At F, MP = AP. When firm raises wages from W_1 to W_2, MP > AP, implying that percentage increase in output is greater than percentage increase in wages. The firm should keep increasing wages till F where percentage increase in output is equal to percentage increase in wages, i.e. MP = AP. If the firm keeps increasing wages beyond F, AP > MP, the firm's ULC will be higher. The wage level at F is known as efficiency wage, W_E, as the elasticity of output with respect to wage $(\%\Delta Q/\%\Delta W) = 1$. It is common to observe that firms pay different efficiency wages because each firm will have its own TP curve. It is possible that both firms pay the same level of efficiency but they have different levels of Q_E. We will examine how efficiency wage can influence involuntary unemployment in the chapter on unemployment.

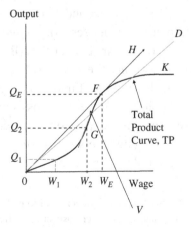

- TP curve shows how firm's output depends on wage paid by firm to workers
- Slope at G = gradient at G = Marginal Product (MP) of wages
- Hence, MP changes as we move up the curve
- Slope of OD at V = Average Product (AP) of wages at V,
- Slope of OH at F = AP of wages
- At G, MP of wages > AP of wages
- At F, MP = AP
- At G, we increase wages till F where MP = AP
  The wage at F is Efficiency Wage (W_E)

Figure 8.5:   The Determination of Efficiency Wage (W_E)

Efficiency Wages and Dual Labour Markets[1]

Efficiency wage theory can be applied to the whole economy and also to big firms. Suppose there are two sectors in an economy. Sector 1 may consist of professionals whose output cannot be easily measured and the cost of monitoring is high.[2] In this case, employers of Sector 1 may pay efficiency wage to elicit the right effort from these professionals. On the other hand, Sector 2 consists of workers performing repetitive and monotonous jobs and the cost of monitoring is low. In this case, firms need not pay good wages to discouraging workers from shirking. Hence, there exist dual labour markets in the economy.

Similarly, for a big firm, due to asymmetric information, the trusted employees are insiders who receive high wages and are recipients of firm sponsored training activities. On the other hand, the outsiders are dispensable. Generally, new employees are outsiders and there is probation requirement for new employees before they are given more permanent employment contracts.

Seniority-based Wage System

Due to traditions and perhaps inertia, many firms pay workers according to seniority. Hence, older workers will receive higher wages. There is no vicious competition among workers. More experienced workers are more eager to teach younger workers. Figure 8.6 shows such a seniority-based wage system. Workers, say, start working at age 25 and retire from the firm at age 62. Of course, there is no pension under seniority-based system. The AB curve is known as the wage curve. Area under the AB curve (*OABG*) is equal to total wages over the working life with this firm. The seniority-based wage system has some limitations. Firstly, the age of worker may not be the same as the VMP, implying there is cross subsidy among workers which may not have a positive impact on work effort. Secondly, there is no mechanism whereby employers can reduce wage costs if there is a recession. In this case, employers have to retrench some

---

[1]This is also known as Internal Labour Market Theory. See Doeringer and Piore (1971).
[2]We will explore cost of monitoring when we examine the macro aspects of efficiency wage theory later in the book.

workers if there is a negative demand shock. Furthermore, under senior-ity-based wage system, employers would likely not employ those workers reaching retirement age.

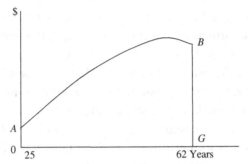

Retirement age is 62. There is no pension from the government

Figure 8.6: Seniority-Based Wage System

How about ULC of workers under seniority-based wage system? To answer this question, we have to bring in VMP. In Figure 8.7, the *CD* line represents the VMP of workers annually (we assume that VMP increases each yearly at the same rate. How should the firm pay the worker? One way is to pay each worker according to his VMP. However, because of the three factors mentioned earlier in this chapter, namely, asymmetric infor-mation, principal-agent problem and the cost of monitoring workers, the firm is likely to pay workers according to the *AB* line.

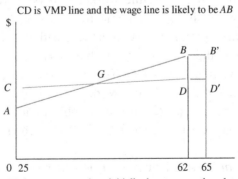

Underpay new workers initially than overpay them later

Figure 8.7: Given VMP Line, What is the Wage Line?

In other words, the firm pays a worker below his VMP initially but promises to pay a worker above VMP after *G*. In this case, the area under the *CD* line is the same under the *AB* line. Paying worker less than his VMP is also known as delayed compensation. If the worker cannot deliver as he promised, to the firm, the ULC is not too high. If the worker leaves the firm after working a few years, the firm will not suffer as the excess of VMP over wages of this worker can be used to train new workers. On the other hand, the workers will work hard as they know that they are being exploited for the time being but the hard work will be rewarded later. Hence, efficiency wage may not be more superior than delayed compensation. If the worker stays with the firm for his entire working life, the ULC is low in the beginning and rises to the value of one at *G* and then ULC will start rising. Note that area *ACG* is equal to area *GBD*. To the firm, taking into account the worker's entire working life, ULC is equal to one. Any increase in the retirement age from 62 to 65 will upset the firm because area *GB'D'* is now greater than area *ACG*. The firm will not object raising the retirement age if the firm is allowed to pay workers according to *DD'* line.

Flexible Wage System

Flexible wage system describes a wage system where worker is paid a relatively low fixed wage component. If the worker works hard, and if the firm makes lots of money, the worker will be rewarded a bonus. Flexible wage system is more suitable for firms in the private sector where prices of their products vary in tandem with business cycles. The VMP of workers is therefore subject to business cycles as is shown in Figure 8.8. The VMP curve is *CD*. The *AB* curve represents the fixed wage component. For instance, the worker is now 42 years. His fixed wage component is *GJ* and *GF* is the variable bonus component. His total earning for the year is *JF*. The ULC is always equal to one for each worker annually.

Wilkinson *et al.* (2015) argue that it is better to reward groups than individuals. They found that group rewards can produce more cooperative, better performing groups and also better performing individuals than

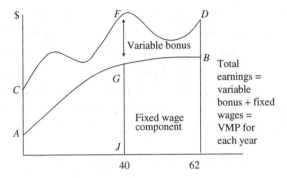

When workers do well, pay them bonus.
So, CFD can be endogenous

Figure 8.8: Flexible Wage System

individual-based reward systems. Of course, when we reward the groups, we worry about free riders. They argue that all are not free riders. Many poor performers are actually self-sacrificers. Hence, if we want to reward groups, we have to improve the appraisal system. In Singapore, as we will examine later in the book, bonus is given to both groups and to individuals.

The difference between efficiency wage and flexible wage is subtle. If the firm is conservative, it will prefer flexible wage system. You show me the result and then I reward you. For efficiency wage, the firm is an optimist. The firm trusts you and the firm gives you a raise and you work hard to earn it. In the final equilibrium, both efficiency wage and flexible wage may bring the same results.

Flexible wage system may be better than seniority-based wage system for the following reasons: if the age of retirement is raised, the firm under flexible wage system will be indifferent. If older workers cannot perform, they will be paid only fixed wage component but no bonus. ULC is still equal to one. When there is a recession, firms under seniority-based wage system will have to retrench some workers as they cannot reduce wage costs. But firms under flexible wage system can reduce wage costs by not giving bonuses.

Suppose John works under seniority-based wage system for some years already but the firm decides to move him from seniority-based wage system to flexible wage system. Is the migration of seniority-based wage system to flexible wage system hassle free? Consider that John has worked for this firm for 10 years as John is at A' in Figure 8.9. He is now aged 35. He has been underpaid by area $ACC'A'$. If the firm wants to move him to a new wage system, the firm has to give him back the delayed compensation amount. If John is now aged 50, then he has the right to demand compensation of area $D'B'BD$. He will get nothing, of course, if he resigns at his own initiative.

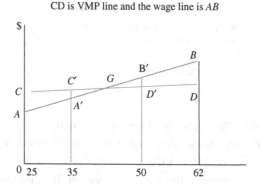

CD is VMP line and the wage line is AB

Figure 8.9:   Undo Delayed Compensation

Suppose John's wage is $1,000 a month and his boss plans to increase his wages by $200. But the firm can place him under the flexible wage system by giving him a raise of $50 in the basic salary and give him a year-end bonus of $150 times 12 = $1,800. Next year, if the firm does not do well or John's performance is below par, John will not get any bonus. John is being disadvantaged by the adoption of the flexible wage system. The good news is, under flexible wage system, John is less likely to get retrenched if the firm does not do well.

Monthly Variable Component Wage System

Flexible wage system is superior to seniority-based wage system but it still has a main limitation. If there is a negative demand shock, the government may want all firms to trim wage costs immediately so that employment level can be maintained. In this situation, flexible wage system may not work well as giving bonus is not a monthly expenditure but annual or semi-annual. We will explain why government is concerned about this aspect of the flexible wage system when we examine public policy in Singapore in Chapter 15.

Consequently, the idea of monthly variable component (MVC) wage system is mooted and in essence, each worker has a fixed wage component and monthly variable component as is shown in Figure 8.10. At the end of the accounting year, the deserving worker will be getting a bonus if the firm does well. MVC is much more flexible than flexible wage system because variable wage component is monthly and therefore it can be reduced or removed almost immediately. The reader may wonder why firms and workers would support this scheme. In the event of a crisis where firms have a choice either to retrench some workers or reduce wage costs across the board, most firms would prefer to reduce wage costs so that the moral of the workforce can be maintained and MVC allows the firms such an option. On the other hand, most firms would not want to be the first groups of firms to remove MVC as the firms may lose their best workers. The workers therefore will not be at the mercy of the employers. Besides, as we will examine later in the book, in Singapore, only a national body has the moral authority to urge firms to reduce or remove MVC.

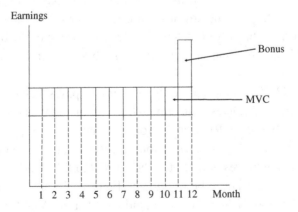

Figure 8.10:   Monthly Variable Component (MVC) Scheme

John is on flexible wage system with a monthly salary of $1,500. For the coming year, based on his past year performance, his employer plans to increase his base salary to $1,700 and give him a bonus of $1,500 for the coming year. How can his employer place him under MVC? From the perspective of flexibility of wage costs, the firm is advised not to raise the based salary. Instead, his employer should give John an MVC of $200. In this case, John will still get a total of $1,700 in monthly wages. The difference is that the MVC will not be factored in by banks when John wants to get a loan to buy a car or a house. And of course, MVC can be a macro instrument to protect jobs.

Tournament Pay

In sports, all winnings seem to go to a few contesters. For instance, the winner of a big tennis tournament gets $1 million and the runner up gets $0.5 million, etc. But the difference in ability between these two contesters is actually quite slim. So, what is the economics behind the tournament pay scheme? In sports, rewards are based on relative performance rather than absolute performance. Hence, this criterion of relying on relative performance has pushed all contesters to go all the way out to perform (of course, sports cheats are common unfortunately).

Instead of relying on various payments system that we mentioned above in this chapter, some firms adopt tournament pay scheme to force their executives to push the envelope of efficiency. It is believed that in a mild competition, the best executive's VMP is a fraction of the best executive's VMP if competition is reduced to one big winner who gets more than his VMP.

Figure 8.11 shows the nature of tournament pay scheme. At the job level 4, the firm stipulates that only a fraction of the executives can be promoted to job level 3. Right at the top, you have only one CEO. If you want to be promoted, you have to outperform your colleagues. In the process, most executives will stretch their VMP to the limit.

But would you want to be promoted? Figure 8.12 answers this question. At job level 4, each executive is paid less than his VMP. At job level 3, the VMP is still larger than the wages but the gap is smaller. But at job level 3, W exceeds VMP and of course for the CEO, his W is much greater

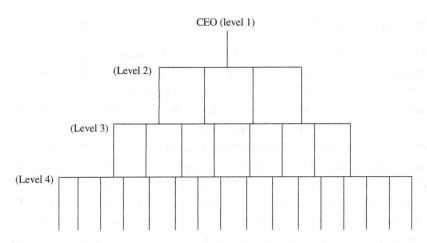

Figure 8.11: Tournament Pay Scheme

than his VMP. The firm which aims to maximize profit will ensure that $\Sigma\text{VMP} = \Sigma W$. Suppose Mike is an executive at G at job level 4 and his chances of moving up are not great. He may leave the firm. But he may not leave the firm because his alternative salary may be less than GF.

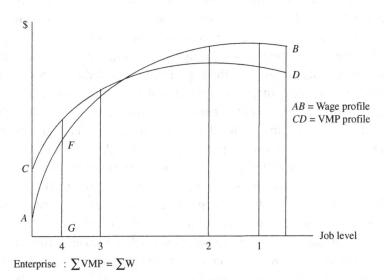

Enterprise : $\Sigma\text{VMP} = \Sigma W$

Figure 8.12: Top Executives Being Subsidized by Lower Executives

How Wages can Compensate for Working Environment

Throughout this book including this chapter, we argue that in a competitive labour market, the market wage is W_C. This implies that all workers receive the same wages. This outcome is true provided all jobs are the same in terms of nature of the job and working environment and all workers have the same skills and same utility function. This set of conditions of course is not met. Working conditions are not the same and workers are different in terms of skills and their preferences towards leisure and the working environment. Consequently, there are substantial amounts of wage differentials in the labour market. It is a common practice that MNCs give hardship allowance when they send their executives to work in poor countries. We will examine how each person can invest in his human capital in the next chapter but now we will focus on how wages can act as an incentive to compensate for unpleasant or risky working conditions.

Adam Smith (1976) argued that wages do not get equated across jobs in the competitive labour market but it is the remuneration which takes, into account, the advantages and disadvantages of the job that is equated. In other words, firms which have an unpleasant working environment must offer more remuneration to attract workers and firms which have a pleasant working environment need not have to offer more remuneration to attract workers. But among the whole set of the remuneration, wage is still the hard currency and firms use high wages to compensate for a bad working environment.

This theory of compensating wage differentials implies that when wage differentials are greater, the bigger are the differences in working environment. Suppose there are two types of jobs in the labour markets, safe jobs with zero probability of injury and risky jobs with high probability of injury. The firms that offer risky jobs must offer higher wages (W_R) to attract workers which are higher than W_S, the wage of safe jobs. The bigger the wage differentials ($W_R - W_S$), the easier it is for the firm to attract workers to accept risky jobs. In Figure 8.13, the supply curve of workers (S_R) in risky jobs has a positive slope because greater wage differentials can attract more workers to accept the risky jobs. On the other hand, the demand for workers in risky jobs will decrease as the relative costs of hiring these workers increase. As the demand curve and supply curve meet, the equilibrium market differential (W_G) is established.

If workers have better appetite for risky jobs, the supply curve will shift down. If the government puts a tax on risky jobs, at the same wage gap, the demand curve will shift down. If technology can reduce risky jobs, the demand curve for risky jobs will shift down.

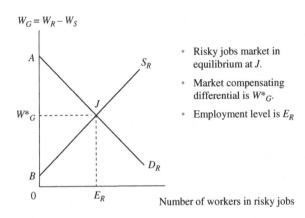

Figure 8.13: Determining Market Compensating Differential (W_G)

Discussion Questions

1. Is trust between management and employees an important factor in implementing flexible wage system?
2. Under the MVC scheme, where is the VMP curve?
3. What is the ULC path under MVC and tournament pay scheme?

Bibliography

Doeringer, P. and Piore, M. (1971). *Internal Labor Markets and Manpower Analysis*. Lexington, MA: DC Heath.

Smith, A. (1976). *The Wealth of Nations*. Chicago: University of Chicago Press.

Wilkinson, I. F., Ladley, D. and Young, L. C. (2015). "Bonus Time? Research shows It's Better to Reward Groups than Individuals", *The ADAPT International Bulletin: An Ongoing Project*, Bulletin No. 16/2015.

Chapter 9

Economics of Labour Unions

When we bring in government minimum wage law into a labour market, the labour market is no longer competitive. Similarly, when we bring in a labour union into a labour market, the labour market is no longer competitive. However, unions have much more impact than the minimum wage law in the labour markets.

What Do Labour Unions Do?

Consider a firm with 100 workers. These 100 workers have freedom to decide whether to join the labour movement as union members. If more than 50% of the workers decide to join the union, under the Trade Union Act in most countries, the labour movement is able to set up a union branch to represent the 100 workers to negotiate with the management over wages (W) and fringe benefits (FN) of the workers. This is known as collective bargaining and the terms of agreements will be put in writing in the form of collective bargaining agreement. Union members can then enjoy collective bargaining benefits (B_C). Better B_C per union member will increase employment cost per worker.

Union leaders or union representatives are elected by union members periodically. Union members have to pay a fee (union due) per month and therefore expect the union to negotiate a good collective bargaining package that will put most union members on the higher indifference curves. In other words, unions have to obtain higher wages (union wage premium)

123

and better welfare. Hirsch and Macpherson (2009) find that the union wage premium averaged 20% over the years 1983 to 2008. It was down to 17% in 2010 (McConnell *et al.*, 2010).

Of course, collective bargaining benefits will increase the cost of employing workers. A generous collective bargaining package will force employers to move up the demand curve for labour, causing some workers to be retrenched.

In some countries, unions themselves compete for union members. There is inter-union rivalry where workers in a factory can choose, say an electrical union or electronic union. Similarly, there is infra-union rivalry where workers in a factory can choose Branch *A* or Branch *B* of Electrical Union as union members. Union rivalry will cause union wage premium to increase consequently forcing employers to move higher on the labour demand curve.

There is economics of scale in organizing a union. As a result, many big firms are unionized but it is not the same with small firms. For a big firm, the Theory of Internal Labour Market argues that employees can be categorized into insiders and outsiders.[1] Insiders enjoy higher wages and employment stability and are recipients of firm sponsored training programmes. On the other hand, outsiders are paid at competitive wages and they are dispensable workforce when the product demand falls. Consequently, there is little human capital investment in them. All union officials are thought to be insiders.

Minimum Wage of Labour Unions

Without labour unions, the equilibrium point in the competitive labour market is at *J* (see Figure 9.1). The whole aim of a labour union is to change the labour supply curve to $W_U KS_L$ by imposing a minimum wage (W_U) for all the union members. The firm will choose *U* and cut employment to E_U. Some workers among the outsiders will be retrenched.

Union officials are well aware of the law of labour demand and hence, they will not blindly raise wages as it will hurt the employment base for

---

[1]This is also known as Dual Labour Market Theory (see Doeringer and Piore, 1971).

Unions raise wages at W_U and employers chose E_U. There is a
trade-off between wage increases and employment.

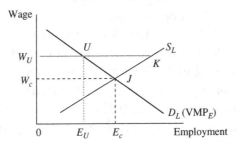

Figure 9.1: Union Minimum Wage (W_U) with Competitive Product Market

organizing the union. As Figure 9.2 shows, given the same minimum wage
(W_U), the loss in employment is bigger with more elastic labour demand
curve, D_{L2}.

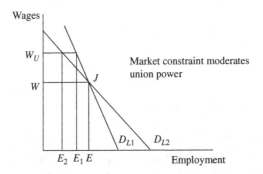

Figure 9.2: Elasticity of Labour Demand Limits Union's Push for Higher Wages

Remuneration

In Figure 9.1, the wages are presented on the vertical axis. In all economics textbooks, although we put wages on the vertical axis, it is actually
wage costs on the vertical axis. But it has served the purpose well in terms
of analysis except when we want to analyze fringe benefits. Wage is part
of labour cost. Payroll tax is also part of wage costs. Firms also provide
FN to the workforce. Examples of FN are free transport from certain loca-
tions to the plant, a clinic at the plant, common eating area for the

workers, etc. But all these will increase the cost of employment. Hence, remuneration is the sum of wage costs and FN.

If we hold remuneration constant, firms can decide the combination of wage bill and FN at the firm level. Of course, in practice, most Employment Acts have a limit to this composition in the sense that firms cannot pay workers all in the form of FN. However, from the analytical perspective, we can draw Isoremuneration (Iso-R) line in the way we conceptualize Isocost line. In Figure 9.3, the total cost of remuneration is $100,000 represented by Iso-R$_1$, represented by $Y_C X_C$. Hence, there is a map of Iso-R lines.

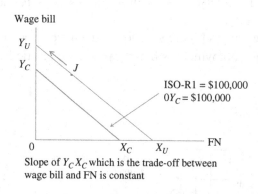

Figure 9.3:   Iso-Remuneration (ISO-R) Line

Suppose, in the absence of a union, $0Y_C$ in Figure 9.3 is the remuneration which is equal to $100,000. A typical union's strategy is two folds: First is to move to $Y_U X_U$, a higher Iso-R line. But there is a limit to the upward move as the labour demand curve is downward sloping. At the $Y_U X_U$ line, the union's next strategy is to push from J towards Y_C as most workers want more wages instead of FN. In essence, collective bargaining benefits (B_C) under a monopoly union are higher but this is achieved at the expense of employment.

However, one can argue that certain amount and certain aspect of FN could raise efficiency of the firms. As Figure 9.4 shows, the relation between efficiency is not a straight line. As FN increases, the overall efficiency of the firm will increase but beyond G, marginal increase in efficiency is zero. Hence, if unions want to move from R to V, that is acceptable but firms would not want FN to be less than G.

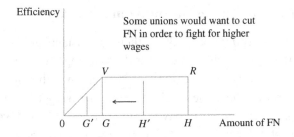

Figure 9.4:   FN Can Affect Efficiency at the Plant Level as Shown by OVR Line

Impact of Labour Unions on Economy

Figure 9.5 shows that the equilibrium wage (W^*) is the same in Sector 1 and Sector 2. Suppose Sector 1 is unionized, the new equilibrium point is U, the wage is now W_U and employment level is E_U. Suppose all the workers who lost their jobs move to Sector 2. The new equilibrium point is N, the new wage and employment levels in Sector 2 are now W_N and E_N respectively. The loss in output in the unionized sector is $E_U UJ E_U^*$ and the gain in output in the non-unionized sector is $E_N^* KN E_N$. Assume that both the labour demand curves have the same slope, area $E_U VJ E_U^*$ is the same as area $E_N^* KNE_N$, the loss in output of the economy is area UJV. Thus, formation of union in a sector can cause overall output loss equal to half of union wage premium ($W_U - W_N$) times employment loss in the unionized sector.

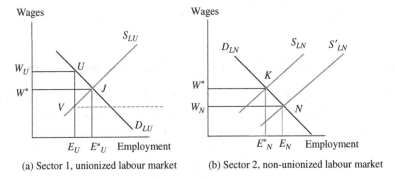

Figure 9.5:   Unionized and Non-unionized Sectors

Impact of Labour Unions on Individual Workers

Assume a firm has 100 workers, 30 of them are insiders and 70 outsiders. Figure 9.6 shows that each worker is at J^*, working the same number of hours and resting on indifference curve, U^*. A union at this firm is formed and the union raised the wage level, changing the budget line from AT to $A'T$. Each union member has to pay a union due monthly and we can consider the slope of $A'T$ as net wage. Of course, the firm will react with cutting the number of hours in total. We assume that union officials are insiders and they manage to strike a deal with the management such that each insider is at J_1, resting on a higher indifference curve, U_1. 40 outsiders are at J_0 resting on a lower indifference curve, U_0. The remaining 30 outsiders will be retrenched. They are at T, collecting unemployment benefits.

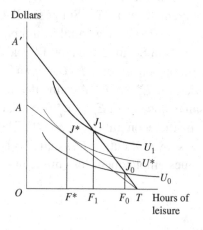

- Formation of the union will alter the budget line from AT to $A'T$
- Each worker starts at the same point at J^* but outcome is different

Figure 9.6:   Formation of Union Affects Workers Differently

Union Maximizes Utility Subject to Labour demand Curve

Earlier in this chapter, we argued that union officials will raise wages but how high? We need a theory to explain union wage strategy. Assume that labour union has the following utility function:

$$U_U = f(E, W),\qquad (9.1)$$

where E = level of employment and W = wage rate.

Figure 9.7 shows two indifference curves of the union. This monopoly union is expected to maximize utility subject to the budget constraint which is the labour demand curve (D_L). The starting point for the union is J which is the equilibrium point in the competitive labour market. Under the assumption of utility maximization, the union will choose K and set wages to be equal to W_K. The firm will then reduce employment to E_K. Hence, we can see that there is a trade-off between wage gain and employment as the union moves from J to K. If the labour demand curve is D'_L, the union would be much better off at K', as compared to K, because the union has bigger wage gain, smaller employment loss and rests on higher indifference.

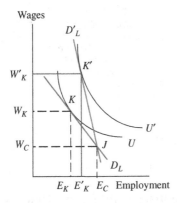

- Competitive wage = W_C
- Monopoly union maximizes utility by choosing K
- Union demands wage = W_K and employer cuts back employment to E_K
- With inelastic demand D'_L union could demand higher wage and get more utility (reference point is J)

Figure 9.7:   Monopoly Union Maximizes Utility Subject to Labour Demand Curve

Firms Maximize Profit Subject to Union Minimum Wage and Labour demand Curve

In Chapter 5, we show that, at each market wage, the firm will choose profit maximizing level of employment based on VMP. The segment of VMP which is below VAP constitutes the labour demand curve. Figure 9.8 shows an iso-profit curve map of peaking at the labour demand curve. If the wage level is W_0, the firm's profit maximizing level of employment is E_0 and the profit level is π_0. The firm is at J on iso-profit curve represented by π_0. If we want the firm to have either less than optimal employment level (E_K) or more than optimal employment level (E_F), and at the same time to keep the same profit level, the wage has to be lower. This explains why K, J and F are on the same iso-profit curve and the wage level for K and F is W', which is lower than W_0. In the same figure, we also draw another iso-profit curve which represents profit level, π_1. When iso-profit curve is lower, its profit level is higher. In this case, $\pi_1 > \pi_0$. The explanation is simple. Comparing J and V, both points have the same employment level and therefore same output level, but at V, the wage level is lower and therefore profit level is higher.

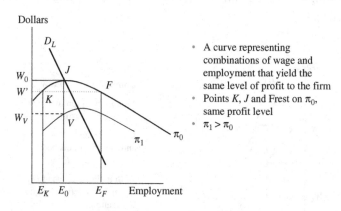

Figure 9.8:   A Map of Iso-profit Curves

The monopoly union will negotiate with a firm. Union wants to maximize utility and the firm wants to maximize profit. Figure 9.9 shows how monopoly union interacts with the firm. Without union, the firm is at J. As expected, the union will choose M, demanding W_m which is higher than W_C. Contract M indicates that the union wants wage level to be at W_M and the firm's employment level is E_M (which is not drawn). Is contract M efficient and socially optimal? Contract M is allocatively efficient as it contains profit maximizing level of employment, indicating that M is on the labour demand curve. But is M Pareto optimal? The answer is no. If the union can manage to persuade the firm to move from M to B, the union is better off as it is on higher indifference curve and the firm is no worse off as the firm is on the same iso-profit curve. Similarly, if the firm can persuade the union to move from *M* to *F*, the firm is better off as its profit level is higher and the union is no worse off as it is on the same indifference curve. Hence, *M* is not Pareto efficient.

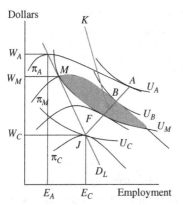

* Monopoly union chose contract *M* which is allocatively efficient

* Moving from *M* to *B* will make the union better off without making the firm worse off

* Moving from *M* to *F* will make the firm better off without making union worse off

* From *M* to *K*, both union and the firm are better off.

* Any contract along *FB* is superior to *M*

* *JA* is the contract curve

* But if we move from *F* to *B* along the contract curve, we make the union better off at the expense of the firm and vice versa.

* Hence, any contract along the contract curve is Pareto efficient

Figure 9.9: Efficient Contracts and the Contract Curve

It is obvious that any contract such as *K* which is between *B* and *F*, will make both parties better off. Hence, *BF* is known as the contract curve as we start the analysis at W_M. The union will want to push the contract towards *B* while the management would want to push the outcome towards *F*. Generally, the contract curve is *JA*. Any contract along *JA* is efficient as we cannot make one party better off without making the other party worse off. Note that the contract curve is off the labour demand curve except at *J*. This implies that the firm employs more workers than necessary. This is known as featherbedding which is a common practice under monopoly union.

The contract curve in Figure 9.9 has a positive slope. Theoretically, it is possible that the contract curve is vertical as is shown in Figure 9.10. In other words, all contracts such as *A*, *B* and *F* are on the same vertical curve, employing the same level of employment. In this case, all points on the vertical contract curve are both allocatively efficient and Pareto optimal. There is no featherbedding.

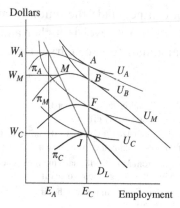

- Vertical contract curve *JA*
- Firm hires same no. of workers as in absence of union
- Union and firm split fixed-size pie along contract curve
- At *J*, employer keeps all the rents
- At *A*, union gets all the rents
- A contract on vertical contract curve is called a strongly efficient contract and all contracts are allocatively efficient as well as Pareto efficient

Figure 9.10:   Strongly Efficient Contracts

Strikes

When there is a breakdown in collective bargaining between union and management and neither party wants to give in, the union may call a strike to force the matter forward. So, union workers will refuse to work. The union will try its best to prevent other workers from working and will try to stop the firm from bringing outside workers to come in to work. Hence, strikes are messy and costly to both parties. Reder and Neumann (1984) find that for a listed firm, a strike can reduce the value of shareholders' wealth by about 3%.

Strike can be analyzed in terms of wanting to share the rent of a business between the union and the management. Borjas (2013, p. 434) uses Figure 9.11 to show Hicks paradox with regard to strike. Suppose there is $100 in rent to be shared between the union and the management. *Y* represents the union getting all the rent and *X* represents the management getting all the rent. Union's position is at *A* and the management's position is at *B*. If either parties refuses to give in, there will be a strike and the rent available will be reduced to, say $80. As strike is costly to both parties, there is greater willingness to change the initial position. Some facing changing settlement will emerge. In this case, *S* is the outcome after a strike with both getting $40 each. This is irrational in economics as both could have got $50 each without a strike. This dilemma which is known as Hicks Paradox arises because of asymmetric information. The Hicks Paradox is based on a zero sum game. We will examine a win–win framework in Chapter 10.

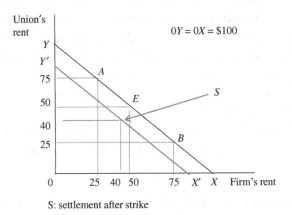

S: settlement after strike

Figure 9.11:   The Hicks Paradox

Many models have been advanced to explain why a strike takes place. One of the common methods is Asymmetric Information. We present two versions of Asymmetric Information.

Version 1: Union officials know about the firm's market and profit conditions better than the union members. But union members want higher wages. Union officials realize it is unproductive to ask for higher wages, but since members insist on it, they have no choice but to go ahead and demand for higher wages. The consequence is a strike because union officials cannot afford to offend union members.

Version 2: The firm knows about its profit conditions better than the union officials. Union officials would demand for higher wages on the assumption that the firm has made a good profit. But the firm did not do well and therefore would not give in for higher wages. Thus, a strike would take place. The union would then settle for a lower wage demand as the strike progresses.

With regard to the firm's bargaining strength, if the firm is caught by extremely low inventory, it is more likely to give in to higher wage demands because not meeting delivery deadlines can be costly in terms of money and reputation. On the other hand, strikes are less likely to take place if labour demand curve is elastic, which is the outcome of capital mobility. When unions are militant, demanding higher wages forcing firms to enjoy only normal profits, firms can move the plant out of the country. Unions have no choice but to moderate on wage demands. Borjas (2013) observes strike activity has been declining in the USA because of capital mobility, among other factors.

In many countries ranging from Indonesia, India to Germany to developing countries, we see the following newspaper headlines involving union activity:

(i) Rising labour costs have led three electronics plants to leave Batam (S.T., 16/09/2013).
(ii) Toyota suspends assembly in India (S.T. 18/03/2014).
(iii) Germany seeks to rein in union power after the cockpit pilots union (Lufthansa) grounded biggest airline over pay disputes (S.T. 7/04/2014).

Monopsony and Labour Unions in the Labour Markets

In Chapter 7, we examine the economics of monopsony and how it copes with government minimum wage law. In this section, we also take into account the interaction between monopsony and labour unions. Labour unions affect the labour market by imposing union minimum wage (W_U) in the same way as government imposing minimum wage law (W_L). Hence, the analysis and conclusion are the same. Figure 9.12 shows that the labour unions have introduced minimum wage changing the labour supply curve and marginal cost of employment curve. The monopsonist will maximize profit at F. Labour unions can remove labour exploitation in the labour market but cannot remove labour exploitation in the product market. Note that Figure 9.12 is identical to Figure 7.9 of Chapter 7 except that in Chapter

7, it is W_L and in this chapter, it is W_U. The only way union officials can remove labour exploitation in the product market is to join politics and be elected as members of Parliament and change the law to ban monopoly.

- Monopsonist maximizes profit at F where VMP = MC_E.
- Employment level is E_L.
- There is still labour exploitation (VF) in the product market

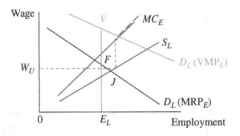

Figure 9.12:   Union Minimum Wage (W_U) and Monopsony with Monopolistic Product Market

Marshall's Rules of Derived Demand Revisited

Based on Marshallian rules of labour demand, we would like to analyze the following situations:

(i) Labour demand curve for textile industry vs labour demand curve for public sector employees.

Textile industry is labour intensive and very competitive. Hence, its product demand curve is D_T and its labour demand curve is D_{LT} (see Figure 9.13). When labour unions push wages higher from W to W_U, demand for textile workers will fall substantially from E to E_T. The rise in wages will push product prices higher to maintain same (but low) profit margin. Hence, the increase in price from P to P'_T is substantial, causing big reduction in demand for output from Q to Q'_T. This fall in product demand explains why D_{LT} is very elastic. This is why unions in labour intensive industries are helpless in raising wages.

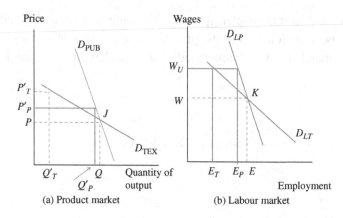

Figure 9.13:   Demand for Labour in Textile Industry and in Public Sector

In the same figure, we show the product demand curve and labour demand curve for a government ministry represented by D_P and D_{LP}, respectively. Both demand curves are inelastic. When public sector wages rise, reduction in labour demand is small from E to E_P. When wages rise, the Ministry is likely to raise the product price marginally from P to P'_P. (This will cause a budget deficit, of course). Hence, the reduction in product demand in the Ministry is small and explains why D_{LP} is not elastic. This is why public sector unions dare to raise wages for public sector employees but not the unions in the textile sector. Eventually, the market constraint and globalization limit union militancy which is lacking in the public sector.

(ii) Labour demand curve for Traded Sector vs labour demand curve for Non-traded Sector.

The traded sector is very competitive. Hence, its product demand curve is D_T and its labour demand curve is D_{LT} as is shown in Figure 9.14. When labour unions push wages higher from W to W_U, labour demand for traded sector will fall substantially from E to E_T. The rise in wages will push product prices higher to maintain same but low profit margin. Hence, the increase in price from P to P' is substantial, causing big reduction in demand for output from Q to Q'_T. This explains why D_{LT} is very elastic. This is why unions in traded sector are helpless in raising wages.

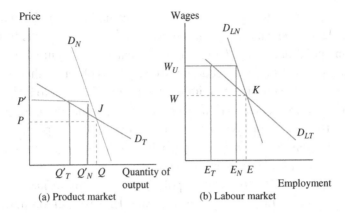

Figure 9.14: Demand for Labour in Traded Sector and in Non-traded Sector

The product demand curve and labour demand curve for non-traded sector are D_N and D_{LN} respectively, both are inelastic. When labour unions in non-traded sector push wages higher from W to W_U, labour demand for non-traded sector will fall marginally from E to E_N. The increase in wages will be passed on to consumers by raising the price from P to P', the fall in output in the non-traded sector is smaller from Q to Q_N and this explains why the labour demand curve for the non-traded sector is less elastic. Hence, unions in non-traded sector can be more militant than the unions in traded sector.

Featherbedding

Traditional labour unions would want to maximize the well-being of union members. Labour unions are against outsourcing and against using technology to replace workers. They support government's policy to increase minimum wage so that they can push union minimum wage higher. As labour demand curve is downward sloping, they redistribute income from non-union members to union members. They obtain higher wages at the expense of employment, causing income inequity to increase. These unions are indifferent to the blight of the unemployed.

Throughout this chapter, we assert that unions can decide on wage level for union members and the employment can decide on level of employment. But in many cases, because of featherbedding, the employer is off the labour demand curve. In other words, the employer is forced to accept any point other than *J* on the contract curve (see Figure 9.9). Below are some examples of featherbedding. Allen (1986) observes that over half the contracts in the construction industry require a foreman to be hired for as few as three workers. Johnson (1990) reports that the union for painters prohibits the use of spray guns or limits the width of paint brushes. Johnson also reports that unions for teachers will also insist on minimum teacher–student ratio or maximum class size.

Consequently, due to its monopoly power, unions influence practically all aspects of the employment contract. However, union power and militancy is limited by the market constraint and capital mobility. The kinds of unions examined in this chapter can be regarded as micro-focused unions. In Chapter 10, we will explore macro-focused unions which take into account macro impact of their actions.

Discussion Questions

1. Show that labour unions can raise wages and employment in a situation where there is a monopsony. You may have to read Chapter 7 to refresh your memory.
2. Is the labour demand curve in the informal sector elastic?

Bibliography

Allen, S. G. (1986). Union Work Rules and Efficiency in the Building Trades. *Journal of Labour Economics*, April, pp. 212–242.

Borjas, G. J. (2013). *Labor Economics*, Seventh edition. New York: McGraw-Hill.

Doeringer, P. and Piore, M. (1971). *Internal Labor Markets and Manpower Analysis*. Lexington, MA: DC Heath.

Hirsch, B. T. and Macpherson, D. A. (2009). *Union Membership and Earnings Data Book: Compilations from the Current Population Survey*, 2009 edition. Washington, DC: Bureau of National Affairs (2009).

Johnson, G. E. (1990). Work Rules, Featherbedding, and Pateto Optimal Union-Management Bargaining, *Journal of Labour Economics*, Jan, pp. S237–S259.

McConnell, C. R., Brue, S. L. and MacPherson, D. A. (2010). *Contemporary Labor Economics*, Nineth edition. New York: McGraw-Hill.

Reder, M. W. and Neumann, G. R. (1984). Output and Strike Activity in the U.S. Manufacturing: How Large are the Losses. *Industrial and Labour Relations Review*, 37, pp. 197–211.

Chapter 10

Economics of Macro-focused Unions

In Chapter 9, we explained why labour unions want better wages, better fringe benefits and job security for their union members. But globalization makes their effort less effective if not totally useless. Greek economy is in trouble and the Greek government is forced to impose austerity measures and the Greek unions naturally protest viciously. But is there a better way for the Greek labour unions to react? Or more importantly, can the Greek labour unions prevent the Greek economy from getting into this mess in the first place? This chapter is not about the Greek economy but it is a chapter on how a good union can help an economy cope with globalization where demand for products is price elastic and demand for social spending at home is excessive.

Chew and Chew (2010) moot the idea of a macro-focused union where the union takes into account the national health of the economy. Typically, a macro-focused union will not ask for higher wages at the expense of employment and the economy. A macro-focused union will work with the management and the government so that higher wages can be obtained without any adverse impact on employment. Hence, macro-focused unions look after the interest of all workers and consequently, they face free ridership. In other words, the macro-focused union puts interest of the economy above its interest in the form of providing a public good. To counter free ridership, the macro-focused union has to provide non-collective bargaining benefits for workers to enjoy exclusive benefits or else workers would want to free ride. These non-collective bargaining benefits which can be regarded as country club benefits are paid for by the union and are at the discretion of the union. Of course, most unions are too poor to provide significant country club benefits but the government is willing to provide assistance such that the macro-focused unions can provide country club benefits. This chapter examines the dynamics of a macro-focused union in the labour market and the economy.

What Do Macro-focused Unions Do?

Figure 10.1 shows the equilibrium point (J) in the competitive labour market. A macro-focused union would want to maximize employment and hence, the union would want the wage level to be at W_C, which is the competitive wage level without the union in the first place. At this point, the macro-focused union adds value neither in the production process nor in the labour market. However, the macro-focused union would work with the management and the government to shift labour demand curve to D'_L, thereby raising competitive wage to be W'_C. This is how the macro-focused union adds value to the economy, by raising wages for all workers. If there is a negative demand shock, shifting the labour demand curve from D_L to D_{LR}, the macro-focused union would fight for the wage level to be at W_R, thereby protecting employment level at E_C. This is another way how the macro-focused union adds value to the economy by protecting all workers. The macro-focused union contributes to the economy in the form of union social responsibility but at its own expense as it now faces free ridership. We will examine how this free ridership can be overcome later in the chapter.

- Macro-focused union would raise wages by shifting labour demand curve and protect employment by lowering wages when labour demand curve shifts down due to recession.

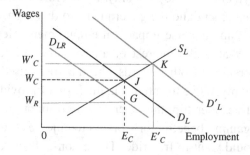

Figure 10.1:   Macro-focused Union's Behaviour in the Labour Market

Adversarial and Strategic Collective Bargaining

In Chapter 9, we used Figure 9.11 to show collective bargaining outcomes under the Hicks Paradox. This is adversarial collective bargaining taking advantage of the other's weaknesses to get a bigger share of the rent. An alternative to adversarial collective bargaining is strategic collective bargaining which aims to get what you want but not at the expense of the other party. Figure 10.2 shows the meaning of strategic collective bargaining. Both macro-focused unions and management work to increase the rent by shifting the XY line to $X'Y'$ line. Then, both sides can substantiate their contribution to push the outcome in their favour between J and K. An outcome closer to K means the management gets a bigger share of the rent and vice versa. The level of trust between the union and management is higher under strategic collective bargaining than under adversarial collective bargaining.

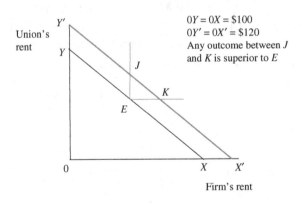

Figure 10.2:   Strategic Collective Bargaining

Would macro-focused unions ask for excessive wage increases? It is likely that a macro-focused union would want greater wage increases than what the management is prepared to give, which is the essence of collective bargaining. Figure 10.3 presents such a situation where the union wants A and the management wants B. Under strategic collective bargaining, both the union and management must work to shift XY line to $X'Y'$ line. E represents the final outcome where the needs of the union and the needs of the management can be met at the same time. The bigger gap of

AB means that the union has to do more work. Hence, it is not likely that a macro-focused union will ask for excessive wage increases.

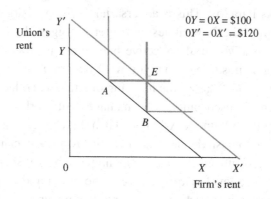

Figure 10.3:   Initial Gap Bigger, the Union has to Work Harder

During a recession where the *XY* line shifts downwards to *X'Y'* line as is shown in Figure 10.4, the macro-focused union would settle for either *K* where the workers bear the cost of the burden but remain employed or *J* where workers bear most of the recession pain.

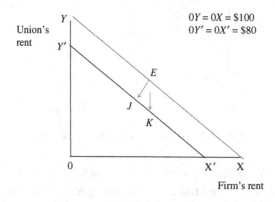

Figure 10.4:   Recession would Shift *XY* Line Downward

Collective Bargaining Benefits and Remuneration

In Figure 10.5, under perfect competitive labour market, $0Y_C$ is the remuneration which is equal to $100,000. A micro-focused union will raise wage and wage costs at the expense of employment. $0Y_U$ is the remuneration which is equal to \$130,000 in the presence of a micro-focused union. Workers thus enjoy higher collective bargaining benefits (B_C) but the firm will retrench some workers. A macro-focused union will not seek higher wages at the expense of employment. If the macro-focused union does not contribute to productivity growth, $0Y_C$ is the remuneration which is the same as that without the presence of a union. Suppose, the macro-focused union has contributed to productivity growth in terms of shifting labour demand curve upward, workers get more wages and B_C, the remuneration is now equal to \$120,000. In this case, the macro-focused union might be the sole loser as workers can free ride.

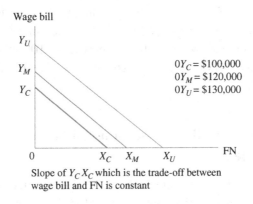

Slope of $Y_C X_C$ which is the trade-off between wage bill and FN is constant

Figure 10.5: Iso-Remuneration (Iso-R) Lines

We shall now examine the following three situations with regard to union membership and free ridership:

(i) Consider Firm X with 100 workers. This firm is unionized with 80 union members. The union is micro-focused. The collective bargaining benefits (B_C) is generous. The firm will retrench some workers. The probability of being retrenched is high among non-union members as they are not represented by the union. In other words, there is incentive for workers to join a micro-focused union as members.

(ii) Consider Firm Y with 100 workers. This firm is also unionized with 80 union members. The union is macro-focused. The collective bargaining benefits (B_C) is higher than that under competitive labour market but without any impact on employment. The firm will not retrench workers due to productivity growth. As the macro-focused union delivers a public good, there is no incentive for non-union members to join the union. On the other hand, some union members may opt out of union membership to save from paying the union due. As we will discuss later in the chapter, the macro-focused union must provide significant union benefits so that the non-union members will consider joining the union. These union benefits are regarded as non-collective bargaining benefits (B_N) which are paid for by the union and not by the employer. In this case, we can conclude that union members can enjoy B_C and B_N. An increase in B_N does not force the firm to move up the labour demand curve as it is paid for by the union.

(iii) Consider Firm Z with 100 workers but this firm is not unionized. These 100 workers might want to join the union in order to enjoy B_N. Later in the chapter, we will discuss how these 100 workers can join as social members of the union and therefore be entitled to B_N but not B_C.

Union Social Responsibility and Non-collective Bargaining Benefits

In the literature, there is extensive discussion on Corporate Social Responsibility. But in this chapter, the focus is on Union Social Responsibility (USR). USR is being carried out when a union puts the interest of the economy above the interest of the institution. What are the gains to the union in conducting USR? The general public will appreciate its efforts and the government certainly will embrace this effort. We can therefore draw the marginal benefit (MR) line of USR to the union as is shown in Figure 10.6. The MR line is downward sloping, indicating diminishing marginal returns to USR. The cost of USR comes from the need to remove free ridership problem by offering non-collective bargaining benefits (B_N).

Examples of B_N are: unions give scholarships and bursaries to children of union members. Union members get a big discount when they use union facilities such as swimming pools, holiday resorts and golf courses. Union members and general public do shop at supermarkets run by the

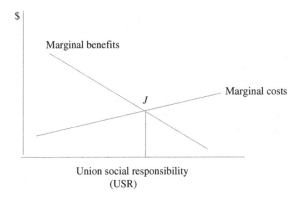

Figure 10.6: Optimal Level of USR

unions. Union members enjoy cash rebates when they buy from a specific list of merchandize items. Hence, if the union knows workers' preference well, the union members can get more cash rebates, meaning more B_N. From this perspective, the cash rebate a union member gets depends on how much he buys from the approved list of merchandize items. In other words, unions provide B_N to induce workers to join the union. In a way, we can perceive that workers joining the union is like joining a country club and hence they receive country club benefits, B_N in return for a fee which is the monthly union due.

Country club benefits are not free of cost. The MC of providing B_N is assumed to be upward sloping, indicating rising cost as the amount of USR increases. As MR line meets MC line, we can determine the optimal amount of USR at J. The government can provide financial assistance so that the MC line of the union can shift down thereby increasing the optimal amount of USR. We will provide some examples from Singapore to discuss on how the government can shift MC line down later in the book. However, various attempts to quantify USR have been in vain. This is a topic for future research.

In the next two figures, we want to present B_N in comparison with market wages. In Figure 10.7, the macro-focused union will shift the demand upward and all workers including union members will get market wages, W_C'. But to counter free ridership, union members will get B_N which is equal to GK.

- Macro-focused union would raise market wages to W'_C by shifting labour demand curve. Only union members get B_N which is equal to GK.

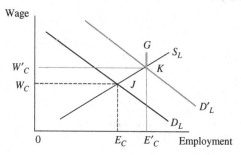

Figure 10.7:   During Good Times, Union Members get GK in Addition to W'_C

During a recession, the union would support cost cutting measures to reduce market wages to W_R, as is shown in Figure 10.8. All workers suffer a wage cut but only union members can get B_N, which is equal to GK, to partially offset the fall in wages. How much is B_N per union member? Chew (2014) estimated B_N to be $65 monthly per union member in contrast to monthly union due of $9 for Singapore.[1]

- During a recession, macro-focused union supports wages to be reduced to W_R. All workers including union members receive less wages but only union members get B_N which is equal to GK

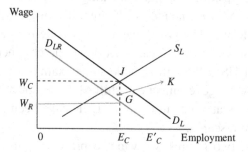

Figure 10.8:   During Recession, Union Members get KG to Offset Fall in Wages

---

[1] See Chew (2014) on how B_N is estimated.

Using B_N to increase union membership

Under a macro-focused union, workers need not worry about retrenchment due to collective bargaining outcome. This repeatedly explains why macro-focused union faces free ridership and the use of B_N to counter free ridership problem. Hence, for a worker eager to join a union is similar to him joining a country club. If the benefits of union membership exceed the cost, then, the worker will be a union member. Suppose a worker plans to work for "t" months. The cost of the ith worker becoming a union member is

$$C_i = R_i + \Sigma\, U_{it}/(1 + r)^t,$$

where

$t = 0$ to m (length of employment in terms of months),
C_i = cost of union membership per period of the ith worker,
R_i = registration fee of the ith worker,
U_i = union dues per worker; $9 per month in Singapore,
m = expected length of time of employment in the labour market,
r = rate of time preference.

Looking at the cost equation, the main component of cost is the monthly union due. Registration fee is insignificant. Later on, we will drop registration fee from the cost equation.

The benefits of becoming a union member for the ith worker is

$$B_i = \Sigma\, (B_{Cit} + B_{Nit} + B_{Pit})/(1 + r)^t,$$

where

B_i = the ith worker's benefits of joining a union,
B_{Ci} = collective bargaining benefits of ith worker per month
B_{Ni} = non-collective bargaining benefits of the ith worker enjoyed by the union members per month. B_{Ni} varies from worker to worker but in some figures later, we assume that it is the same for each worker for ease of exposition,

and B_{Pi} = the monetary equivalent of the psychic value of the ith worker's ideology regarding the labour movement in general.

If $B_{Pi} > 0$, monetary value of worker's preference is positive towards the union. In other words, if $B_{Pi} = \$20$, it means that being associated with the labour movement is equivalent to getting \$20 in cash. On the other hand, if B_{Pi} is negative and say, $B_{Pi} = -\$30$, this implies that being associated with the labour movement is costing him \$30 per month. It is obvious that B_{Pi} varies from worker to worker.

On the benefits equation, collective bargaining benefits are not important for two reasons. Firstly, under a macro-focused union, collective bargaining benefits are not excessive. And secondly, most employers will extend the collective bargaining benefits to non-union members as well. Hence, we will drop collective bargaining benefits from the benefits equation.

Hence, the net benefit of becoming a union member is as follows:

$$D_i = B_i - C_i = \Sigma \, (B_{Nit} + B_{Pit} - U_{it}) / \, (1 + r)^t, \qquad (10.1)$$

where D_i is the net gain of becoming a union member for the ith worker.

If D_{Bob} is positive for Bob, then he will join the union. As far as the union is concerned, they want to increase union membership. The immediate instrument is to enable union members to get more country club benefits per month, (B_{Nit}). U_i is union due per month and it is the only monthly cost of union membership. Hence, $U_i = C_i$. In other words, given B_{Pit} and C_{it}, an increase in B_{Nit} will induce more workers to join the union.

For ease of illustration, we examine the net benefits on per month basis (and we can then put the discount rate aside). Consider John whose particulars are as follows:

$$C_J = \$9; \quad B_{NJ} = \$6; \quad B_{PJ} = \$2 \quad \text{and} \quad B_J = \$8.$$

As $C_J > B_J$, John will not join the union and become a union member.

For ease of exposition, we define B'_{NJ} where John will be indifferent between joining and not joining the union as follows:

$$B'_{NJ} + B_{PJ} = C_{it} = \$9. \qquad (10.2)$$

Rearranging, we get $B'_{NJ} = C_{it} - B'_{PJ} = \$9 - \$2 = \$7.$

If the union is able to increase B'_{NJ} by one dollar and label it as B^*_{NJ}, then John will join the union now, as $B_J > C_J$. Of course, if we have 100 workers, we should be able to find B'_{NJ} for each worker and OR line in Figure 10.9 shows such a relationship.

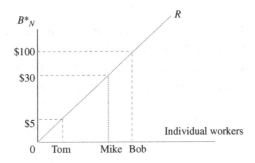

Figure 10.9:   Country Club Benefits Curve to Buy Union Membership

For instance, Tom's B^*_{NT} is $5 and Mike's is $30. Both of them pay the same union due. Their B^*_N varies due to the difference in B_P, implying that Tom is in more support of the labour movement than Mike. Suppose Mike is the 100th worker to join the union and he is also the last worker to join the union, then we can conclude that union membership is 100. For ease of presentation, we assume that OR is a straight line although it can take various shapes.

In the short run, the macro-focused union has to accept OR line and find ways to increase B_N. But if the labour movement is able to resolve work disputes at the plant level, workers' B_P will improve and OR curve will shift down. If union officials are found to be corrupt, then B_P will fall in value if there are positives and increase in value if they are negatives. In this case, OR curve will shift up.

Provision of B_N

Unions need financial resources to provide B_N. Suppose TF is the total funds available to provide country club benefit then the following can be stated as follows:

TF = Total union dues per month + total registration fees
    + donations + other incomes − (wage bill + business costs).

152   *Labour Economics and Public Policy in Labour Markets*

Total union dues per month will increase if there is an increase in union due or increase in union membership. The actual country club benefits received by each union member is

$$B_{Ni} = \text{TF/union membership.} \qquad (10.3)$$

In Figure 10.10, the supply curve of country club benefits is labelled as KK curve. Note that on the vertical axis, it is B_N and not B_N^*. The KK curve allows us to determine actual country club benefits per member. For instance, if there are 200 union members, then, the actual country club per member is $100 per month.

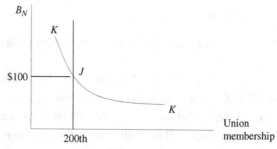

If we have 200 union members, then $B_N = \$100$

Figure 10.10:   Supply Curve of Country Club Benefits Per Member

KK curve has a negative slope because we assume that there are no increasing returns to scale in the provision of country club benefits. If the union is able to obtain more donation, KK curve will shift up. If the union increases the monthly union due, KK curve will shift up. If the union is good in managing the union funds such that for each million dollars in business cost, B_N is higher, then KK curve will shift up. If the union knows what the workers want in terms of lifestyle and consumer demand, for a given level of expenses, B_N is higher, then KK curve will shift up.

A model to determine union membership

In Figure 10.11, we have the OR curve and also KK curve (which is assumed to be a straight line for simplicity). Note that on the vertical axis, we have

B^*_N for the *OR* curve and B_N for the *KK* curve. AT *J*, the actual amount of country club benefits (B_N) is determined which is equal to $30 a month in this simple example. Note that Mike's B^*_N is $30, and hence there is no consumer surplus for Mike but for the remaining workers, the total consumer surplus is area *0GJ*. Mike is the last worker to join the union. If Mike is the 100th worker, then we can conclude that union membership is 100.

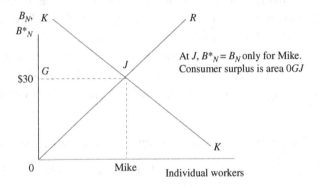

Figure 10.11:   Model of Union Membership Country

All unions would like to increase union membership. For a macro-focused union, the officials have to find ways to shift the *OR* curve downward and the *KK* curve upward.

We would like to examine the situation where monthly union due is raised, say from $9 to $12. In Figure 10.12, *J* is the original equilibrium point. When monthly union due is raised, the *KK* curve will shift up to become the *FF* curve.

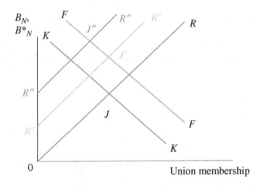

Figure 10.12:   Raising Union Due

Following Equation (10.2), we put in new union due and it becomes:

$$B'_{NJ} + B_{PJ} = C_{it} = \$12. \tag{10.4}$$

The B'_N will be higher by \$3 and hence B^*_N will be higher by \$3 too. In this case, the *OR* curve will become $R'R'$ curve. From R to $R¢$ is known as the statistical effect. Comparing J' to J, there is no change in union membership. If union members and workers at large are annoyed by the raising of union due, B_P will deteriorate and the $R'R'$ curve will become the $R''R''$ curve (assume that each person is annoyed by the same amount of pain). From R' to R'' is known as psychological effect. Hence, this model concludes that raising union due will not increase union membership.

Factors influencing unions to be micro or macro-focused (USA)

Using the American Federation of Labor and Congress of Industrial Organizations, as an example, AFL-CIO is a loose and voluntary federation of independent and autonomous national unions (McConnell *et al.*, 2010, p. 299). The loose relationship is presented in Figure 10.13. The AFL-CIO does not engage in collective bargaining for its own employees

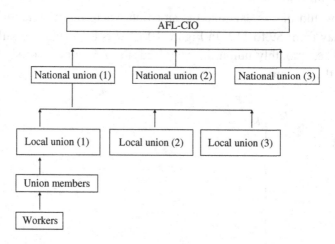

Figure 10.13:   Structure of AFL-CIO

Source: This slide is modified from a figure on p. 299, McConnell, *et al.* (2010).

or the unions under their charge. The AFL-CIO formulates from the labour perspectives on a spectrum of political issues ranging from the minimum wage to foreign policy and engages in political lobbying. The AFL-CIO also has the power to settle jurisdictional disputes with the objective of minimizing inter- and infra-union rivalry. The AFL-CIO can be a micro-focused or macro-focused labour movement.

The national unions are federations of local unions that are typically in either the same industry or the same skilled occupation. A national union has two basic functions: (1) to increase union membership and (2) to negotiate collective bargaining agreements at the local union level. The collective bargaining strategy of the national union is to standardize wages so that local unions will not compete in lowering wages. The national unions are independent of the firms which employ their union official and union members, which is not the case in many developing countries.

In the USA, both AFL-CIO and national unions are very independent of each other and also of the society at large. But local unions are subservient to their national unions. Both AFL-CIO and national unions have the sole power of deciding whether to be micro-focused or macro-focused. But the gravity is on the side of micro-focused. When a national union is micro-focused, its local unions are also micro-focused union. It is easy to be micro-focused as union officials need to be elected periodically.

The AFL-CIO would face a challenge if it wants to be macro-focused but national unions want to remain micro-focused. But there is very little reason or rationale for AFL-CIO to be macro-focused. Later in the book, we will examine the orientation of the labour movement in Singapore, which is macro-focused.

Factors influencing unions to be micro- or macro-focused (Singapore)

Singapore was a British colony. After World War II, during the 1950s, the pro-leftist trade unions in Singapore were engaged in a struggle for power with the colonial government. In 1954, Lee Kuan Yew (LKY), together with a few unionists such as Devan Nair, founded the People's Action Party (PAP). Under the leadership of LKY, the PAP won the

General Election in 1959 and set up self-government. As the youngest prime minister in the world, LKY lost no time in taming the leftist unions and changing the militant labour movement into one that is macro-focused.[2]

Since 1963, the labour movement in Singapore has been represented by the National Trades Union Congress (NTUC). Chew and Chew (1995) argue that the NTUC is a macro-focused union as it looks after the interests of all workers in Singapore. The NTUC is a social as well as political partner with the PAP government in promoting the economic development of Singapore. As the NTUC is macro-focused, it needs a second instrument to promote trade union membership: non-collective bargaining benefits (B_N) as we have mentioned above. Chew and Chew (2011) also argue that NTUC uses strategic collective bargaining in striking a good balance in the distribution of rent between the NTUC and the management.

As mentioned earlier in this chapter, very few unions, if at all, can provide sufficiently substantial non-collective bargaining benefits. NTUC is in a position to provide sufficiently substantial non-collective bargaining benefits because the Singapore government has been willing to help NTUC to provide such non-collective benefits by fiscal transfers. The Singapore government treats the NTUC as a strategic partner in economic development because the NTUC is a macro-focused union. The NTUC regards the government as a good partner as it can achieve its objectives of serving the country.[3]

Because NTUC is macro-focused, tripartism in Singapore under name of the National Wages Council (NWC) reinforces the principle of setting wages to maximize the employment level. Set up in 1972, all major decisions concerning wage increases and wage cuts are examined and endorsed by the NWC.[4] In July each year, the NWC would announce the non-mandatory wage guidelines, which are based on market forces. The basic principle of wage guideline is that wage

---

[2]See Chew (1991) for a history of the labour movement in Singapore.
[3]At the same time, it helps the government to get elected.
[4]See Lim Chong Yah and Chew (1998), for a discussion on the NWC.

increases should be supported by productivity growth. In other words, inflation rate is not an important consideration in the wage increase equation.[5]

But what makes NTUC a macro-focused union? What are the political conditions for the NTUC to operate as a macro-focused union? As mentioned in Chew (2014), the leaders of NTUC are also leaders of the PAP which governs Singapore since 1959. By being a macro-focused union, the NTUC helps their political party to manage Singapore well in terms of full employment and price stability. This political condition will prevail as long as there is no change in government.

The apex of the labour movement in Singapore is the Central Committee which governs the orientation of the NTUC. Members of the Central Committee are elected by delegates from the affiliated unions. Each affiliated unions normally would have many branch unions. The affiliated and branch union officials are elected by the union members periodically, normal every three years.

At least a few central committee members are Members of Parliament (MPs) from the PAP. The union chief who is the Secretary General is usually an MP and most importantly a Cabinet Minister. Hence, the labour movement in Singapore and the Singapore government can work as a team in attracting foreign investment, boosting training of workers and involving in reform of the wage system which aims to maintain competitive unit labour cost (ULC) while allowing wages to rise. This strategic advantage is hard to replicate in other countries.

Although the Central Committee of the NTUC is macro-focused, it does not automatically imply that the affiliated unions and branch unions are macro-focused. As Figure 10.14 shows, due to direct elections, the affiliated and branch union officials can be micro-focused. However, the fact of the matter is that in Singapore, union officials at all levels would not adopt micro-focused orientation because of the remuneration system. The full time members of the Central Committee members are either paid

---

[5]Of course, the Singapore government has to ensure that inflation rate in Singapore is low via strong Sing dollar.

by the government or the NTUC. The affiliated and branch union officials are either paid by the NTUC or the employers concerned. This is very different compared to AFL-CIO in the US. As mentioned above, AFL-CIO can be micro-focused because it is a loose and voluntary federation of independent and autonomous national unions.

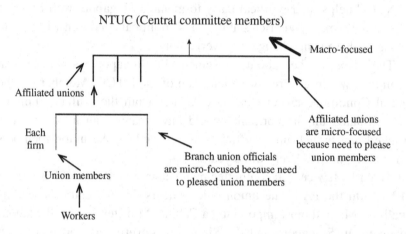

Figure 10.14:   Which is Macro-focused and Micro-focused?

Concept of being Macro-focused Applicable to other Fields

If a newspaper is micro-focused, the sole objective is to increase circulation of the newspaper. In the reporting, it will be profitable for the newspaper to sensationalize an issue. If there is big controversy or racial tension in the society because of the reporting style, this newspaper will benefit at the expense of the country. Hence, following the labour movement, all newspapers should be macro-focused in the sense that they should report the events with the purpose of reporting news and educating the public with no hidden agenda except to benefit the country. Again, similar to the labour movement, a macro-focused newspaper can be a government-run newspaper which ultimately will be rejected by the society at large.

In some countries, there is no religious harmony. A religion that is micro-focused does not allow public space for other religions. A micro-focused religion will attack other religions. On the contrary, a macro-focused religion will respect other religions. In promoting its religion and to its increase membership, a macro-focused religion will put the interest of the country above the interest of that religion. In Singapore, we promote inter-faith meetings. Figure 10.15 shows that such an activity where leaders of all religions pray together is an important step in promoting religious harmony in Singapore.

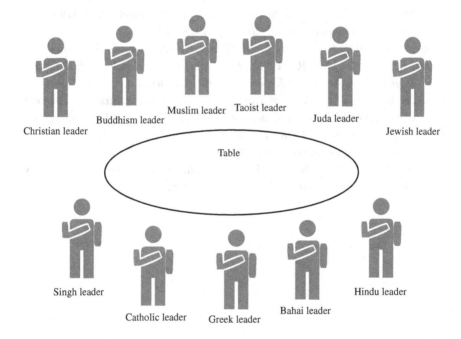

Figure 10.15: Macro-focused Religions Under One Roof

Discussion Questions

1. Discuss where would a macro-focused union want to bargain for the amount of fringe benefits in Figure 9.4 of Chapter 9.
2. Discuss what would be the shape of the contract curve under a macro-focused union in Figure 9.10?

3. What happens to NTUC in terms of economic and political orientation if there is a change in government in Singapore?

Bibliography

Chew, R. and Chew, S. B. (2010). Union Social Responsibility: A Necessary Public Good in a Globalised World. *International Journal of Comparative Labour Law and Industrial Relations (Netherlands)*, Vol. 26, No. 4, pp. 435–446.

Chew, R. and Chew, S. B. (2011). From Adversarial Collective Bargaining To Strategic Collective Bargaining: The Case of a Small-Open Economy. *Bulletin of Comparative Labour Relations*, pp. 59–68.

Chew, S. B. (1991). *Trade Unionism in Singapore*. Singapore: McGraw-Hill.

Chew, S. B. and Chew, R. (1995). *Employment-Driven Industrial Relations Regimes: The Singapore Experience*. UK: Avebury.

Chew, S. B. (2014). "Influence of Trade Unions on Economic Strategy: The case of Singapore", *Singapore Economic Review*, Vol. 59, No. 4, 1450035, pp. 13.

Lim, C. Y. and Chew, R. (1998). *The National Wages Council, Wages and Wage Policies*. Singapore: World Scientific.

McConnell, C. R, Brue, S. L. and Macpherson, D. A. (2010). *Contemporary Labor Economics*, Ninth edition. Irwin: McGraw-Hill.

Chapter 11

Human Capital

When a jobseeker looks for a job, he offers a set of skills for sales in the labour market. He hopes that a prospective employer might find his skills useful as a factor of production. In Chapter 2, we showed that the jobseeker would want to maximize his utility given his skill set and utility function. In the chapter on unemployment, we will show how a jobseeker can look for the best wage offer. But in this chapter, we focus on the skill sets. If the jobseeker has no skills, he is said to offer a warm body in the labour market. His labour supply curve in terms of hours will be horizontal at the subsistence wage with no worker surplus. If a jobseeker has good skills, his labour supply curve has a positive slope with large worker surplus.

Formal Education

Hence, all people will want to acquire a skill set with formal education and improve the skills set with retraining and on-the-job training. The starting point of this chapter is that a person has completed 12 years of education. He is now a high school leaver. He has to decide whether to work and earn a yearly wage of W_{HS} or to go to university to become a degree holder and earn a yearly wage of W_{Uni}. If he decides to go to the university, his decision to study is an activity in investment in human capital. He hopes that, although he incurs cost in terms of foregone earnings and actual expenses, he will be financially better off because $W_{Uni} > W_{HS}$ hopefully for as many as 30 years or more. Education is not the only form of investment in human capital. Training is just as important. Job search, health, migration and networking are only important forms of investment. This chapter focuses on education and training.

Present Value of Future Costs and Earnings

How to compute whether it pays to get a university degree? Suppose W_{HS} = $24,000. The foregone earnings of four years are therefore $96,000. The yearly expense, say, is $10,000 and for four years, are is $40,000. Hence, we know the total cost for Year 0 (the present), for Year 1 to Year 3. Let us say, W_{Uni} = $36,000 starting from Year 4. Hence the yearly earnings differential, D, is $ 12,000 a year for Year 4 onwards for the next 30 years. Can we just add and subtract the numbers and reach a conclusion on whether to go to university is a right decision? The answer of course is no, you cannot. Apart from year zero, all these numbers are future costs and earnings. We need to compute the present value of the future costs and earnings.

If someone promises to give you $1,000 a year from now, what is the present value of this amount? Is it bigger than if you have $1,000 now, today? Your $1,000 now, if you put in a bank and earn a rate of interest, say, 10%, it will be $1,100 a year from today. Hence, the present value of $1,100 a year from today, is equal to $1,000. So, the present value of $1,000 a year from now is worth less than $1,000. The formula for calculating present value (E_{PV}) of E_1 a year from today is:

$$E_{PV} = E_1 / (1 + r),$$

and 30 years from now will be

$$E_{PV} = E_{30} / (1 + r)^{30},$$

where r is rate of interest or rate of discount.

Figure 11.1 shows that this person has completed his basic education and he is 18 years old. If he chooses to work, his earnings line is AB. If he chooses to study, his foregone earnings are represented by W and actual expenses are represented by T. FG is his earnings line as a uni graduate. His total earnings differentials is E.

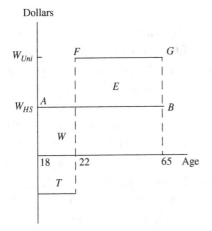

Figure 11.1: Potential Earnings Streams Faced by a High School Leaver

AB is earnings line of a high school leaver and FG is the earning line of a uni graduate
E is total earnings differential
W is foregone earnings of a uni student
T is education expenses for four years

The present value of going to study for a degree instead of working as a high school leaver is as follows:

$$\text{PV}_{\text{Uni-HS}} = -(W + T) - (W_1 + T_1)/(1 + r)^1 - (W_2 + T_2)/(1 + r)^2$$
$$- (W_3 + T_3)/(1 + r)^3 + E_4/(1 + r)^4 + \cdots + E_{47}/(1 + r)^{47},$$
$$\text{PV}_{\text{Uni-HS}} = \sum -(W_j + T_j)/(1 + r)^j + \sum (E_j)/(1 + r)^j, \tag{11.1}$$

where W_j = Foregone earnings for the jth year, $j = 0, 1, 2$ and 3

T_j = Actual expenses for the jth year, $j = 0, 1, 2$ and 3

E_j = Earnings differential between W_{Uni} and W_{HS} for the jth year, $j = 4,$ 5,…, 47 and

r = rate of interest or discount rate.

In sum, we can re-express as follows:

$$\text{PV}_{\text{Uni-HS}} = \sum (D_j)/(1 + r)^j, \tag{11.2}$$

where $D_j = - (W_j + T_j)$ where $j = 0, 1, 2$ to 3
and $D_j = (E_j)$ where $j = 4, 5$ to 47.

Based on Equation (11.2), we have data on D_j s and if we use the right interest rate or the discount rate, we can estimate $\text{PV}_{\text{Uni-HS}}$. If $\text{PV}_{\text{Uni-HS}}$ is positive, then university education is profitable. But how profitable? If the high school leaver chose to start a business instead. And the present value of his business is larger than the present value of university education, then university education is not so profitable for the high school leaver. The issue here is we should also compare the present value of similar investment in terms of riskiness. Going into business is a high risk which only a high rate of return can justify.

Economists of course prefer to use rate of returns for analysis. If we set $PV_{Uni\text{-}HS} = 0$ from Equation (11.2), as we know Ds, we can solve for r, and this r is now regarded as i which is regarded as internal rate of return. What is the economics of internal rate of return? Suppose we estimate that $i = 5\%$. It means that if the relevant interest rate is 4%, $PV_{Uni\text{-}HS}$ will be positive at 4%, which means it is a profitable investment to acquire a university degree instead of working as a high school leaver. Hence, economists like to compare i with the rate of return on investment which has a similar degree of risk as university education.

Rate of Discount

Based on Equation (11.2), we can see that a high rate of interest will make university investment less profitable. Market rate of interest is relevant as we can earn interest payments at the market rate. In Equation (11.2), we often calculate present value using rate of discount which is more emotional or personal. A person with a higher rate of discount will not give up present consumption at the expense of his future consumption. An older person or a sick person will have high rate of discount. Married people with children will have lower rate of discount than a married couple with no children.

Given the rate of discount, people can decide how much they should invest in schooling. A person should continue to study as long as rate of return is greater than the rate of discount. He should stop studying the moment the rate of return is equal to rate of discount. We will now use the wage–schooling curve to examine the stopping rule.

The Wage–schooling Curve

Figure 11.2 shows that a high school leaver has an annual net earnings of $24,000. If he is a degree holder, his annual net earnings are $36,000.

With a master degree and a PhD, his respective annual net earnings are $46,000 and $50,000. *GV* is the wage–schooling curve. Given this curve, we can estimate the marginal rate of return (MRR) to education. The MRR for university education is $6,000/$24,000 which is 25%. For the master degree and PhD degree, the respective MRRs are 20% and 11% as is shown in the Panel A of Figure 11.2. As the *GV* curve is concave, there is law of diminishing MRR. Given the MRR curve, a person will stop studying when his discount rate is equal to MRR. The discount rate which represents the marginal cost cannot exceed MRR as he is assumed to maximize present value of his investment. If his discount rate is 15%, he would stop at the master degree level. If his rate of discount is 10%, then, he would complete the PhD degree. Hence, the stopping rule is that MRR is either greater or equal to the rate of discount.

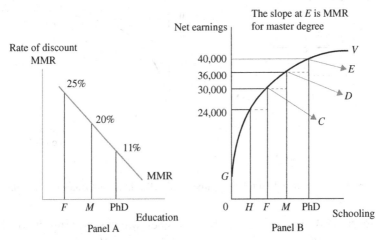

Figure 11.2: The Wage–schooling Curve

Obviously, all people would want to have a high wage–schooling curve. Different people of course would have a different wage–schooling curve. If John is more able than Mike in the labour market, his net earnings will be higher than Mike's as his wage–schooling curve will be higher. Hence, the wage–schooling curve is determined by the ability of each person. If John has a greater ability, this means that he can earn more than others per unit of education. His higher income could be because

(i) he spent less money in studying, (ii) his networking is better, (iii) he is better looking, (iv) he speaks well, or any combination of the above, etc. If there is high income tax rate or higher tuition fee, the wage–schooling curve will shift down as net earnings to present wages.

Figure 11.3 shows that John and Tom have the same wage–schooling curve. The question is do they have the same investment in schooling? The answer lies in the respective discount rate. Since both have the same wage–schooling curve, both have the same MRR line. In Panel A, we show that Tom's rate of discount is higher than John's rate of discount. Hence, using the stopping rule, John's years of schooling is Y compared to X for Tom. Back to Panel B, John will therefore have higher net earnings than Tom.

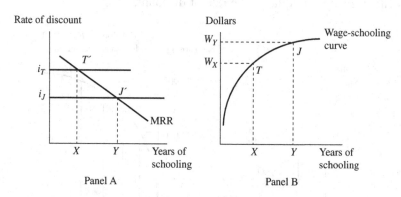

Figure 11.3:   John and Tom Have Same Ability But Different Rates of Discount

Figure 11.4 shows that Tan has a higher wage–schooling curve than Wong. Hence, Tan's MRR line is also higher than Wong's as is shown in Panel A because $JG > KG$. In this example, we assume that both have the same rate of discount. Using the stopping rule, Tan would have acquired Y years of schooling and his net earnings are represented by W_Y. For Wong, his net earnings are represented by W_X. The difference between W_Y and W_X in this simple framework is clearly determined by difference in ability and investment in education. If Wong has the same schooling as Tan, Wong's net earnings would be W^*, but W^* is not observable. We need to use econometrics to estimate W^*. Once W^* is available, then we can estimate JK, the difference of W_Y and W^*, to be attributed to difference in ability.

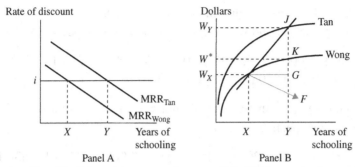

From X to Y, tan got more money than wong ($JG > KG$) because tan is more able.

Figure 11.4:   When Workers Have Different Abilities but same Discount

Selection Bias

Sometimes we observe that people do not accept jobs that pay well. We use the following example to explain how selection bias can lead to choice of careers which are seemingly not rational.

Suppose Lee is good as a worker in a blue-collar job and Chen is good as a worker in a white-collar job. The payouts matrix is given in Table 11.1.

Table 11.1:   Payouts Matrix

Worker	Net earnings per period in blue-collar job	Net earnings per period in white-collar job
Lee	$24,000	$40,000
Chen	$20,000	$45,000

For a blue-collar job, Lee earns more than Chen but reverse is true for a white-collar job. Suppose we use a two period model.[1] The cost of schooling is only foregone earnings. Both have the same discount rate at 10%. For a person to accept a blue-collar job, no additional schooling is necessary and hence, this worker can work for two periods. But to accept a white-collar job, the first period must be devoted to schooling. This worker can only work for one period.

---

[1]This example is modified from Borjas (2013, p. 255). One can consider more periods but the message is the same.

For Lee, the present value of working immediately and of going to school for one period and working for one period is respectively:

$PV_{Blue, Lee}$ = \$24,000 + \$24,000/(1 + 0.1) = \$24,000 + \$21,818 = \$45,818,
$PV_{White, Lee}$ = 0 + \$40,000/(1 + 0.1) = \$36,364.

The choice is obvious that Lee would not want a white-collar job.
For Chen, the respective figure is:

$PV_{Blue, Chen}$ = \$20,000 + \$20,000/(1 + 0.1) = \$20,000 + \$18,181 = \$38,181,
$PV_{White, Chen}$ = 0 + \$45,000/(1 + 0.1) = \$40,909.

Chen would want a white-collar job.

Hence, both are rational. But we often compare the observed data which are $PV_{Blue, Lee}$ and $PV_{White, Chen}$. And we conclude that Chen is not rational because Chen would have made more as $PV_{Blue, Lee}$ is greater than $PV_{White, Chen}$. But $PV_{Blue, Lee}$ is not relevant to Chen. $PV_{Blue, Chen}$ is relevant to Chen but $PV_{Blue, Chen}$ is not observable. This problem is often cited as selection bias but it can be corrected.[2]

Education as a Signalling Device

Imagine an employer wants to employ 10 workers but he has to screen 1,000 job applicants. How is he going to effectively choose the right workers at the minimum cost? If he makes a mistake in recruitment, he may have to dismiss some workers or labour turnover is high. He will incur other costs such as retraining costs, etc. This is a problem of asymmetric information which was discussed in the chapter on Incentive Pay.

Spence (1973) has come out with a solution for employers to use a diploma (education) to screen job applicants. It has many simplifying assumptions but the message is strong and simple. The essence of Signalling Model is that a firm treats a worker with the diploma as a high productivity person and one without the diploma as a low productivity person. Accordingly, this firm will pay a high productivity worker a high monthly wage and a low productivity worker a low monthly wage. As is shown in Panel A of Figure 11.5, a worker without the diploma will receive a lifetime earnings of \$100,000 and a worker with the diploma will receive a lifetime earnings of \$200,000. Implicit in the Signalling Model is the

---

[2]See Borjas (2013, p. 256).

assumption that education may add knowledge but basically does not alter a person's ability at the workplace. Of course, the firm will make a strategic mistake if low productivity workers do manage to get the diploma.

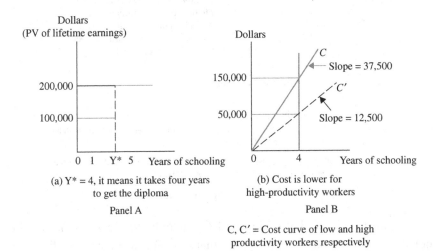

(a) Y* = 4, it means it takes four years to get the diploma

Panel A

(b) Cost is lower for high-productivity workers

Panel B

C, C' = Cost curve of low and high productivity workers respectively

Figure 11.5:   Education as a Signal

The model assumes that the cost of getting the diploma is high for low productivity people and low for high productivity people. Panel B of Figure 11.5 shows that the cost line of getting the diploma for low productivity is C with a slope of $37,500. If it takes four years to get the diploma, the cost of diploma is $150,000 for low productivity person. The cost line of getting the diploma for high productivity worker is C' with a slope of $12,500. If it takes four years to get the diploma, the cost of diploma is $50,000.

We want to show that, for signalling model to work, based on maximization of present value, it is not profitable for low productivity person to study for the diploma. In Figure 11.6, we superimpose the revenues and costs into one figure. For low productivity person, without the diploma, the lifetime earnings are $100,000. But if he gets the diploma, the net lifetime earnings are only $50,000 ($200,000 − $150,000). Hence, low productivity person will not study for the diploma. For high productivity person, without the diploma, his lifetime earnings are $50,000. But with the diploma, his lifetime earnings are $150,000 ($200,000 − $50,000). Hence, for high productivity person, it pays to study for the diploma. In this case, the model is said to have effective separating equilibrium.

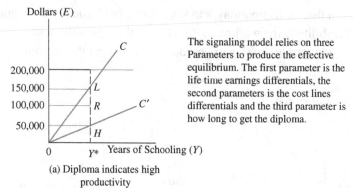

The signaling model relies on three Parameters to produce the effective equilibrium. The first parameter is the life time earnings differentials, the second parameters is the cost lines differentials and the third parameter is how long to get the diploma.

(a) Diploma indicates high
productivity

- For low productivity persons, without a diploma, they receive 100,000. With a diploma, net earning is only 50,000 (200,000–150,000).

- For high productivity persons, without a diploma, they receive 100,000. With a diploma, net earning is only 150,000 (200,000–50,000).

Figure 11.6:   Signaling Model

Figure 11.7 is similar to Figure 11.6. The only difference is that we do not use numbers but notations for analysis. For instance, the lifetime earnings for workers without diploma are represented by E_n and with diploma are represented by E_w. The cost of education for low productivity person is $C_{Low} = Y \cdot S_{Low}$ where Y = number of years to get the diploma and S means slope. Similarly, this also applies for high productivity person.

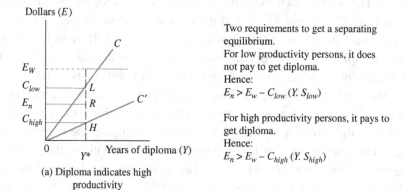

Two requirements to get a separating equilibrium.
For low productivity persons, it does not pay to get diploma.
Hence:
$E_n > E_w - C_{low} (Y. S_{low})$

For high productivity persons, it pays to get diploma.
Hence:
$E_n > E_w - C_{high} (Y. S_{high})$

(a) Diploma indicates high
productivity

- With diploma, workers get E_w. Without diploma, workers get E_n.

- Slow = slope of cost curve for low productivity persons. S_{high} = slope of cost curve for high productivity persons.

- Cost of diploma for low productivity persons, $C_{low.} = Y. S_{low}.$

- Cost of diploma for high productivity persons, $C_{high.} = Y. S_{high}.$

Figure 11.7:   Conditions for Effective Separating Equilibrium

The conditions for effective separating equilibrium are $E_n > E_w - C_{low}$ $(Y \cdot S_{low})$ and $E_n < E_w - C_{high}$ $(Y \cdot S_{high})$.

Dual Labour Markets as a Substitute for Signalling Model

It is expected that many economists have attacked the Signalling Model. The main criticism is there are cheaper ways to solve the problem created by asymmetric information. For instance, *Dual Labour Market Theory* by Doeringer and Pior (1985) suggests that for a large enterprise, there are so-called insiders and outsiders. Insiders are workers trusted by the firm and therefore enjoy job stability and high salary and are recipients of company-sponsored training. On the other hand, outsiders are basically treated as a buffer against cyclical factors. Consequently, they do not have job stability and are dispensable. When a firm recruits workers, new workers are put on probation and therefore treated as outsiders.

Training

Training is as important as education as an investment in human capital. Training and retraining is essential for workers to remain employed. There are two types of training. One is general training where training will increase productivity of workers in any firm. Firm specific training, as the term implies, will increase productivity provided the worker works for the firm which trains him. It is hard to find firm specific training. We will consider, for the time being, general training. In Figure 11.8, the VMP of a worker without training is $1,000 per period. Assuming no depreciation of skills, *ABCD* line is the VMP line of a worker without training. Consequently, the *ABCD* line is also the wage line of the worker.

We want to examine the economics of on-the-job training. When the worker receives training which takes place in one period from 0 to 1 in Figure 11.8, his VMP is only $600 during that period. The cost of training is $600. The decrease in VMP is to be expected as the worker must devote time to learn. After training, the VMP of the worker is $1,400 per period. Hence, the VMP line of a trained worker is *GHI*. The training is useful from the society's point of view and also from the point of view of the worker, as the worker can work for more periods at higher level of VMP.

If the worker bears the cost of training, he will receive $600 during training and earn $1,400 per period for many more periods to come. His

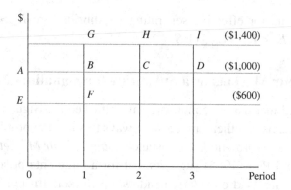

Figure 11.8:   Wage and VMP Lines with Training

wage line is therefore *EFGHI*. However, most workers do not bear the cost of training. They do not want to have smaller take home pay. In any case, if they cannot complete the training or quit the job for one reason or another, they cannot recoup the cost of training.

If the firm bears the cost of training, the firm will pay the worker the same wage which is $1,000 per period. But during the period of training, the VMP of the worker under training is only $600. Hence, the firm bears $400 in cost of training. From period 1 to 2, the firm would want to take back the cost of training and therefore continues to pay the worker $1,000 per period although this period, the VMP of the worker is $1,400. Hence, when the firm bears the cost of training, the wage line of the worker is *ABCHI*. This however presents a problem. The worker is at *B* but his VMP to other firms is at *G* as this is general training. Other firms will offer this worker $1,400 at *G*. If the worker leaves, the firm cannot recoup the cost of training. The bigger the distance between *G* and *B*, the higher is the probability that the worker will be poached. Hence, no firms want to be caught at *B* and all firms want to be in the position to attract workers at *G*. Consequently, the amount of training is less than optimal both at the firm and society level. This is market failure in training.

Market failure calls for government intervention. In Singapore, a training scheme in the name of Skills Development Fund (SDF) which was set up in 1979 aims to reduce market failure in training. All firms in

Singapore are required by law to pay training tax known as SDF levy.[3] The SDF revenue will then be used to subsidize, ranging from 30% to 70%, of training cost to encouraging firms to train their workers. SDF levy is not resented by firms as SDF is a tripartite in nature, supported by the government, employers and the NTUC. SDF scheme is effective as each year about 400,000 workers are sponsored by SDF funding.[4] SDF aims to encourage general training. SDF will not be involved in firm specific training as there is no market failure in firm specific training. Chew (1988) shows that SMEs did not make full use of the SDF funding. At the same time, SDF funding cannot be used to train those who are unemployed.

Hence, Singapore's Workforce Development Agency (WDA) is tasked to train those who are unemployed, those who work for SMEs and those who want to change careers. As technology changes so fast, WDA has outsourced the training schemes to the private sector. Training institutes need to work with employers to map out the training schemes and there is some obligation for employers to employ them after training under the scheme known as Train and Place.[5] Those who are in the informal sector in Singapore will be trained by the self-help organizations such as Chinese Development Assistance Council (CDAC).

With effect from March 2016, citizens above the age of 25 have been given $500 in SkillsFuture credit.[6] This is virtual individual account. I would like to propose that we can encourage Singaporeans to put money in this account and the government can match the amount equally subject to a ceiling. If this proposal is implemented, this SkillsFuture account can be another account under the Central Provident Fund scheme which will be discussed later in the book.

We can see that there has been an attempt to ensure that those who want to learn new skills will be able to select the appropriate training scheme with training subsidy. Singapore has the resources and will to

---

[3]It is a small percentage of total pay roll.
[4]See Year Book of Statistics, Dept of Statistics, Singapore (2014).
[5]See https://www.google.com.sg/webhp?sourceid=chrome-instant&ion=1&espv=2&ie=UTF-8#q=train%20and%20place%20singapore.
[6]See http://brightfuture.sg/what-is-skillsfuture/?gclid=CMS-xvzYsM8CFdGHaAodLs4NQg for SkillsFuture scheme.

ensure that each adult citizen is able to attend a training scheme each year. Hence, although Singapore is small in size, it is big on training.

Private Tuition as a Form of Training

In many countries, parents ensure that their children have private tuition to improve the grades of their children in schools. This is an arms race in education. In Figure 11.9, we show that the amount of time spent on studies is *OA* per period and the school grade is *X*. If the parents arrange for private tuition and assume that the time spent on studies is the same, *KA* is equal to *OE*. The school grade has improved by *Y*. This is a good outcome. But the trade-off behind this narrative is that the time for rest or play is reduced. As long as the grade has improved, the trade-off is acceptable at least in the short run. However, if the parents keep increasing the time spent on tuition, the time to study, the time to rest or to play will be compromised. The child may suffer a burn out and the grade will eventually fall. By then, it may be too late as the child may hate schooling.

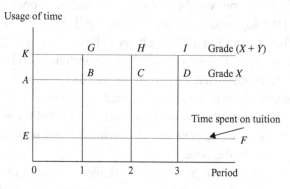

Figure 11.9:   School Grades and Private Tuition

Discussion Questions

1. How to take into account when university education is not fully an investment?
2. Use Figure 11.7 to show that if it takes less than half the time to get the diploma, the diploma would not be useful as a signalling device.

3. You are given the following facts. Derive the range of Y to get an effective separating equilibrium:

$$E_n = \$100,000; \ E_w = \$200,000; \ S_{high} = 12,500; \ S_{low} = 37,500.$$

4. If the firm bears \$300 in training cost and the worker bears \$100, what is the wage line of this co-cost sharing situation based on Figure 11.8?
5. Use a figure similar to Figure 11.8 to analyze how SDF scheme can alleviate market failure in training.

Bibliography

Borjas, G. J. (2013). *Labor Economics*, Seventh edition. New York: McGraw-Hill.

Chew, S. B. (1988). *Small Firms in Singapore*. Singapore: Oxford University Press.

Doeringer, P. B. and Pior, M. J. (1985). *Internal Labor Markets and Manpower Analysis*, books.google.com.

Spence, M. (1973). "Job Market Signalling", *The Quarterly Journal of Economics*, Vol. 87, No. 3, Aug, pp. 355–374.

Chapter 12

Labour Market Discrimination and Values in Society

In a competitive labour market, two persons with the same skills set and same utility function may receive different wages because of differences in race and gender. These differences are often attributed to labour market discrimination. In this chapter, we want to examine how economists analyze labour market discrimination.[1] In particular, we want to distinguish four types of discrimination, namely employer discrimination, employee discrimination, customer discrimination and statistical discrimination.

Employer Discrimination

In the labour market, there are black workers and white workers. Suppose both are equally productive and the market wages for both are $1,000 per month. An employer by the name of Armstrong discriminates against employing black workers. It means that when he employs a black worker, he suffers an emotional cost of $100. Hence, the cost of employing a black worker is $1,100 although the actual outlay is only $1,000 ($W_b$). Armstrong acts as if the cost of employing black worker is not W_b but is $W_b (1 + d)$ dollars where d = discrimination coefficient which is 0.1.[2]

If all employers are like Armstrong who discriminates against black workers, then no firms will employ black workers at the wage of $1,000

---

[1]The basic framework is based on Becker (1971).

[2]In the case of nepotism, the coefficient is negative.

a month. If black workers have to find work to pay bills and raise families, black workers have to accept lower wages. Employers would pay \$1,000 for a white worker and therefore employers would employ a black worker if the total cost is also \$1,000. This means that the actual wage for black workers, W_{ba}, cannot exceed \$1,000. We can derive W_{ba} as W_{ba} $(1 + 0.1) = \$1,000$. Hence, $W_{ba} = \$909$. The higher the discrimination coefficient, the lower will be the wages for the black workers.

Suppose that black workers and white workers are equally productive but they face different market wages such as $W_w = \$1,100$ and $W_b = \$1,000$. Since black and white workers are perfectly substitutable, any employers without prejudiced would employ black workers as is shown in Panel B of Figure 12.1. The VMP_E line is the same for white as well as for black workers. As $W_b < W_w$, non-discriminating firm will employ E_b number of black workers. Suppose a firm discriminates against black workers mildly. Its discrimination coefficient (d_m) is only 0.05, the total cost of hiring black workers is $W_b (1 + d_m) = \$1,050$ which is still lower than W_w, the mildly discriminating firm will still employ all black workers but a smaller number of black workers as $E_{bm} < E_b$. Even though the actual outlay of employing black workers is still the same which is \$1,000, the total cost is higher due to emotional cost. The increase in total cost has hurt the black workers as the demand for black workers is reduced. If discriminating coefficient (d_s) is 0.1, then this discriminating firm will employ either white workers (E_w) or black workers (E_{bs}) or any combination because $W_w = W_b (1 + d_s)$. If the strongly discriminating firm employs

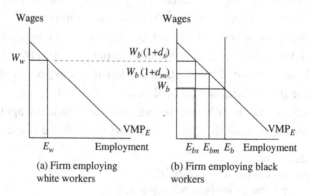

(a) Firm employing
white workers

(b) Firm employing black
workers

Figure 12.1:   Employer Discrimination

only white workers, we can conclude that the discriminating coefficient is greater than 0.1. In Panel A of Figure 12.1, strongly discriminating firm employs E_w number of white workers. W_w is either equal to or smaller than $W_b (1 + d_s)$.

It is intuitive that a firm which discriminates against any workers is against profit maximization. The reason is simple. Both black and white workers are equally productive and black workers are cheaper. Profit (π) will be maximized when the firm employs black workers till W_b = VMP. This situation is depicted at j in Figure 12.2 where E_n is the number of black workers employed. The total output is equal to area *agjh* and total wage bill is equal to area *egjh*. Assume no other cost of production. Profit is equal to:

$$\Pi = \text{Total output} - \text{Total wage bill} = \text{area } agjh - \text{area } egjh = \text{area } age.$$

If the firm discriminates against black workers mildly and therefore the firm will still employ black workers but a smaller number of black workers as $E_d < E_n$. In this case, the profit is smaller as is shown below:

$$\Pi_m = \text{Total output} - \text{Total wage bill} = \text{area } acih - \text{area } efih$$
$$= \text{area } acfe < \text{area } age.$$

Emotional cost (area *bcfe*) which has caused employment of black workers to be smaller is included in Π_m.

- At E_n, Π = Total output – total wage bill = area *agjh* – area *egjh* = area *age*

- At E_d, Π_m = Total output – total wage bill = area *acih* – area *efih* = area *acfe* < area *age*.

- Profit is reduced by area *cgf*

- At E_d, Π_s = Total output – total wage bill = area *acih* – area *bcih* = area *acb* < area *acfe*.

- Profit is reduced by *bcge*

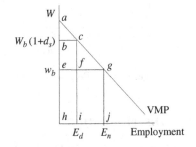

Figure 12.2:   Employer Discrimination and Its Effects on Profit

If the firm employs all white workers even though white workers are more expensive, this means that the discrimination coefficient is high such that W_w is either equal to or smaller than $W_b(1 + d_s)$. In this case, the profit is even smaller as shown below:

$$\Pi_s = \text{Total output} - \text{Total wage bill} = \text{area } acih - \text{area } bcih$$
$$= \text{area } acb < \text{area } acfe.$$

The only difference between Π_s and Π_m is that the emotional cost has been converted into a component for W_w.

In Figure 12.3, we present the relation between profit and discrimination coefficient. Using the same example where $w_b < w_w$ and black and white workers are equally productive. When d_b is zero, the firm will employ only black workers and receive π_{MAX}. As d_b increases from zero to a positive number, the firm will still employ only black workers but fewer black because of emotional cost and p will decrease as the employment level is not at profit maximizing level. When discrimination coefficient reaches a threshold level at d_s, the firm will start employing only white workers. The profit (π_s) is low because the firm employs a much smaller workforce (all white workers) and pays a much higher wage per worker ($W_w > W_b$).

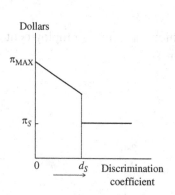

- Assume $W_b < W_w$
- When d_b is zero, the firm will employ only black workers and receives π_{MAX}.
- As d_b increases from zero to a positive number, the firm will still employ only black workers but π will decrease.
- At d_s, the firm will start employing only white workers and receives lower profits of π_s

Figure 12.3:   Profits (π) and Discrimination Coefficient

Employee Discrimination

Armstrong is a white worker. His market wage is $W_w = \$1,000$. However, if one of his colleagues is a black worker, he will suffer an emotional cost of $100. To him, he is paid only $900. His perceived wage is $W_{wp} = W_w (1 - d_b) = \$1,000 (1 - 0.1) = \$900$.

Suppose they are two employers and in the labour markets, we have black and white workers and all are equally productivity and the market wages are the same for white and black workers at $1,000 a month. If a firm employs all white workers, then profits can be maximized. If a firm employs all black workers, then profits can be maximized too. Any rational employer will not have an integrated workforce as this employer has to pay white worker more than $1,000 to get him to work with black workers. The above illustration leads us to conclude that employee discrimination will lead to segregated workforce. As long as firms can employ segregated workforce, there is no impact on profits.

However, if the firms need to have an integrated workforce due to scarcity of white workers and black workers need to find work, then the employer has to compensate white workers for working with black workers. The perceived wage (W_{wp}) of a white worker has to be $1,000. This means that the market wage of a white worker is $W_w = W_{wp}/(1 - d_b)$. Hence, W_w is greater than $1,000 in this example. There is a wage gap now between white and black workers. If d_b is bigger, W_w is higher. The profits of this employer who employs an integrated workforce will fall. Furthermore, if this employer is able to reduce wages of black workers to pay the emotional cost of the white worker such that the average wage per worker is the same to the firm and employ the same total number of workers in the integrated workforce, his profits will not fall. But this outcome is at the expense of black workers. The wage gap between white and black workers will be bigger.

Customer Discrimination

A store sells a product at the price of $1. A customer by the name of Bob goes to this store and makes a purchase of the product at $P = \$1$. However, when Bob is served by a black employee, he will suffer an emotional cost of 10 cents. Hence, to Bob, the perceived price (P_p) of the product is no longer $1 but $1.1 which is equal to $P_p = P(1 + d)$ where d is the customer discrimination coefficient . Other things being equal, Bob will buy fewer units as the demand curve for the product is downward sloping. The store will suffer in sales and therefore profits. What can the store do? The store would prefer to employ white employees to serve Bob.

If the store employs a black worker, in order to attract customers such as Bob to buy the same quantity of the product, P_p has to be equal to $1. The actual price (P) is therefore equal to $P = P_p/(1 + d) = 1/(1 + d) < \$1$. The firm has to lower the price. Either the firm lowers the price or makes arrangements such that all black workers will not be visible to the customers. All these considerations and options will lead to one solid outcome which is employing black workers is more costly than simply the wages of black workers.

Suppose again black and white workers are equally productive and $W_w = \$1,200$ and $W_b = \$1,000$. In the presence of customer discrimination, to the store, although $W_b = \$1,000$, the store's actual cost of employing the black worker (W_{ba}) is $1,100 if d_{bc} is equal to 0.1. $W_{ba} = \$1,200$ if d_{bc} is equal to 0.2. The black workers will therefore suffer in terms of lower wages and smaller employment as long as d_{bc} is greater than zero.

Statistical Discrimination[3]

Due to asymmetric information, employers always have difficulty in identifying job applicants who will turn out to be productive workers. Suppose William is an employer who aims to recruit a few workers whom he hopes that they are productive and will not resign within a year. He has hundreds of job applicants. Obviously, he will examine the personal characteristics which he thinks will help him to decide who is a good worker for his firm. However, due to past experience, he is also interested in examining the group statistics of all job applicants in terms of race, gender, marital status, number of grown up children, schools they studied, current place of residence, etc.

Suppose William observes that a job applicant who is married with grown up children and lives near the location of William's firm, has the record of staying with his firm for at least more than a year. If William takes the group statistics into account, his decision of hiring is based on statistical discrimination (SD).

---

[3] See Thurow (1975) for the pioneer work on statistical discrimination.

Figure 12.4 presents the decision making process of an employer using statistical discrimination. Individual statistics are plotted on the Y-axis and group statistics are plotted on the X-axis. Suppose William as an employer decided to recruit workers based on Y only. And, he chose Y_1, then this is not SD.

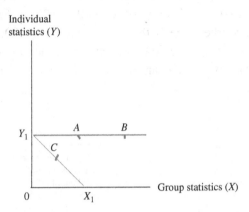

Figure 12.4:   Statistical Discrimination

There are two versions of SD. For Version 1, William's requirement for a job applicant is Y_1. Hence, he will choose a candidate either at A or B. So, group statistics count. In this case, group statistics is an added advantage. For Version 2, William does not have any minimum requirement with respect to Y. He will choose either C or X_1. There is a trade-off between Y and X in Version 2.

SD is different from employer discrimination as William does not bear emotional cost of employing any job applicants based on group statistics. His profit is not promised. SD is also different from signalling model. In the signalling model, job applicants will acquire "diploma" to indicate that they are productive. In the case of SD, the job applicants' group statistics are not 'investment goods".

William can make mistakes using group statistics but these are plain mistakes and not due to discrimination. Statistical outliers can fall victims or benefit from SD. For instance, if a married woman with grown up children plans to quit within a year but did not inform William at the interview. In this case, she benefited from SD. A single woman who is not a job hopper, is not employed by William as he concludes that she will quit soon. She is a victim of SD.

Figure 12.5 shows that most employers use the *OR* line to determine wages of workers according to the group statistics. Mary, a job applicant is at *M* which is above the *OR* line. Mary is a statistical outlier and she is paid more than the average worker. She therefore benefits from SD. Jane, another job applicant is at *J* which is below the *OR* line. She is paid less than the average worker. She is therefore a victim of SD. Of course, if statistical outliers become a common occurrence, then the *OR* line is not reliable and ultimately not relevant. In this case, there is no SD.

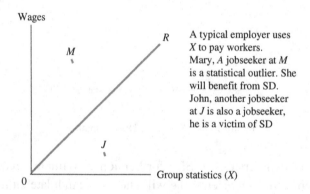

Figure 12.5:   Statistical Outliers and Statistical Discrimination

Labour Market Equilibrium

Implicitly in many examples we use in this chapter, there was a condition that if black workers have to find work they have to accept lower wages due to lack of choice. By implication, if there are more black workers in the labour markets, the wages of black workers will be lower. Figure 12.6 presents this perspective.[4] The demand curve for black workers is a function of R_{BW} which is the ratio of W_B over W_W. When R_{BW} is greater than one, implying that black workers are more expensive, there is very little demand for black workers. Hence, employers who employ N_F of black

---

[4]This figure is modified from Figure 12.4, Ehrenberg and Smith (2003, p. 410).

workers have a negative discrimination coefficient against black. When R_{BW} is equal to one, non-discriminating employers will employ $N_G - N_F$ for black workers. When black workers are cheaper than white workers, demand for black workers is strong. Given the supply curve of black workers (S_{LB}), the equilibrium R_{BW} is determined at J. If the supply curve of black workers shifts to the right, the wages of black workers relative to the wages of white workers will decrease.

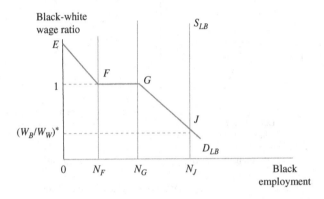

Figure 12.6: Determination of Black/White Wage Ratio

The slope of EF portion of the labour demand curve for black workers reflects the degree of negative discrimination in the labour markets. The FG portion shows no discrimination and the slope of GJ portion reflects discrimination against black workers. If GJ portion is flatter, the relative wages for black workers will be higher given the labour supply curve of black workers.

Now we consider discrimination against black women. In Figure 12.7, the demand curve for white male lawyers and for black female lawyers are D_{WM} and D_{BF}, respectively. The supply curve of white male lawyers and of black female lawyers are S_{WM} and S_{BF}, respectively. If there is no discrimination and both types of lawyers are equally productive, all the lawyers regardless of gender and race should receive the same salary. However, due to discrimination against black female lawyers, the demand curve for white male lawyers will shift upward and the demand curve for black female lawyers will shift downward. The equilibrium point for white male lawyers is at *J* while that of black female lawyers is at *K*. There is a salary gap now between white male lawyers and black female lawyers. If there is more supply of black female lawyers, the wages of black female lawyers will be lower.

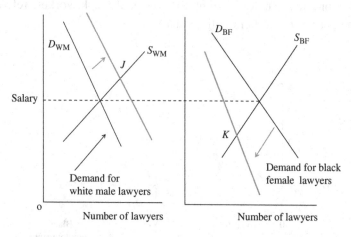

Figure 12.7:   White Male Lawyers vs Black Female Lawyers

Occupational Crowding

In certain occupations such as kindergarten teachers, more than 95% of the workforce is women. It is tempting to conclude that this occupational crowding is caused by discrimination. According to Borjas (2013, p. 401), the occupational crowding need not be the outcome of discrimination by employers but the results of social norm that girls are taught to believe that certain occupations are meant and good for girls. As more girls join these few occupations and therefore increase the supply of labour, the wages of women decrease. At the same time, these occupations cannot grow in size as most of these occupations are not traded sectors. Consequently, the demand for women workers in these female dominated occupations does not increase despite competitive wages for women. We therefore observe that R_{mf} which is the ratio of male wages over female wages, being greater than one.

Explaining Male–Female Wage Gap (R_{mf}) as Outcome of Specialization in Household Production

Consider James and Mary as two individual employees. If they get married with each other, we expect James to continue to work in the labour market and Mary perhaps quits work especially if they have children. We want to examine the decision making process of James and Mary as a couple. Due to perhaps, occupational crowding, James' wage is $300 and Mary's wage is $250 as is shown in Figure 12.8. Due to gender difference in biology, Mary's productivity in the household sector is $200 and James' productivity in the household sector is $150. Hence, both face different opportunity sets and in this example, we begin by assuming that R_{mf} is greater than one if both James and Mary are fully time employees.[5] Whether James and Mary would work in the labour market and if so, for how many hours is the outcome of utility maximization.

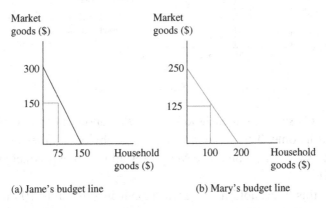

(a) Jame's budget line	(b) Mary's budget line

Figure 12.8:   James and Mary — Unmarried Opportunity Sets

As a married couple, James and Mary would only have one opportunity set as shown in Figure 12.9. As a couple, the total labour income is $550 at N and the total value of the household sector is $350 at H. However, it is obvious that James has a comparative advantage in the

---

[5] We can start with R_{mf} being less than one and still get the same conclusion.

labour market and Mary has a comparative advantage in the household sector. There is clear division of labour in the sense that James will be the one who starts work in the labour market and Mary in the household sector. The household's opportunity set is NFG. If this couple choose G, this household has $150 in labour income and $275 in household income. Hence, the division of labour dictates that Mary's contribution in household income is $200 and James' is $75. James' labour income is $150. James works in the labour market and also contributes to household production and Mary is full time at home.

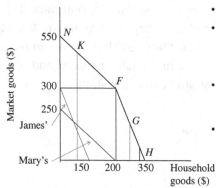

• At *H*: James and Mary allocate all

• At *G*, Mary is full time in household sector and James allocates his time between work and household.

• At *F*, James full time in labour market and Mary full time in household sector.

• At *K*, James full time in labour market and Mary allocates her time between work and household.

Figure 12.9:   Opportunity Set of Married Couple

If *F* is chosen, this household has $300 in labour income and $200 in household income. The division of labour is obvious. James uses all his time earning labour income and Mary uses all her time producing household goods.

At *K*, this household has $425 in labour income and $100 in household goods. To earn $425 in labour income, James works full time earning $300 in labour income and Mary contributes $125 in labour income. Mary also contributes $100 in household production.

Given the utility function of the household, James and Mary will decide the utility maximization point on the household opportunity set. Figure 12.10 shows three situations. In Panel A, the couple chose *G*, resting on the indifference curve, *U*. At *G*, James has a part time job and Mary does not work in the labour market. In Panel B, the couple chose *K*, implying that James has a full time job and Mary has a part time job. In Panel C, there is clear division of labour between James and Mary.

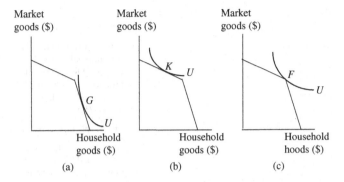

Figure 12.10:   Who Works Where?

Figure 12.11 presents a situation where there is an increase in wages. *G* is the original equilibrium point for the household, resting on indifference curve, *U*. At *G*, James has a part time job. As the household opportunity set expands, the new equilibrium point is either *K* or *F*. James will become a full time worker. Mary may be a part time worker if *K* is chosen.

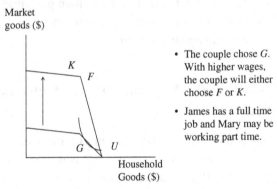

- The couple chose *G*. With higher wages, the couple will either choose *F* or *K*.

- James has a full time job and Mary may be working part time.

Figure 12.11:   Increase in the Wage Rate Leads to More Hours in Labour Market

Figure 12.12 presents a situation where there is an increase in productivity in the household activity due to advanced technology. The original equilibrium point for the couple is *K*. As the technology has expanded the household opportunity set from left to right, the new equilibrium point may be *K′* or *F* or *G*. However, we argue that most households would want a certain required amount of household goods, such as H_R as shown in the figure. *K′* is likely the chosen point, meaning James has a full time job and Mary is still a part time worker but may be working more hours.

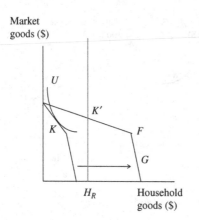

The couple chose *K*.

With higher productivity in household sector, Jane can spend fewer hours to produce the required amount of household goods (H_R).

The couple now chose *K'*.

James is still a full time worker and Mary can put in more hours in labour market.

Figure 12.12:   Increase in Household Productivity Can Lead to More Hours in Labour Market

In sum, our analysis shows that most households will either choose *K* or *K'*. Even without discrimination against women, James will earn more than Mary as most full time workers earn more than part time workers on per hour basis. Gender wage gap therefore lies in job structure even if we can remove discrimination against women.

Explaining Male–Female Wage Gap (R_{mf}) as Outcome of Job Structure

Goldin (2014) has shown that, without relying on discrimination against women, R_{mf} is approaching the value of one but is unlikely to be equal to one on two accounts. Firstly, the job structure is such that full time workers are paid much highly on per hour basis than part time workers. Secondly, most women work on part time basis. Using her methodology, we look at two occupations: cleaners and teaching profession at the university level.

In Figure 12.13, *GK* represents the relations between wages per period and job tenure. A long job tenure implies being associated with the firm for a long time as a full time employee. *GK* is a pretty flat line, implying that job experience is not that important in these occupations. Goldin finds that, for pharmacists, the *GK* line is flat. Due to advanced technology, she argues that this profession has structured the jobs such that it is very easy for a pharmacist to rejoin the profession after a break from the labour market. Hence, for pharmacists and other similar occupations such as cleaners, the *GK* line is flat. It does not matter whether most women have short job tenure and men have long job tenure, the wages of male and females is similar. In this case, R_{mf} is closely to the value of one for these two occupations.

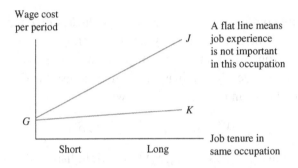

Figure 12.13:   Wage–Job Tenure Line

Goldin uses lawyers as an example to explain why R_{mf} is much greater than the value of one for some occupations where networking is important. For law profession, continuous labour market experience is important. The wage–job tenure line is very steep such as *GJ*. One has to put in long hours in the profession to be productive and discontinuous labour market experience is not tolerated. Given the *GJ* line, those who work full time will receive much higher wages per period than those who work part time. From the household production model discussed above, we know that most women have a short job tenure and men have a long job tenure. She therefore concludes that R_{mf} is very high for the law profession without relying on gender discrimination.

What can we do to narrow R_{mf}? If technology can allow women to work from home and be as efficient as those in the office, the wage–job tenure line will be flat and R_{mf} is likely to move closer to one. However, if networking is important and you need to meet clients and socialize away from home, there is little chance that R_{mf} is equal to one.

Measuring Gender Discrimination

Assume that wages are a function of schooling plus all other statistics. Ignoring all other variables, the male earnings function and female earnings functions can be stated as follows:

$$\text{Male workers: } W_M = \alpha_M + \beta_M S_M,$$

$$\text{Female workers: } W_F = \alpha_F + \beta_F S_F.$$

All α's are coefficients. For instance, β_M indicates how much a man's wage increases if he gets one more year of schooling.

It will be wrong to attribute $\Delta W = W_M - W_F$ as gender discrimination.

To measure gender discrimination, we need to use the Oaxaca (1973) composition which can be expressed below:

$$\Delta W = \alpha_M + \beta_M S_M - \alpha_F - \beta_F S_F.$$

By adding and subtracting $(\beta_M S_F)$ to the right hand side of the above equation, we get:

$$\Delta W = \alpha_M + \beta_M S_M - \alpha_F - \beta_F S_F + \beta_M S_F - \beta_M S_F.$$

Rearranging, we obtain

$$\Delta W = \alpha_M - \alpha_F + (\beta_M - \beta_F) S_F + \beta_M (S_M - S_F).$$

Let

$$G = \alpha_M - \alpha_F + (\beta_M - \beta_F) S_F \quad \text{and} \quad H = \beta_M (S_M - S_F).$$

G measures the differential in gender wages which is due to discrimination and H measures the differential in gender wages which is due to differences in schooling.

Figure 12.14 shows the earnings function for males and females. A typical male worker is at M, earning W_M in wages. A typical female worker is at F, with less schooling than her counterpart and earns W_F in wages. If we use the statistics provided by the government, we have to compare M and F and the wage differentials are due to differences in schooling and how markets treat male and female workers differently. If the typical female woman was paid as if she were a man, she would earn W_F^*. Hence the correct way to measure gender discrimination is to estimate the difference between W_F^* and W_F.

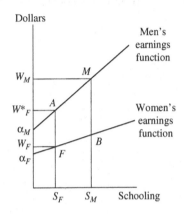

- Average woman has S_F years of schooling and earns W_F

- Average man has S_M years of schooling and earns W_M

- Part of wage differential arises because men have more schooling than women

- If the average woman was paid as if she were a man, she would earn W_F^*

- Measure of discrimination is then given by $(W_F^* - W_F)$.

- A and B are not observable

Figure 12.14:   Measuring Gender Wage Discrimination

Discussion Questions

1. Suppose black and white workers are equally productive and $W_w = \$2,200$ and $W_b = \$2,000$. What is the value of the discrimination of D_S in Figure 12.3?
2. In Figure 12.11, would K' be the utility maximization point in terms of a tangency between the budget line and an indifference curve?
3. Discuss the wage–job tenure line for university teaching profession.
4. If $\alpha_M = \alpha_F$ and $\beta_M = \beta_F$, what is the expression for earnings equation for all workers regardless of gender?

Bibliography

Becker, G. S. (1971). *The Economics of Discrimination*, Second edition. Chicago: University of Chicago Press.

Borjas, G. J. (2013). *Labor Economics*, Seventh edition. New York: McGraw-Hill.

Goldin, C. (2014). "A Grand Gender Convergence: Its Last Chapter", *America Economic Review*, April, Vol. 104, No. 4, 1091–1119.

Ehrenberg, R. G. and Smith, R. S. (2003). *Modern Labor Economics*. Boston: Addison Wesley.

Oaxaca, R. 1973. "Male-Female Wage Differentials in Urban Labor Markets." *International Economic Review* 14: 693–709.

Thurow, L. (1975). *Generating Inequity*. New York: Basic Books.

Chapter 13

Employment and Unemployment

What is full employment and full employment output? How do economists look at unemployment? Is unemployment preventable or involuntary? This chapter will examine all these issues.

Measures of Labour Market Participation

A jobseeker is an unemployed person. He fails to get a job at the prevailing wage and he still actively looks for a job. A person with a job is regarded as an employed person. He may work 10 hours a day. He may work three hours a day as a part time worker, but a part time worker is still considered being employed.

Labour force is the sum of unemployment and employment. Employment rate is the ratio of employment over the labour force and unemployment is the ratio of unemployment over the labour force. Using this definition, we can conclude that the sum of employment rate and unemployment rate is equal to 100%.[1]

Labour force participation rate is defined in terms of labour force over population. Female labour force participation rate is defined in terms of female labour force over female population. Female labour force participation rate in almost all countries have been rising as the purchasing power of wages declines.

---

[1] In many textbooks, employment rate is defined in terms of employment over population.

In the developing countries, they seldom use unemployment rate. Rather, they discuss in terms of labour utilization rate. The labour utilization rate which, has been dictated by the seasons is high during the harvest time.

In many countries, they allow foreign workers to work. Those foreigners, who quality for more stringent criteria are given green cards or accepted as permanent residents, but they are not citizens. If we include foreign workers and permanent residents as part of the labour force, employment rate would be higher and unemployment rate would be lower compared to these measures strictly applicable to citizens. If we want to assess effectiveness of public policy in the labour markets, we should not include foreign workers and permanent residents in the measurement of employment and unemployment rates.

Economists like to discuss and compare unemployment rate across countries. Table 1.1 of Chapter 1 shows how unemployment rates differ across selected countries. The reader would ponder why unemployment rates differ so much. The answer lies in the labour market dynamics but it is increasingly being affected by populist policies.

Labour Supply over the Business Cycle

Labour supply is sum of employment and unemployment. During a recession, some workers lost their jobs and many more workers saw their take home pay reduced. Do we have more labour supply during a recession? In a typical household, some main bread winners have earned less during a recession. Consequently, the secondary workforce such as the wife and adult children may join the labour market to look for a job to supplement family income. As they enter the labour market as jobseekers, the labour supply increases. This is known as added worker effect. On the other hand, during a recession, some jobseekers get so discouraged of not being able to get a job, quit the labour market. They are therefore not counted as part of the labour force, although they still want to work. This is known as discouraged worker effect, which reduces labour supply. Hence, whether labour supply would increase over the business cycle depends on the strength of these two opposing forces.

During an economic recovery, the workers' earnings have increased. The secondary workforce may opt to quit the labour market either to look after the household or back to school. This is known as withdrawal effect, which reduces labour supply. On the other hand, many people who quit the labour markets on the account of discouraged worker effect now want to enter the labour market because of economic recovery. This is known as encouraged worker effect. During the first year of economic recovery, where encouraged worker effect is strong, we may see the situation where both employment level and unemployment level increase.

Black Employment and Unemployment

It has been observed by many scholars that male labour force participation rate for whites and blacks have been declining in the past five decades.[2] In particular, the male labour force participation rate for blacks has declined from 85% in the 1960s to 65% in 2010. At the same time, due to affirmative action programs, many large firms have to employ black workers and large firms provide good wage jobs, the wages of black workers have increased over the similar period.[3] These findings do not contradict our conclusion that if there are more black workers in the labour market, wages of black workers would fall. An explanation has been put forward to explain falling labour participation rate and higher wages of black workers.[4] Suppose the medium wages of black workers is W_{BM} which is a weightage average of low wages (W_{BL}) and high wages (W_{BH}) of black workers. However, due to generous cash grants and other welfare programs, the reservation wage of black workers has increased. Consequently, many low wage black workers quit the labour market. As many black workers earning low wages have quit the labour markets and there is about the same number of black workers earning high wages, we therefore observe a higher medium wage (W_{BM}) of black workers, although wages of black workers were about the same.

In Table 13.1, we show that if young blacks live in less segregated city, the percentage of idle young blacks is 15.4%. However, if they live in very segregated city, the percentage of idle young blacks is 21.6%.

---

[2]See Borjas (2013, p. 392).
[3]This issue is complex. See Freeman (1973) for some discussion.
[4]See Borjas (2013, p. 391).

Table 13.1:   Relation between Black Residential Segregation and Percentage of Blacks Who are Idle, 1990

Group	City is not very segregated	City is very segregated
Blacks aged 20–24	15.4	21.6
Whites aged 20–24	7.0	6.6

Source: Borjas (2013, Table 12.2, p. 502).

We know the causality is complex but all governments must implement policy to avoid segregation by race, age or income levels. We will examine public policy of Singapore in this regard later in the book.

Types of Unemployment

Figure 13.1 presents a typical competitive labour market where wages are fully flexible, the equilibrium point is J and there is full employment. Unemployment is zero because all jobseekers who are willing to work at W_C have found work. This is what we said in the previous chapters. But this narrative is not completely correct. Even in a full employment situation, there will be some "long-term" unemployment. There can be two types of long-term unemployment even when the economy is at full employment. First type of long-term unemployment is known as frictional unemployment. Information flows in the labour markets are never perfect.

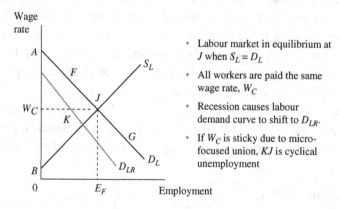

* Labour market in equilibrium at J when $S_L = D_L$
* All workers are paid the same wage rate, W_C
* Recession causes labour demand curve to shift to D_{LR}.
* If W_C is sticky due to micro-focused union, KJ is cyclical unemployment

Figure 13.1:   Equilibrium in Competitive Labour Market

Consequently, it takes time and effort for unemployed workers and employers with job vacancies to find each other. Consider a jobseeker who has five wage offers but he decides to continue job search for an even higher wage offer. He is between F and G on the labour demand curve, D_L. He is unemployed till he accepts a wage offer. He is regarded as frictionally unemployed. Frictional unemployment is not visible in Figure 13.1. It is not short-term unemployment and it can be reduced effectively by only increasing the efficiency of the labour markets.

The second type of long-term unemployment is structural unemployment. Structural unemployment arises when there is a mismatch between the skills demanded and supplied in an occupation or in a locality. In other words, the labour demand curve in Figure 13.1 only indicates the demand for workers with the right skills. Structural unemployment is not visible in the figure. It is not a short-term unemployment because structure unemployment can be reduced only by effective training schemes and by reducing monitoring cost of worker performance. Later in this chapter, we will present efficiency wage model to explain structural unemployment.

When a recession comes, besides the two types of long-term unemployment, there is short-term unemployment which is known as cyclical unemployment. In Figure 13.1, we show that, when there is a recession, the demand curve for labour will shift down to D_{LR}. If wages are sticky due to perhaps micro-focused union, there will be KJ amount of cyclical unemployment.

In this book, we define frictional and structural unemployment as long-term unemployment. By implication, the long-term unemployment cannot be reduced by demand management policy. On the other hand, cyclical unemployment is regarded as short-term unemployment which is avoidable because it can be removed by expansionary Keynesian policy.

Full Employment, Full Employment Output and Natural Unemployment

In an economy at any moment, actual unemployment is therefore the sum of frictional, structural and cyclical unemployment. But economists often discuss policy options in terms of full employment output. What is full employment and what is full employment output? Answers to these two related questions lie in the definition of natural unemployment.[5] In this book, full employment is defined in terms of no short term unemployment in the economy. Hence, in Figure 13.1, E_F is full employment level and $OAJE_F$ is full employment output. Natural unemployment is the sum of frictional and structural unemployment as cyclical unemployment by definition is zero.

In terms of percentages, actual unemployment (U_A) in an economy is the sum of frictional rate (U_F), structural rate (U_S) and cyclical unemployment rate (U_C). When the economy is in full employment, actual unemployment which is the sum of only frictional and structural unemployment with no cyclical unemployment is then defined as natural unemployment rate (U_N).

In Figure 13.2, we show the relation between actual GDP (GDP_A) and employment level. At the full employment level (E_F), the full employment output is GDP_F. If employment level is E_1 which is less than E_F, the actual GDP (GDP_1) is less than GDP_F. This indicates that cyclical unemployment is positive. Actual unemployment rate is greater than natural unemployment

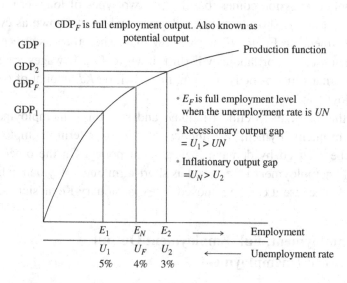

Figure 13.2:   Full Employment Output

<hr>

[5]There is an extensive discussion on how to define natural unemployment. See Tobin (1972) for the pioneer definition.

rate, which implies that there is a recession and the economy is under performing. If employment level is E_2 which is greater than E_F, GDP_2 is greater than GDP_F. This indicates that the economy is overheating and the cyclical unemployment is negative. In the same figure, we also include another X axis representing unemployment rate. There is a fixed relation between employment level and unemployment rate. At the full employment level (E_F), actual unemployment rate is U_F. When employment level is E_1, actual unemployment rate is U_1. When employment level is E_2, actual unemployment rate is U_2.

We can now express the relationships among these unemployment rates and GDPs as follows:

At a given level of GDP_A, $U_A = U_F + U_S + U_C$.
At the full employment GDP, $GDP_A = GDP_F$ and $U_N = U_F + U_S$.

Based on Figure 13.2, an economy is said to suffer from deflationary output when $GDP_1 < GDP_F$ or $U_A > U_N$. An economy is said to suffer from overheating when $GDP_1 > GDP_F$ or $U_A < U_N$. Inflationary pressure gains momentum when U_A is much lower than U_N. All governments aim to ensure that GDP_A is equal to GDP_F, or U_A is equal to U_N, as there is no social cost when the economy is at full employment level.

Figure 13.3 shows a hypothetical situation where Country ABC's natural rate of unemployment (U_N) is stable from year to year. However, its actual unemployment (U_A) fluctuates a lot according to business cycle. The hypothetical economy suffers from Keynesian unemployment since 1997 and again in 2008. We shall now examine the macro-economic performance in terms of U_A and U_N for Hong Kong, South Korea, Taiwan and Singapore.

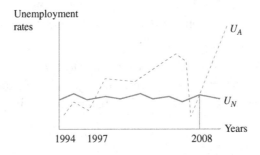

Figure 13.3: This Economy Suffers from Cyclical Unemployment

A Study of Actual Unemployment Rate vs Natural Unemployment Across Four Economies

When there is a recession, three macro variables namely, the exchange rate, the wage costs and the employment level, will reflect the severity of the recession. If an economy is under fixed exchange rate, then the wage costs and the employment will bear the burden of the recession in the sense that wage costs and the employment level will fall significantly. Needless to say, if the wage costs are inflexible, an economy under fixed exchange rate, the only variable, which is the employment level, will fall sharply, causing U_A to be much higher than U_N.

Groenewold, N and Tang SHK examine the gap between U_N and U_A for Hong Kong, Korea, Taiwan and Singapore. Their results on Hong Kong can be captured by Figure 13.4 which shows the gap between U_N and U_A from 1980 to 2000. Hong Kong suffered from overheating from 1986 to 1996. The 1997 East Asian Currency Crisis hit Hong Kong badly. As Hong Kong has been under fixed exchange rate with regard to the US dollar and its wage costs are not so flexible, Hong Kong's U_A is at least twice the level of U_N from 1997 to 2000.

Figure 13.4:   This Economy Suffers both Overheating and then Cyclical Unemployment

Figure 13.4 can also represent Korean situation. Before the 1997 Currency Crisis, the macro-economic management of Korea has been excellent. However, Korea needed IMF bailout to stabilize its currency during the Currency Crisis. One of the conditions was to allow foreign capital to buy local firms. The outcome was extensive retrenchment. Thus, U_A is twice as high as U_N during 1997–2000.

Again, the Taiwanese situation can be represented by Figure 13.4. The Taiwanese economy suffered overheating during 1986–1995. But wage costs in Taiwan were not flexible enough to cope with the 1997 Currency Crisis, its U_A is higher than its U_N from 1997 to 2000. But Taiwanese labour markets still performed much better than Korean and Hong Kong's labour markets during the Currency Crisis.

Figure 13.5 shows that the gap U_A between U_N has been very small for Singapore as it was a deliberate policy on the part of Singapore government to protect the employment level. Among the three macro variables, one is fixed and Singapore exchange rate has to be quite stable as Singapore is a regional financial centre, the wage costs were adjusted downwards. As will be examined in Chapter 15, Singapore's wages costs are to a large extent fully flexible to keep U_A to be close to UN. Diagram 13.5 only shows the relationship between U_A and U_N. Changes in wage costs and the exchange rate are not in the picture. The main reason Singapore has been able to keep unemployment rate low is because its labour movement is macro-focused, which was extensively examined in Chapter 10.

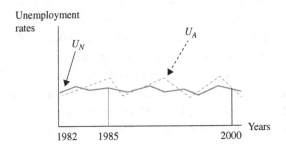

Figure 13.5: This Economy has Managed to Keep Actual Unemployment Rate (UA) Close to Natural Unemployment Rate (UN)

Figure 13.6 shows U_A was much higher than U_N from 2000 to 2005 for Singapore. But from 2006 to 2012, except for 2008 which was the World Financial Meltdown, U_A was below U_N, implying overheating in Singapore.[6]

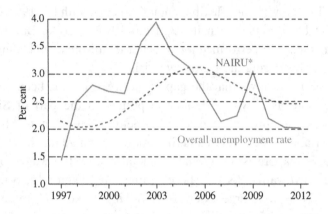

Figure 13.6: Natural Rate of Unemployment (NAIRU) and Actual Unemployment (Overall Unemployment Rate) from 1997 to 2012

Source: MAS annual reports, Singapore.

Okun Law and Cyclical Unemployment

According to "Okun's Law", when unemployment rate falls by 1%, GDP will rise by 2%.[7] The percentage by which GDP changes when unemployment rate changes by 1% is called Okun coefficient. Countries with less flexible labour markets will have higher Okun coefficient. Okun law can be extended to imply that if there is 1% increase in cyclical unemployment rate, the gap between potential GDP and actual GDP will increase by 2%. For instance, if USA's cyclical unemployment rate is 1% and USA's potential GDP is 8,000. Then the difference between the

---

[6]The overheating caused the government to suffer a minor election defeat in 2011 General Election.

[7]This law only holds true for the U.S. economy, and only applies when unemployment rate is between 3% and 7.5%. See Fuhrmann (2015) for more discussion.

actual GDP and the potential GDP is 2% times 8,000 which is equal to 160. In this way, we can estimate the cost of GDP foregone when cyclical unemployment is 1%.[8]

Table 13.2 provides another example where the actual unemployment rate (U_A), natural unemployment rate (U_N) and potential GDP (GDP_F) is given for three years. We can use Okun law to estimate the cost when actual unemployment rate is not equal to natural rate.

Table 13.2: Actual unemployment rate, natural unemployment rate and potential GDP, country XYZ

Year	U_A	U_N	GDP_F
2002	9.7	6.1	3,433
2006	6.8	5.8	6,093
2010	4.5	5.2	8,563

For 2002, the cyclical unemployment rate is 9.7–6.1% which is 3.6%. Hence, the GDP foregone is (3.6% times 2% times 3,433) equal to 247. For 2006, the GDP foregone is much smaller as actual unemployment rate is close to natural unemployment rate. For 2010, there is overheating as actual unemployment rate is lower than the natural unemployment. This means that the cyclical unemployment rate is negative, the difference between 5.2% and 4.5%. The inflationary pressure measured in terms of the amount by which actual GDP exceeds potential GDP is equal to −120 (−0.7% times 2 times 8,563).

Theory of Job Search and Frictional Unemployment

There are two types of people looking for a job. The first type of people looking for a job is those already employed. It is difficult to model the behaviour of job search because they can wait and look for the perfect job.

---

[8]Of course, one can use this law to estimate the cost of any type of unemployment on GDP loss.

In this chapter, we only want to consider the behaviour of job search of those who are unemployed and actively looking for a job.

Consider John who graduated from the Institute for Education is actively looking for a job. We assume that John is aware that he will get many wage offers, given his human capital, K^*. The lowest wage offer is $1,000 a month and the highest wage offer is $2,500 a month as is shown in Figure 13.7. In other words, John has a wage offer distribution (*FGH*) which provides a probability distribution of wage offers to John. The area under the wage offer distribution is equal to one. But based on information from the labour markets, John is aware that there is a high probability that he will get a job paying between $1,200 and $1,800 and a low probability that he might end up get a job paying less than $1,200 or more than $1,800.

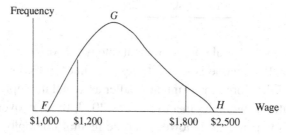

- The wage offer distribution (FGH) gives frequency distribution of potential job offers to John, an ITE graduate

- If John is a poly graduate, the FGH will shift to the right by $500. If John is a university graduate, his FGH will shift to the right by another $1,000.

Figure 13.7:   The Wage Offer Distribution

What is John's strategy? John will increase his human capital (K^*) such that the *FGH* curve will shift to the right. But what is John's search strategy? If job search is costless, then John will wait till he gets a job paying him $1,800 or $2,500. But job search is costly. We have to model John's job search behaviour.

In the literature, there are two approaches to job search. The first type of job search is known as non-sequential search. In this approach, John will collect 20 wage offers and then choose the job that pays the highest.

This approach may take a long time because a job offer normally has an expiry date. To get 20 valid wage offers may not be possible.

The second approach is known as sequential search.[9] In this approach, John first must establish an asking wage (W_A). When John receives a wage offer which is either equal to or more than the asking wage, John will accept the job offer and stop the job search. If the wage offer is below the asking wage, either he reviews W_A or reject the wage offer. If he rejects the job offer, he will continue with his job search.

In Figure 13.8, we see that $W_A > W_R$ which is reservation wage. But W_A is generally lower than W_H because there is a low probability that John will get a wage offer that is around or above W_H. The total probability of getting a wage offer between W_A and W_H is area $W_A YX W_H$. If W_A is close to W_H, John's duration of job search will be long because the total probability of getting a wage offer within that range is much smaller. During the job search, John is unemployed frictionally and therefore this unemployment is voluntary.

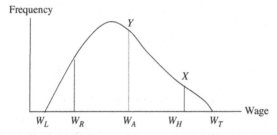

* W_L = Lowest wage offer; W_R = Reservation wage; W_A = Asking wage; W_H = High wage; W_T = Top wage offer

Figure 13.8: The Wage Offer Distribution with W_R and W_A

Determination of Asking Wage

What affects John's W_A? If he asks for a high asking wage, he is likely to reject many job offers. So, he is also likely to experience longer period of job search. Hence, there is cost of wanting a high asking wage. But the

---

[9]See Stigler (1962) for non-sequential search and McCall (1970) for sequential search. The presentation of the wage offer distribution is modified from Figure 12.8, of Borjas (2013, p. 508).

benefit is that, if he succeeds in getting a job offer that matches his high asking wage, he can enjoy higher wages for more periods. Figure 13.9 presents a framework to determine the asking wage based on marginal benefits (MR) and marginal cost (MC) of rejecting job offer.

When John receives a low wage offer, he knows that the next wage offer is likely to be higher. Hence, if he rejects the low wage offer, the MR of additional job search will not only be positive but high in value. However, when John rejects a high wage offer, the next wage offer is not likely to be much higher. The MR of rejecting a high wage offer may be positive but is small in value. This explains why the MR line is downward sloping in Figure 13.9.

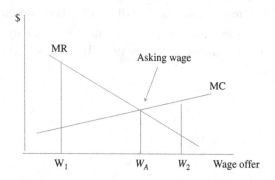

Figure 13.9:   Determination of Asking Wage

When John rejects a low wage offer, the cost is low. When John rejects a high wage offer, the cost is therefore high. Hence, the MC line is upward sloping. Consider a wage offer at W_1, MR > MC. John will not accept W_1 and will continue to search. When John receives a wage offer equal to W_A, MR = MC, he will stop the job search and accept the job offer. If John receives a wage offer at W_2, John will grab it because MC is greater than MR. So, asking wage is John's minimum wage expectations.

One main factor affecting MR line is the discount rate. When a worker has a high discount rate, he is known to be a present-oriented person. Future gains from additional job searches are discounted more.

The MR line will shift down for a person with high discount rate. Hence, in Figure 13.9, the MR line will shift down, and the Asking wage is lower.

The MC of job search is very much affected by unemployment benefits. Borjas (2013, p. 516) observes that, using US data, when unemployment benefits run out, the probability of finding a new job jumps up. Furthermore, when unemployment benefits increase significantly, the MC of additional job search is lower and the MC line will shift down, increasing the worker's asking wage.

Financing Unemployment Benefits Scheme

In the USA, when a worker is retrenched, he is entitled to get unemployment benefits if he had been employed for at least six months for a limited period.[10] According to Borjas (2013), 70% of laid-off workers return to their former employer at the end of the unemployment spell. This is a large percentage. But it happens for a reason. In the USA, a firm that had high lay-off rates in the past are normally assessed higher tax rates. When a firm faces excess labour, the firm can retrench the redundant workers and save on labour costs. Although, the firm has to pay higher tax rates later, the extra cost is still lower than the savings on payroll. When the unemployment benefits run out, the firm will recall these workers back. This is known as temporary lay-off, which is being encouraged by the way unemployment benefits is being operated. The firm is taking a risk. The firm may suffer if these workers acquire bad habits during the unemployment spell or they leave for other firms.

Temporary lay-offs or lay-offs are cyclical unemployment which can be reduced by demand management policy. The best approach is to encourage training of redundant workers during recession. Later in the book, we will show that in Singapore, we have a scheme to encourage firms to train redundant workers during recession.

---

[10]For details on entitlement of unemployment benefits, see Borjas (2013, p. 513).

The Sectoral Shifts Hypothesis and Structural Unemployment

How to account for structure unemployment? Chapter 1 shows us that many jobs will be lost due to changes in technology. In Singapore, in 1980, for each cessation of company there were 13 new companies but the ratio in 2014 was only 2.[11] Globalization will increase trade. Those sectors which benefit from globalization will demand for labour and those sectors which could not compete will retrench workers. Change in demand structure, technology and globalization will disrupt the labour market and those economies which under-estimate these market forces will face serious structural unemployment. Figure 13.10 presents the sectoral shifts hypothesis to highlight the importance of skill mismatches. The expanding sector will need workers of certain skills and the contracting sector will release workers of old skills. Unless there is low cost and market oriented training schemes, unfilled job vacancies (V) and unemployed workers (U) will rise in tandem although V may be equal to U.[12]

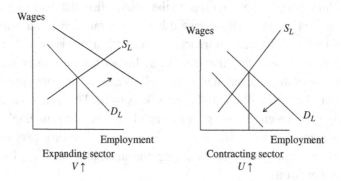

Figure 13.10:   The Sectoral Shifts Hypothesis

The Macro Theory of Efficiency Wage and Involuntary Unemployment

In Chapter 10, we argue that firms pay efficiency wage to buy "compliance" so that workers will not shirk. Underlying this reasoning is that the

---

[11]We will examine this aspect in detail in Chapter 16.

[12]We again will examine a market-oriented training scheme later in the book.

cost of monitoring workers is not low. Given the cost of monitoring, the efficiency wage is the profit-maximizing wage because the increased efficiency (MR) is equal to higher wage cost (MC).

In this chapter, we want to examine the link between efficiency wage and market conditions. In Figure 13.11, the competitive market wage is W_C. When unemployment rate is very high at around A, it is not easy to get a job if workers lose their jobs at A. Hence, efficiency wage is slightly above the competitive wage. However, if the unemployment rate is low, implying that it is easy to get a job with a good wages, the efficiency wage has to be very high to buy "compliance" from the workers. If the cost of monitoring is lower significantly, the curve will shift down and the level of efficiency wage will be reduced.

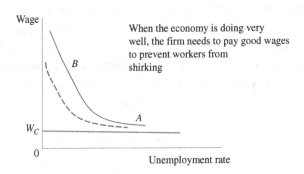

Figure 13.11: Efficiency Wage and Labour Markets Conditions

Figure 13.12 shows that the competitive labour market with W_C as the competitive wage level. S_L is the labour supply curve which shows the number of people with the right skills wanting to work at various wage levels. But the workers may shirk. To ensure workers will not shirk, we pay efficiency wage. At F, employment level is low, hence, the required efficiency wage is slightly above W_C. As employment level is high around G, the required efficiency wage will be much higher than W_C. Hence, NS is the no shirk labour supply curve. At each efficiency wage, the number of people willing to work (S_L) exceeds the number of people willing to work hard (NS). This "excess labour supply" makes workers work hard as no-shirk workers can be replaced with ease.

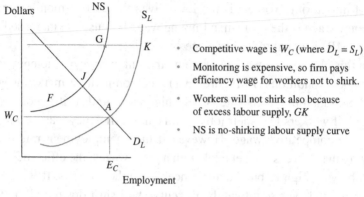

Figure 13.12:   The No-shirking Supply Curve (NS)

The intersection point between NS and the labour demand curve (D_L) will determine the equilibrium efficiency wage which is W_{EFF} (see Figure 13.13). Workers will not shirk at J because they are paid efficiency wage and also there is excess supply of labour at J. In this context, we can conclude that efficiency wage creates involuntary unemployment which is costly. The only way to decrease this kind of involuntary unemployment is to use technology to lower the cost of monitoring workers so that we can lower efficiency wage.

In the event of a recession, the labour demand curve will shift to D_{LR}. Recession will depress wages but competitive wages will fall more than efficiency wage as is shown in Figure 13.13.

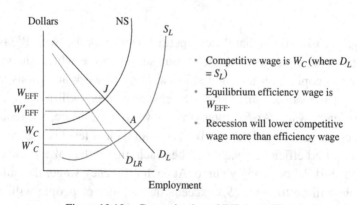

Figure 13.13:   Determination of Efficiency Wage

Implicit Contracts with Union and the Impact on Employment

Union density has never been very high, ranging from 36% in the public sector to 10% in manufacturing sector in the USA in 2013.[13] However, even without union presentation, there are still labour contracts specifying wages and number of hours of work. These labour contracts are known as implicit contracts which can be unwritten and unspoken. We will use Figure 13.14 to explain the essence of implicit contracts. *A* is the competitive labour market equilibrium point with W_C and E_C as the respective wage and employment. In the event of a recession, the labour demand cure will shift to D_{LR}. Although there are no written policy, there are three possible outcomes in terms of implicit contracts. From *A* to *G* is the fixed wage contract. Workers on this fixed wage contract realize that wages generally would not be affected but there will be big retrenchment. Of course, insiders would benefit. From *A* To *F* is the fixed employment contract. Workers on this contract know that their jobs are protected but they will face a wage cut. From *A* to *M* is the moderate contract, implying that both wages and employment level would decrease according to the slope of the labour supply curve. Micro-focused unions

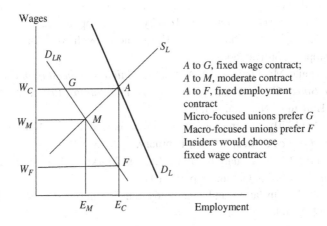

Figure 13.14: Implicit Contracts and Employment

---

[13] See Tables 3a and 7a from Hirsch and MacPherson (2013) for details.

would prefer fixed wage contract and macro-focused unions would prefer fixed employment contracts. Most employers would prefer fixed employment contract because if the economy picks up, they can resume full capacity very soon. However, there may be some employers who prefer fixed wage contract as they can take the opportunity to remove unwanted workers. Obviously, all governments would like fixed employment contract for two reasons. Firstly, the employment is stable and secondly as the wage cost is lower, it can increase exports and will encourage investment.

Discussion Questions

1. Is it practical or desirable to aim at zero unemployment rates for a government?
2. If a country suddenly withdraws unemployment benefits scheme, will unemployment rate increase?

Bibliography

Borjas, G. J. (2013). *Labor Economics*, Seventh edition. New York: McGraw-Hill.

Freeman, R. B. (1973). "Changes in the labour market for Black American", *Brookings Papers on Economic Activity*, Vol. 20, pp. 67–120.

Fuhrmann, R. C. (2015). Okun's Law: Economic Growth And Unemployment, Investopedia on Facebook.

Hirsch, B. T. and MacPherson, D. A. (2013). *Union Membership and Earnings Data Book: Compilations from Current Population Survey*. Washington, DC: Bureau of National Affairs.

McCall, J. J. (1970). "Economics of Information and Job Search", *Quarterly Journal of Economics*, Vol. 84, February, pp. 113–126.

Stigler, S. (1962). "Information in the Labour Market", *Journal of Political Economy*, Vol. 70, October, pp. 94–104.

Tobin, J. (1972). "Inflation and Unemployment", *America Economic Review*, Vol. 62, March, pp. 1–18.

Chapter 14

Economic Inequality

Economic inequality is important in two ways. First, rising economic inequality can cause unrest in a society. Any unrest can put an economy in vicious–poverty cycle which will also hurt the rich. Secondly, because economic inequality can cause damage to society and the economy, most governments will increase welfare spending to improve income inequality. This will lead to increase in government spending and thereby affecting people's behaviour in the labour markets because of moral hazard and other issues. This chapter will provide the analytical framework to understand the earnings distribution and factors affecting earnings.

The Earnings Distribution

In any society, the bulk of workers earn relatively low wages and a small number of people earn extremely high wages. A typical wage distribution is presented in Figure 14.1 which shows that the wage distribution is positively skewed. How can we account for a positively skewed wage distribution? Chapter 11 on human capital provides some answers. If a person has a high wage–schooling curve, and if he also has a low discount rate, he is likely to invest more in human capital and therefore earn more than the rest of the workers.

Table 14.1 shows economic inequity from another perspective. If there is no income inequity, figures in columns (II) and (III) will be the same. But in most societies, the lowest 20% of households account for less than 5% of the total income. And the lowest 40% of households

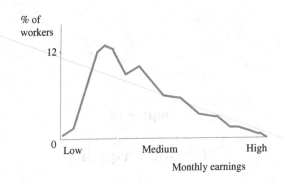

Figure 14.1:   The Wage Distribution in a Typical Country

account for about 10% of total income. Most of the income is earned by the highest 20% of households.

Table 14.1:   Distribution of Income (in %)

Percentage of households (I)	Cumulative percentage of households (II)	Cumulative percentage of income if there is no equality (III)	Cumulative percentage of Income in a typical society (IV)
A Lowest 20	20	20	3
B Second 20	40	40	10
C Middle 20	60	60	20
D Next highest 20	80	80	50
E Highest 20	100	100	100

Economists use the income Lorenz curve to explain income inequity. Putting cumulative percentage of households on the X-axis and cumulative percentage of income on the Y-axis, we can draw the Lorenz curve as is shown in Figure 14.2. If there is no income inequity, as the figures in columns (II) and (III) are the same, the income Lorenz curve is XY line, representing perfect equity. But based on figures from column (IV) the actual Lorenz curve is XGY. Hence, if area XGYX is bigger, there is more income inequity. Many developed countries have generous transfer payments to help the poor and those who are unemployed. With retribution, the typical

The *BC* line indicates that there is no connection between earnings of children and earnings of their parents. The *DE* line shows that there is some connection between earnings of parents and earnings of their children.

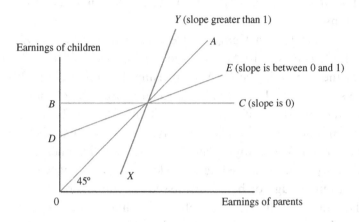

Figure 14.3:   The Intergenerational Link in Income

Borjas cited studies to show that the intergenerational correlation is around 0.4. This implies that a 30% wage gap between two parents translates into a 12% wage gap between the children and a 5% wage gap between the grandchildren. The decline of the differences in income across generations is known as regression toward the mean.

If the intergenerational correlation is around 1.5, as shown by the *XY* line, which implies that a 30 % wage gap between two parents translates into a 45% wage gap between the children and a 67% wage gap between the grandchildren.

The *XY* line shows the relations between the earnings of the first generations of immigrants and the earnings of their children. First generations are generally not well educated but work very hard at low wages. Their children generally earn more than their parents, which explains why, the slope of *XY* is greater than one. However, after two or three generations, the *XY* line disappears and we are back to the *DE* line.

Regression toward the mean can happen due to the following factors: parents do not invest most of their wealth in their children. At the same time, the parents may encounter diminishing marginal returns in investment of their children's human capital. As wealth is substantial, it can increase the reservation wage of the children who parents are rich. If a person is the best mathematician in the country, it is unlikely that any of his children will be the best in the country of their generations.

Despite the fact that empirical evidence points to the *DE* line in Figure 14.3, as Figure 14.4 shows, the income shares of top 1% and top 0.1% of the people in the USA keep rising. For instance, in 2012, the income share of top 1% in the USA accounts for 19% of total incomes and the income share of top 0.1% accounts for 8%. Two hypotheses have been put forward. The first hypothesis is that these people are entrepreneurs, employers and most of their incomes come from capital. They earn money while they sleep. They do not have to worry about retirement age or being dismissed by employers. They are rich and they invest a lot in their children's human capital. They and their children live longer, have more healthy years and therefore they can earn more than the average person or household in the business world.

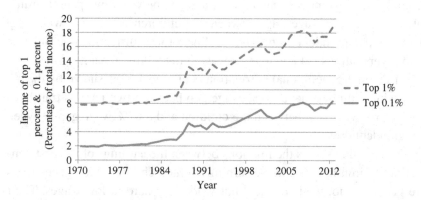

Figure 14.4:   The Income Shares of the Top 1% and Top 0.1% in USA

Source: To generate the above chart, we use data from: The World Top Incomes Database, http://g-mond.parisschoolofeconomics.eu/topincomes, 12/08/2012.

The second hypothesis is wealth concentration through marriage. Rich people tend to marry rich people. This phenomenon is known as assortative mating. Because of assortative mating, coupled with the first hypothesis, wealth is more concentrated in a small number of families.

Discussion Questions

1. Draw the Lorenz curve based on wealth and compare it with the Lorenz curve based on income using Figure 14.2.
2. How do we find the Gini coefficient after redistribution using Figure 14.2?

Reference

Borjas, G. J. (2013). *Labor Economics*, Seventh edition. New York: McGraw-Hill.
Parkin, M. (2015). *Economics*, Eleventh edition. Boston: Pearson.

Chapter 15

Labour Income and Savings in Singapore

In a typical poor society, we can see the damage of vicious poverty cycle to the residents of the country. People are poor and not educated. There are no jobs. The government is poor. Poor people cannot save and therefore do not have capability to invest in human capital and in living environment. Foreign aids can help provided the aids can enhance the capacity building to promote economic development. On the other extreme, in some societies, workers have income but the majority of workers do not save sufficiently such that either they do not invest sufficiently in human capital of themselves and that of their children or the government has to bail them out. This will produce entitlement mentality and consequently a persistent budget deficit and the budget deficit will get bigger due to moral hazard, among other factors.

Hence, poor countries have high population rate, low literary rate and high unemployment rate, which is a recipe for social unrest. For some high income countries in which entitlement mentality strives, they have high unemployment rate, high income tax rate and high national debt-GDP ratio. Neither outcome is good. As we will examine later, citizen-government partnership may produce a better outcome using Singapore as a case study. But first let us look at the wages of residents in Singapore.

Figure 15.1 shows the rising income shares of top 1% and top 5% of residents in Singapore from the 1970s to the 2000s. In 2012, the income share of top 1% of residents was almost 13% which is high but not as well as in the USA where top 1% of residents earn more than 18% of total incomes (see Figure 14.6). The income share of top 5% of residents in

Singapore is more than 30% of total incomes, indicating that the remaining 95% of residents earn less than 70% of total incomes in Singapore.[1] The Gini coefficient for Singapore is expected to be high.[2]

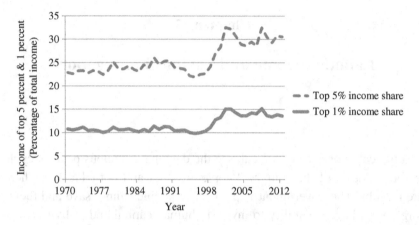

Figure 15.1:   The Income Shares of the Top 5% and 1% in Singapore

Source: To produce the above chart, we use data from: The World Top Incomes Database, http://g-mond.parisschoolofeconomics.eu/topincomes, 12/08/2012.

   Table 15.1 shows the number of residents and their monthly wages for three years, 2005, 2009 and 2013. Residents earning less than $1,000 a month account for about 10% in 2013. Most residents in this category are either below 25 or above 60 in age. Those who earn between $1,000 and $2,000 account for 21% while those who earn between $2,000 and $3,000 account for 18%. The two high income categories are those earn between $4,000 and $5,000 and those earning more than $5,000 account for 23% and 28%, respectively. Hence, more than 70% of residents earn below $5,000 a month in 2013. Does each worker save sufficiently?

---

[1]An attempt to get the income shares of the bottom 5% or 10% was not successful.
[2]We will discuss this later in the chapter.

Table 15.1: Number of Employed and Monthly Wage, 2005–2013

Wages ($)	2005	2009	2013
<500	58,311 (4.2%)	85,520 (5.2%)	44,300 (2.2%)
500–999	168,580 (12.2%)	200,864 (12.2%)	162,800 (8.1%)
1,000–1,999	367,383 (26.6%)	370,421 (22.5%)	420,700 (21%)
2,000–2,999	315,050 (22.8%)	339,826 (20.7%)	360,400 (18.%)
3,000–4,999	275,379 (19.9%)	293,976 (17.8%)	466,00 (23%)
>5,000	196,348 (14.2%)	354,492 (20.6%)	550,400 (27.7%)
Total	1,381,068 (100%)	1,644,610 (100%)	2,004,600 (100%)

Source: *Singapore Year Book of Statistics*, various years.

Propensity to save varies from person to person but to a large extent, it is dependent on wage level. In Figure 15.2, we show three hypothetical saving functions, one for high income workers (F_H), one for average worker (F_A) and one for low income (F_L).[3] Suppose the society's optimum saving is S_M,[4] then the average and low income workers would have less than optimal saving.[5] There will be individual and social consequences if people do not save sufficiently. So, there may be a market failure in saving which calls for government intervention to correct the bad externality.

---

[3]We assume that marginal propensity to consume is high for low income workers.
[4]We will define optimal saving later.
[5]In Figure 15.2, we did not show the saving of average worker.

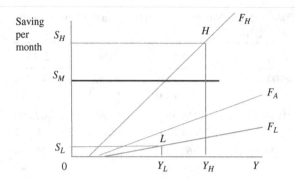

Figure 15.2:   Savings (*S*) as a Function of Labour Income (*Y*)

Compulsory Savings Scheme via Central Provident Fund in Singapore

The Central Provident Fund (CPF) was set up in 1955 as the main social security scheme for residents of Singapore by then the Colonial Government from London. It is a compulsory saving scheme required by law for all employees with no exception. An employee with a monthly pay of, for example, $1000, is required to contribute a certain percentage, say 20%, towards his CPF personal account. His take home pay is therefore $800. At the same time, his employer is required to contribute a certain percentage, say 17%, of the worker's pay towards the same account for the worker. Hence, each month, the worker has $370 in his CPF personal account. The monthly cost of employing this worker in this example therefore amounts to $1,170 and is affected by the employer's CPF contribution rate. Consequently, a wage ceiling was put in place to limit the amount of employer CPF contributions set at S$6,000 in the 1980s and 1990s, but in the last 10 years, it has been $5,000. But from January 1, 2016, it is back to $6,000.

Table 15.2 shows the amount of savings in the CPF personal account for employees in Singapore. An employee with a monthly wage of $5,000 works for 30 years non-stop, his total consolidated wages will be $1,800,000.[6]

---

[6]We do not take into account bonus. Hence, one year's of labour income is equal to 12 times monthly wage. The figures in column (i) are smaller than the actual amount because employees do get more than 12 months of wages. The CPF rules changes each year. The figures presented here and in this chapter are for the purpose of understanding the CPF scheme. The reader should find out the actual figures from the CPF Board with specific purpose.

His total consolidated CPF balances (without interest payments) is $666,000, which is 37% of the consolidated wages. For employees earning $3,000, $2,000 and $1,000 monthly, the respective CPF balances are $399,600, $266,400 and $133,200. Are the sums sufficient from the perspective of the individual and the society? To answer these questions, we need to know the purpose of savings and the purchasing power of savings.

Table 15.2:   Compulsory Savings in Singapore (in Dollars)

Wages	Accumulated wages after 30 years (i)	Accumulated CPF balances (ii)	Ordinary account (iii)	Special account (iv)	Medi-save account (v)	Retirement account (vi)
5,000	1,800,000	666,000	426,240	119,880	119,880	190,860
3,000	1,080,000	399,600	255,744	71,928	71,928	94,056
2,000	720,000	266,400	170,496	47,952	47,952	47,952
1,000	360,000	133,200	85,248	23,976	23,976	23,976

Note: The figures for (vi) are based on two conditions: The ceiling for Medi-save account is $49,800 and all money in the ordinary account have been utilized at age 55.

What are Savings for?

Why do we want people to save? If they save, they can look after themselves in terms of owning a flat, pay for their medical bills, ensure that each of their children has a good education and when they stop working, they have money to support themselves. If they can be independent financially, the government can spend less on social welfare and more on investment in human capital and infrastructure. So, we need to fix the proportion of CPF savings to meet the specific goals.

Figure 15.3 shows that the CPF balances are divided into three accounts, namely Ordinary account, Special account and Medi-save account. The balances in the Ordinary account can be used to pay monthly mortgage payments, pay for tertiary tuition fees, buy shares and gold certificates. The balances in Special account is not for investment but for old age expenses while the balances in the Medi-save account is meant to pay for hospitalization bills for the employee, the spouses, the children and the parents and also pay for annual premium of medical insurance. The proportion of the CPF balances in the three accounts keeps changing according to the needs of the country and also the needs of the family.

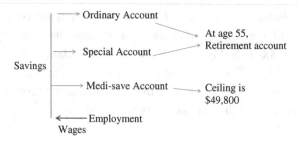

Figure 15.3:   CPF Scheme

In Table 15.2, we compute the balances of an employee after working 30 years in each account using the following proportion: 64% for Ordinary account, 18% each for Special account and Medi-save account.[7] For instance, for a Singaporean after working 30 years at $3,000 a month, the balances in his Ordinary account, Special account and Medi-save account are $255,744, $71,928 and $71,928, respectively. The actual balance in the Ordinary account would be much less, as close to 90% would be invested in housing, shares, etc. The actual balance in Special account would be more as interest payments are not included in the computation. The actual balance in the Medi-save account would be smaller than the indicated amount due to usage of the money to pay for hospitalization, etc. From Table 15.2, we see that the CPF balance of each resident in Singapore depends on the average wage over the working life span. If wages are higher and work for more years, the CPF balances will be bigger. Can Singaporeans withdraw their CPF money if so, when?

Minimum Sum Schemes

As mentioned above, the CPF scheme was introduced in 1955. In the beginning, the rule governing CPF usage was not stringent. When an employee reaches the age of 55, he can withdraw all the CPF money. But since the early 1980s, the government has noticed that some Singapore citizens, particularly men, squandered the lump sum money within a few years when they withdrew all the CPF money at age 55. Consequently, the

---

[7]Currently, the respective proportions are 67%, 15% and 18%.

government has implemented the so-called Minimum Sum Scheme, started in 1987, that all Singapore residents could withdraw all the CPF money but keep \$30,000 in the CPF account. The minimum sum has been raised gradually and today, the minimum sum is \$155,000.

The minimum sum scheme is also implemented in the Medi-save account. Most residents in Singapore are employees and therefore entitled to employer's medical benefits coverage. Hence, the balance in the Medi-save account will keep increasing. However, the ceiling in the Medi-save account is now \$48,900. Any excess of 48,900 will go to Special account. In 2013, the average balance per resident in Medi-save account at age 55 is about \$30,000. The residents are told to keep this balance in the Medi-save account at age 55 for future medical expenses and therefore not allowed to withdraw.

The Singapore government has promised that the annual interest rate on CPF balances will not be less than 2.5%. Specifically, the annual interest rate on the balances in Ordinary account, Special account, Medi-save account and Retirement account are 2.5%, 4%, 4% and 4% respectively. If a resident does not withdraw any excess of \$155,000 in the Retirement account, the annual interest rate is 5%. The weighted average rate of return to CPF balances is higher than the inflation rate in past few decades except 2008–2010 period.

The CPF Board is tasked to look after the day to day operations.[8] For instance, if a Singaporean sells his house, the proceeds of the sale which contain his CPF money will have to be returned to his CPF personal account. The citizen can withdraw the profit but the balance in his Ordinary account should not be affected by the sale of the property. This explains why the usage of CPF money is only applicable to properties in Singapore.

The CPF scheme works provided people have jobs and when the government forces people to save, the government must protect the purchasing power of saving in terms of real rate of return. Let us first examine how does the CPF scheme help Singaporeans to look after post-retirement needs.

---

[8]The government does not want the CPF Board to invest the CPF money. Consequently, as a matter of accounting, about 90% of the CPF balance is used to purchase Singapore government bonds. The proceeds of the sale of the government bonds will be forwarded to a highly specialized institute for the purpose of investment.

In many countries, rich and poor, public sector employees are entitled to receiving a monthly pension when they retire from the public sector.[9] This is lacking in Singapore. Currently, no employees, regardless of been in the private or public sectors in Singapore, is on pension scheme.[10] As we will show now, the Singapore government has converted a fraction of compulsory saving into an annuity for each individual.

Converting Retirement Account into an Annuity Scheme

When an employee reaches the age of 55, he has a new account, called Retirement account, co-existing with the other CPF accounts as is shown in Figure 15.3. The amount of money in the Retirement account is the sum of remaining balance in the Ordinary account and all the accumulated balance in the Special account. To explain the Retirement account, we go back to Table 15.2. Consider an employee whose average wage per month is $5,000 and now he is 55 years in age. His balances in his Ordinary account, Special account and Medi-save account are $426,240, $ 119,880 and $119,880 respectively. For ease of computation, assume that he has utilized all the money in the Ordinary account at age 55.[11] As mentioned earlier, the ceiling in the Medi-save account is $48,900. Hence, at age 55, his Special account would have the balance of $119,880 + $ 70,980, the sum of these two is equal to $190,860. This explains why his Retirement account has the balance of $190,860 in Table 15.2. He is at liberty to withdraw any amount in excess of $155,000 any time. Using the same method, those who earn $3,000 a month, the balance in the Retirement account is $94,056. Notice that the balance in the Special account is the same as the balance in the retirement account for those earn $2,000 and $1,000 as the actual balance in the respective Medi-save account is less than the ceiling. It is estimated that most residents when

---

[9]See Chapter 3 for some theoretical models on pension scheme.
[10]This statement applies to new civil servants. Ex-civil servants do enjoy the benefits of the pension scheme in Singapore.
[11]Usually, there will be a fraction left in the Ordinary account to be carried over to the Retirement account.

they reach 55 in age, the balance in the Retirement account is less than the minimum sum.[12]

We shall show how this balance in the Retirement account will be converted into an annuity scheme for Singaporean employees. For ease of exposition, consider John who has reached 55 years in age and he has $90,000 in the retirement account. He cannot withdraw this amount as it is below the minimum sum scheme. Table 15.3 shows how John's balance in his retirement account can benefit him in a scheme known as CPF Life.

Table 15.3: CPF Life Basic Plan[13]

Retirement account 55 in age	When to collect money	Die at 75	Die at 85
$90,000	At 65, $677 per month Upon death, the bequest is $129,670	$677 per month Bequest is bequest $94,704	$677 per month Bequest is $43,176
	At 66 $679 per month Bequest is $139781	$679 per month Bequest is $99,912	$679 per month Bequest $48,301
	At 70 $852 per month Bequest is $166,058	$852 per month Bequest $131,421	$852 per month Bequest $65,632

Source: www.cpf.gov.sg/eSvc/Web/Schemes/LifePayoutEstimator/LifePayoutEstimator.

John's $90,000 has been converted into an annuity scheme where he can start getting an income a month from age 66 for life. The amount is $677 per month for life. If he dies at age 66, the bequest is $129,670. If he dies at age 75, the bequest is of course reduced to $94,704 . If John chose to collect his CPF Life income from age 70, then both monthly income and bequest are much bigger.

As mentioned in Chapter 1, Thailand, a low per capita income country in Southeast Asia, has a universal health scheme and a universal pension

---

[12]But almost all Singaporeans use the balance in the Ordinary account to pay monthly mortgage over many years. The required sum to keep in the Retirement account is about half of the official minimum sum.

[13]There are many schemes. We use Basic Plan as an example. Please see the source for details.

scheme in which every elderly citizen reaching 65 years in age gets S$20 per month.[14] Such a socially funded pension scheme is not available in Singapore. Hence, Singaporeans have to work hard and continue to work in their 1970s because the CPF Life is not handouts from the government but a motivating factor for citizens to work. Figure 15.4 presents such a situation. As the balance in the retirement account is based on past wages, the low wage workers would not have much in the retirement account. When they reach around age 62, due to retirement age at 62, almost all low wage workers have to change jobs to lower wage jobs, increasing the need to work when they are in their 1970s.

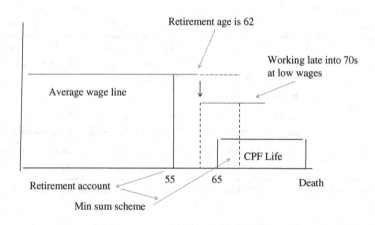

Figure 15.4:   Working in the 70s to Supplement Income from CPF Life

Protecting Purchasing Power of Wages

Figure 15.5 shows that under the CPF scheme, an employee in Singapore is forced to save for post-retirement living expenses (*A*), for children's education expenses (*B*), for healthcare expenses (*C*) and for buying a flat (*D*). The balances in Ordinary account would go mostly to (*D*). There is a provision to invest in shares (*I*) using Ordinary account balance. The balance in Special account strictly goes to (*A*) and those in Medi-save

---

[14] A specialist at the Asia-Pacific office of the United Nations Population Fund in Bangkok made this point. See S.T. 16/01/2016 on page A33, "17M in Thailand will be above 65 by 2040: Report".

account to (*C*). Can low wage families in Singapore afford to educate their children in top ranking universities, have access to first rate medical treatment and able to own a flat?

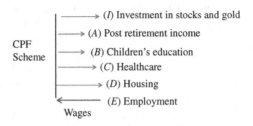

Figure 15.5:   Purpose of Saving

Let us first look at housing. Can a low wage family buy a public flat in Singapore? In most global cities, the answer is no. In Singapore, the government builds public flats for sales. These public flats are known as HDB flats.[15] As HDB flats are meant to be for sales, they have to be affordable. As Table 15.4 shows, there are two prices of HDB flats. P^* is the net price with general subsidy and P is the net price after taking into account the specific conditions of each family. As lower income families buy smaller flats, the Round 2 subsidies are much bigger for smaller flats. As Y is annual earning of a family, the Singapore government's strategy is that the ratio (R) of P/Y should range from 2 to 6 times. Table 15.4 shows that, for a 2-room flat, R is 0.44. Hence, the 2-room flats are very affordable to low income families. All buyers are able to get a subsidized housing loan from the HDB. For a 5-room flat, R is 4.8 times. The ratio is higher because most of these buyers are degree holders and therefore they earn more.[16] It is still very affordable compared to the prices in most global cities. The key strategy here is that wages have good purchasing power for home ownership. The unit housing cost (UHC) is affordable by world standards. This will motivate Singaporeans to work hard and unit

---

[15]HDB is known as Housing Development Board.

[16] Singaporean families can make money from buying HDB flats as each family is able to sell its HDB flat in the open market and buy a second unit from HDB. Bigger flats may generate more capital gains. Hence, higher R is fair too.

labour cost (ULC) (unit labour cost) to the firms is competitive. It is a win–win outcome for individual families, firms and the Society.

Table 15.4:   Ratio of Public Housing Prices and Annual Household Income (11/2015)

Size	HDB prices with round 1 subsidy (P^*) ($)	HDB prices with round 2 subsidy (P) ($)	Annual household income (Y) ($)	$R = P/Y$ ratio
2-room	88,000	8,000	18,000	0.44
3-room	182,000	112,000	30,000	3.73
4-room	284,000	234,000	49,000	4.76
5-room	364,000	334,000	69,000	4.80

Source: http://esales.hdb.gov.sg/hdbvsf/eampu05p.nsf/0/15MAYBTO_page_1905/$file/about0.html.

Ownership of HDB flats is very unique in Singapore. HDB owners cannot sell the flats till they have stayed in the flats for at least five years. When they want to sell the HDB flats in the resale markets, there are restrictions in terms of income ceiling and race. In Chapter 13, we noted that when young blacks live in less segregated city, the percentage of idle young blacks is high. In Singapore, the government does not allow racial segregation in HDB flats. When HDB sells flats or in the resale HDB markets, the government does not allow any HDB block to be exclusively purchased by Chinese families, or Malays or Indians.

How About Unit Education Cost (UDC)
for Singaporean Families?

Quality of education from primary to upper secondary in Singapore has been known to be high. With regard to quality of university education, for 2015, National University of Singapore (NUS) and Nanyang Technological University (NTU) have been ranked 12th and 13th respectively world-wide.[17] Despite the high quality of education, the tuition fees from primary school to university have been very affordable to Singaporean families due to extensive investment on the part of the government in

---

[17] See www.topuniversities.com/university-rankings.

education.[18] Table 15.5 shows the amount spent by government on each student per year. Singaporean families now face a dilemma. They can afford to send their children to abroad for a degree course but the chosen university in USA, UK or Australia may not rank higher than NUS or NTU. In sum, the UDC in Singapore is very affordable even to low income families at all levels of education. This is in part also because there is plenty of financial assistance schemes to help low income families to finance the education of their children.

Table 15.5:   Expenditure Per Student (S$)

Years in School	1996	2000	2013
Primary (6)	2,837	3,137	8,669
Secondary (4)	4,152	5,104	11,606
Junior College (2)	6,726	7,304	14,517
Vocational School (ITE) (1–2)	11,646	8,076	12,227
Polytechnics (3)	8,406	9,546	15,120
Universities (4)	15,037	15,384	21,839

Source: Singapore Yearbook of Statistics.

How About Unit Medical Cost (UMC) for Singaporean Families?

Quality of healthcare in Singapore has been known to be very high. But medical costs have been high too. Since 2014, healthcare insurance known as Medi-Shield Life has been made compulsory for all citizens. Table 15.6 shows the extent to which the premium has been subsidized. But those currently above the age of 80, the government has decided to pay the premium and those currently above 65, the government has decided to pay half. From Table 15.2, we can see that most working adults have sufficient funds in the Medi-save account which can be used to pay for the premium. Of course, when a person is not working due to bad health or did not work for long like many typical housewives, there will not be much in the Medi-save account. The spouse has to help and the government is the last resort.

---

[18]Tuition fees for a non-lab degree course is about $8,000 per year.

Table 15.6:   Premiums for Medi-Shield Life

Age next birthday	Current annual Medi-Shield premiums ($) with subsidy	Age next birthday	Current annual Medi-Shield premiums ($) with subsidy
>90	—	71–73	560
86–90	1190	66–70	540
86–88	1190	61–65	455
84–85	1150	51–60	345
81–83	1123	41–50	220
79–80	865	31–40	105
76–78	775	21–30	66
74–75	646	1–20	50

Source: www.moh.gov.sg/content/moh_web/medishield-life/premiums---subsidies/how-to-receive-premium-subsidies/subsidy---premium-tables.html.

Of course, there is co-payment when one is hospitalized. Table 15.7 shows the extent to which the patient has to pay. Those who could not pay due to poverty, the government uses Medi-Fund to pay for the cost of hospitalization. In 2014, Medi-Fund paid almost $160 million. [19]

Table 15.7:   Co-Payment Scheme Under Medi-Shield Life

	Medi-Shield benefits (old scheme)	Medi-Shield life benefits
Maximum coverage age	92	No maximum age
Maximum claim limit per policy year	$70,000	$100,000
Maximum claim limit lifetime	$300,000	No limit
Daily ward and treatment charges (normal ward)	$450/per day	$700/per day
Daily ward and treatment charges (psychiatric)	$100/per day	$100/per day
Class B2 ward (per stay)	For Ages 80 and below: $2,000. For Ages 81 and above: $3,000	
Class C ward (per stay)	For Ages 80 and below: $1,500. For Ages 81 and above: $2,000	

Source: www.moh.gov.sg/content/moh_web/medishield-life/about-medishield-life/medishield-life-benefits.html.

---

[19] *Source*: www.moh.gov.sg/content/moh_web/home/pressRoom/pressRoomItemRelease/2015/ Medifund-continues-to-ensure-accessible-and-affordable-healthcare-for-all-singaporeans.html.

How does each society provide for social security defined as *A*, *B*, *C*, *D* and *E*? If the social security is heavily relied upon the government as provider of last resort, there will be budget deficit. If the government is ineffective, the majority of the people will suffer. The common sense approach is that citizen and government partnership to meet the goals of *A*, *B*, *C*, *D* and *E* as we see in Singapore.

Citizen–Government Partnership

We started by arguing that people in Singapore want to save for the four essential goods meaning *A*, *B*, *C* and *D* using *E* (see Figure 15.5). With government subsidy, most people who work full time for at least 30 years should be able to purchase these four essential goods. Of course, not all people can work full time for 30 years. Table 15.8 shows the following six possible situations for Singaporean households whose main bread winner reaches 55 years in age:

Table 15.8:   Six Possible Situations for Singaporean House-holds Living in Public Housing

*F*1   The balance in his retirement account is about $5,000.
    The balance in his Medi-save account is about $50.
    His family lives in a one-room rented flat from the government.
	*G*1 The balance in his retirement account is about $90,000.
	    The balance in his Medi-save account is about $30,000.
	    His family lives in a three-room flat with no mortgage.

*F*2   The balance in his retirement account is about $20,000.
    The balance in his Medi-save account is about $5,000.
    His family lives in a two-room rented flat from the government.
	*G*2 The balance in his retirement account is about $120,000.
	    The balance in his Medi-save account is about $40,000.
	    His family lives in a four-room flat with no mortgage.

*G*0   The balance in his retirement account is about $40,000.
    The balance in his Medi-save account is about $10,000.
    His family lives in a two-room flat hopefully no mortgage.[20]
	*G*3 The balance in his retirement account is about $150,000.
	    The balance in his Medi-save account is about $50,000.
	    His family lives in a five-room flat with no mortgage.

[20] Single people can buy two-room flats if they are above 35 years old.

The number of residents living in *F*1 and *F*2 accounts for 3% of the total resident population. Those who live in *G*0, *G*1, *G*2 and *G*3 account for 79% of the resident population. Those residents who live in private housing account for the remaining 18% of the resident population.

By the world standards, Singapore has done well in terms of meeting *A*, *B*,*C*, *D* and *E*. The basic formula for success lies in citizen-government partnership. Each adult citizen has two individual responsibilities: getting a job and lifelong learning orientation to remain employed as shown in Figure 15.6. Each citizen above the age of 25 is given $500 which can be used to attend a training course. I propose that the government can encourage citizens to put in more money to the respective training account by matching the funds on one dollar to one dollar basis. On the other hand, the government must ensure that there is plenty of jobs availability. This can only be achieved by attracting foreign investment. The second government's responsibility is to force people to save for *A*, *B*, *C* and *D*. The third government responsibility is to protect the purchasing power of savings for the attainment of *A*, *B*, *C* and *D* such that UHC, UEC and UMC are good value for money.

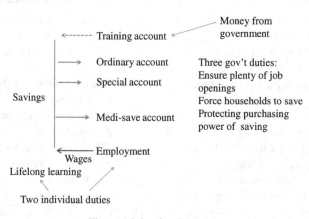

Figure 15.6:   2 + 3 Model

Apart from subsidizing *B*, *C* and *D*, a good fraction of government expenditures aims at helping those who earn $2,000 and those without income due to a variety of reasons other than laziness in the name of Workfare. Generally, there is no moral hazard problem in Singapore. The government of Singapore has been rather careful about not falling into the trap of a welfare state. According to DPM Tharman,[21] after government's social spending, the Singapore's Gini coefficient has decreased from 0.43 to 0.37, a decrease of 0.06. For Demark, the Gini coefficient has decreased from 0.44 to 0.25, a fall of 0.19 and for Finland, a fall of 0.25. Singapore has to increase its social spending by about four times if we want the Gini coefficient to be reduced by 0.25. But this will increase our tax burden because for Demark and Finland, their tax burden is close to 50% while Singapore's tax burden is 16%. It would be difficult for Singapore to attract foreign investment if our tax burden is in the forties.

Discussion Questions

1. Is it possible for Singaporeans to save too much under the CPF scheme?
2. How do we ensure that Singaporeans will use the money in Training account wisely?

Bibliography

Chew, S. B. (2012). "Employment-based Social Protection in Singapore: Issues and Prospects", *ASEAN Economic Bulletin*, Vol. 29, No. 3, pp. 218–229.

Chew, S. B. (2015). Dream Land for Hard Working Singaporeans? In E. Quah (ed.), *Leading Insights on Economy and Environment from 50 Singapore Icon and Beyond*. Singapore: World Scientific, pp. 52–56.

Chew, S. B. and Chew, R. (2012). "An Analysis of Income Inequality, Social Security, and Competitiveness: An Essay on Dr Goh Keng Swee's Contributions to Singapore's Economic Strategy", *Singapore Economic Review*, March, pp. 1250002 (17 pages).

---

[21]*Source*: Economic Society of Singapore Special Distinguished Lecture by DPM Tharman on 14 August 2015.

Chapter 16

Moving Up the Value Chain

In a typical poor society, we can see the damage of vicious poverty cycle to the residents of the country. People are poor and not educated. There are no jobs. The government is not effective. Even if these countries have natural resources, the money will be squandered away. This is why we see evidence that remittances from workers earning money abroad has not helped the country to develop compared to being able to attract foreign investment. This chapter aims to provide a theoretical framework to assess the impact of foreign investment.

Development through Competitive Advantage

Growth of a country needs investment, especially from foreign countries. With the inflow of foreign capital and the accompanying management and technical expertise, a country can slowly develop and hence GDP and employment level will increase.

Figure 16.1 shows that foreign capital is normally attracted to a new country by low wages.[1] This type of labour intensive investment, labelled as M here, implies that providing employment is the pressing objective of the government. When M reaches a critical level relative to the productive capacity of the country, wages will rise and the cost of business will also

---

[1]The figure is modified from a chart in Verma *et al.* (1995).

rise. To the government, this is a mixed blessing. Aiming for high wages and bigger government revenue is the objective of attracting foreign investment but it also implies that a higher level of unit labour cost (ULC) and unit business cost (UBC) can reduce chances of attracting foreign investment and hurt the existing foreign firms.

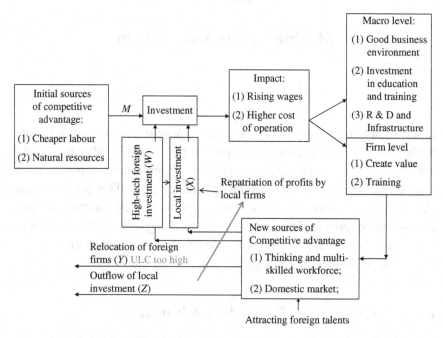

Figure 16.1:   Cycle of Development

At this stage of rising wage costs and business costs, the government can continue to attract foreign investment and help the existing foreign firms by improving business environment and by implementing conducive Employment Acts such that ULC and UBC will not rise although wages and cost of doing business increase.

Sooner and not later, the government has to improve the quality of the workforce by education and training and by importing skilled labour, apart from improving the business environment and infrastructure. This emphasis on quality of the workforce will produce new competitive advantage which is a multi-skilled and disciplined workforce. As the figure shows, this new competitive advantage will attract W, skill intensive foreign investment. When W comes on board, the wages and the cost of doing business will rise at the faster pace. So, the race is on-going between wanting higher wages and higher government revenue and at the same time maintaining ULC and UBC competitive.

As local people learn from economic development and the local GDP expands, the new breed of local entrepreneurs will emerge as shown in Figure 16.1, the local entrepreneurs will invest, labelled as X. Hence, at this moment, there will be three types of investments, M, W (M and W can co-exist if the country is big) and X. W by definition is more skill intensive than M. The W which came in this year will be more skill intensive than those W which can in a decade ago. Eventually, some foreign firms will find ULC and UBC too high. They will relocate to other countries, labelled as Y. Y will first come from M and then from those W which came a decade ago. Also, the local firms will start investing abroad, labelled as Z, for a variety of reasons.

Firms leaving a country or a city to invest in another country are part and parcel of market forces. For a city state like Singapore, labour intensive firms relocate outside Singapore. But for a country like China, relocation of industries can mean moving away from eastern coastal areas to western cities. In fact, Y and Z represent industrial up-grading. As we will discuss later, those firms which relocate are relative labour intensive firms which cannot afford to pay high wages. But Y and Z are two very different situations. For Y, foreign firms leave the country. For Z, local firms invest abroad and repatriate earnings back to the country.

However, for some countries, they could not implement policies to offset the rise in wages and operation business costs. Hence, M would become Y and there is no W. There is no new competitive advantage to attract new investment and to hold on to existing investment. As shown in Figure 16.2, there is limited job opportunity at home. Workers have to seek overseas jobs in large numbers. In this case, instead of local firms sending back the remittances, the workers send back the remittances.

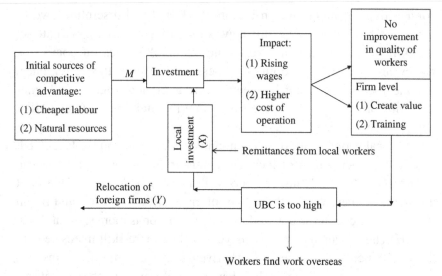

Figure 16.2:   Inability to Hold on to Foreign Investment

However, there is a big difference between foreign aids (FA), remittances (R) from workers and foreign investment (FI). Although all are financial flows to the recipient countries, FI offers working experience, learning opportunity, management know-how. Most important of all, FI forces the government to be disciplined. FA can distort incentives and also lead to corruption. R will boost social spending but can cause asset inflation. There is less incentive to improve governance if the country can rely on R.

For sustainable development, total investment must exceed outflow of funds by the amount required to keep new labour market entrants employed. That is, $M + W + X$ must be greater than $Y + Z$ by the amount necessary to keep the unemployment rate constant.

But if we want higher standard of living for our people, we have to aim for higher wages and at the same time keep ULC and UBC competitive. The only way is to allow W to create Y via higher wages and higher cost of doing business. This is industry upgrading. By using W to chase labour intensive firms away, we move up the value chain. With a large amount of W, our state enterprises can invest overseas and not worry about keeping unemployment rate low locally.

Rising Wages in Singapore

Table 16.1 shows that the nominal wages of an employed resident in Singapore have been rising. As all firms are price takers in the labour markets, firms which do not experience increase in productivity will be forced to shut down. Rising wage costs without significant productivity growth would not encourage formation of new companies.

Table 16.1: Monthly Earnings of Employed Residents in Singapore

Year	Total wages	Including employer CPF	
		Full time	Part time
2003	2,320	2,410	638
2004	2,260	2,326	621
2006	2,260	2,449	565
2007	2,449	2,543	583
2007[a]	2,449	2,543	582
2008	2,708	2,897	600
2009	2,671	2,927	683
2010	2,817	3,000	745
2011	3,000	3,249	800
2012	3,133	3,480	812
2013	3,364	3,705	885

Source: Comprehensive Labour Force Survey, MOM, Singapore.

Figure 16.3 shows the number of formation (the solid line) and cessation (the dashed line) of company in the manufacturing industry in Singapore. When the solid line is above the dashed line, the industry is competitive and labour market is tight and firms are willing to train workers. Relocation of industries will take place and this is good news as the industry forces more labour intensive firms to relocate to other countries. This is one of the objectives of economic development. By moving up the value chain, our standard of living can improve while maintaining the same unemployment rate.

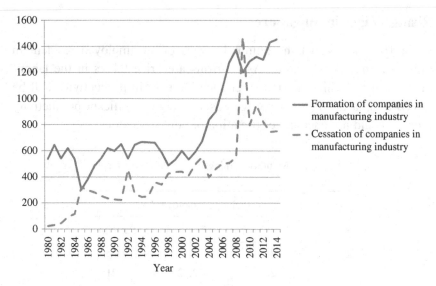

Figure 16.3:   Formation and Cessation of Company in Manufacturing Industry
Source: *Singapore Yearbook of Statistics*, various years.

When the dashed line touches the solid line or exceeds the solid line, then relocation of industries is painful as unemployment will start to increase. And wages and business cost will start to decrease. We do not want to experience this kind of economic adjustment. As we say in economics, we have to stay ahead of the curve.

So, how to enjoy higher wages and bear with higher business cost while being competitive? As is shown in Figure 16.4, the competitive market wage is W_0. A typical firm will employ L_0 of workers. The average surplus per employee for this firm is A_0K_0. Now if market wage rises to W_1, number of employed workers will be reduced to L_1 and the surplus per employed would be reduced to A_1K_1. Hence, if wages keep rising and VMP and VAP remain the same, many firms will be shut down. The economy will be caught at low level equilibrium where unemployment is high and purchasing power of wages is low.

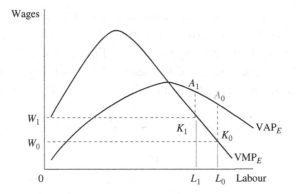

Figure 16.4: Wages and Competitiveness

Hence, we have to attract firms which have higher VAP and VMP curves. Figure 16.5 shows two firms having identical VMP curve but different VAP curves. The market wage rate is W. If wages continue to rise and the two VAPs remain the same. Firm A will be shut down. But how to identify firms with higher VAP curve? We will discuss this issue now.

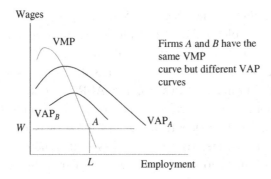

Firms A and B have the same VMP curve but different VAP curves

Figure 16.5: Firms with Different VAP Curves

Annual Surplus Ratio

Annual Surplus Ratio (ASR) is equal to total revenue (TR) minus total business cost (excluding fixed costs). As most firms are price takers, TR is stable. Few firms would dare to increase the price as most products are price-elastic. But operating costs of businesses especially labour costs have been rising continuously.

When labour cost increases, annual surplus is smaller and therefore the ASR will be smaller. Firm *A* in Figure 16.5 has a higher ASR and is able to withstand the rising wage costs than Firm *B*. Table 16.2 shows the labour cost per worker, value added (surplus) per worker and the ASR for a typical firm in each industry within the manufacturing sector.

Table 16.2:   Singapore Manufacturing Sector (2014)

	Labour cost per worker ($)	Surplus/labour costs
Food	38,068	1.85
Textile	27,529	−0.29
Wearing apparel	26,364	0.43
Chemicals	95,364	1.32
Pharmaceutical products	101,100	13.79
Electronics	62,316	2.11
Furniture	28,251	0.13

Source: Census on Manufacturing Activities, 2014, Dept of Statistics.

For Food industry, the ASR is 185%, implying that, any increase in labour cost can be tolerated as the surplus margin is big enough to absorb the rising cost. However, for the textile industry, the surplus ratio is negative, indicates that many firms have negative surpluses. For Apparel industries and Furniture industries, the ASR is less than 50%. Any increase in labour costs will cause some firms in these industries to cease production. But for pharmaceutical industry, the ASR is above 138%. Jobs are protected when wages rise continuously in this industry. At the same time, we can see that those industries with higher ASR also have higher labour costs per workers. Workers on the average are paid three times more in pharmaceutical industry than the workers in Furniture industry. Hence, we want to attract *W* from those industries with high ASR and cost pressure will create *Y* and *Z* from those firms with low ASR.

Over time, Singapore has managed to attract firms with higher ASR and those with lower ASR will be forced to relocate. At the same time, firms with higher ASR increasingly will come from those industries such as pharmaceutical and chemicals.

Table 16.3 shows how ASR varies by firm size in terms of number of workers. For firms employing 50–69 workers, the ASR is 0.7 which is quite low but for firms employing 60–99, the ASR is 2. 05, which is comfortably high. The best firm size in terms of ASR is firms employing 200–2999 workers. From the wages perspective, firms employing 300–499 have the highest wage costs per worker. Hence, small firms are located on the *AB* segment on the ASR curve.

Table 16.3: Singapore Manufacturing Sector (2014)

Firm size by no of workers	Labour cost per worker ($)	Surplus/labour costs
50–69	43,049	0.70
70–99	45,938	2.05
100–149	45,101	1.31
200–299	49,238	3.86
300–499	65,402	2.34
500–999	64,001	2.38
> 999	63,156	1.08

Source: Census on Manufacturing Activities, 2014, Dept of Statistics.

Table 16.4 shows that local firms as a group have low ASR and are located on *BC* segment of the ASR curve. The foreign firms, on the other hand, have much higher ASR. Singapore needs from more investment from USA, UK and France.

Table 16.4: Singapore Manufacturing Sector (2014)

	Labour cost per worker ($)	Surplus ratio
Singapore	39,393	0.54
USA	72,072	3.82
Japan	54,121	0.98
UK	81,370	3.73
Germany	72,069	0.78
France	88,806	1.46
Foreigners	71,453	2.37

Source: Census on Manufacturing Activities, 2014, Dept of Statistics.

Table 16.5 shows the ASR of Singapore manufacturing sector from 2005 to 2014. From 2005 to 2007, as a group, the ASR was around the value of two. But since 2008, the ASR has been around 1.5. In other words, for the whole manufacturing sector, Singapore has moved from K to F on the ASR curve in Figure 16.5. To make the matter worse, the total level of employment has not increased although the ASR has decreased. This is evident from Table 16.5 that the total level of employment in the manufacturing sector has decreased from 424,622 in 2012 to in 416,406, although the decrease in employment is not significant. The only effective way to raise wages for Singaporean workers is to move to industries with higher ASR in terms of speed and scale.

Table 16.5:   Singapore Manufacturing Sector (2005–2014)

Year	Employment	Labour cost per worker ($)	Surplus/labour costs
2005	369,610	38,692	1.88
2006	381,909	39,944	2.08
2007	404,057	41,077	2.00
2008	435,154	40,759	1.34
2009	417,569	40,592	1.53
2010	414,176	43,429	1.94
2011	418,324	45,339	1.83
2012	424,622	46,380	1.75
2013	424,505	48,814	1.52
2014	416,406	52,367	1.55

Source: Census on Manufacturing Activities, various years, Dept of Statistics.

Figure 16.6 shows the surplus ratio for the manufacturing sector from 1980 to 2014. The surplus ratio for the manufacturing sector decreased immediately around 1980 when the labour costs were increased to force the pace of economic restructuring and the ratio increased in 1986 when the employer's CPF contribution rate was cut from 25% to 10%. The surplus ratio went down in 2007 and 2008 due to world financial meltdown. Due to the policy of the Singapore government is using past reserves to pay for 9% of employer's CPF contribution rate, the surplus ratio went up in 2010.

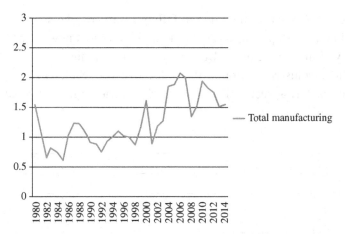

Figure 16.6:   Surplus Ratio for the Manufacturing Sector and Pharmaceutical Products, 1980–2014

Figure 16.7 shows that the surplus ratio for the pharmaceutical products is more than ten times that for the manufacturing sector. But even for the pharmaceutical products, the surplus ratio has decreased since 2012 because the wage costs have increased. Despite the falling surplus ratio, the surplus ratio for the pharmaceutical products is still very high.

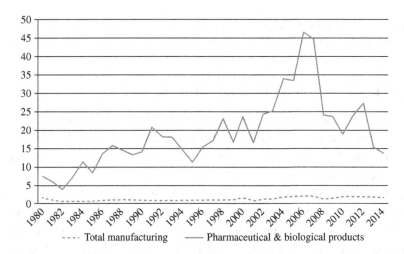

Figure 16.7:   Surplus Ratio for the Manufacturing Sector and Pharmaceutical Products, 1980–2014

Figure 16.8 shows that, due to falling oil prices, the surplus ratio for refined petroleum products fell substantially and it is now in the negative territory. But chemicals and chemical product industry is still healthy with the surplus ratio around the value of two, similar to the value of the manufacturing sector. This goes to show that we need diversity in the manufacturing sector.

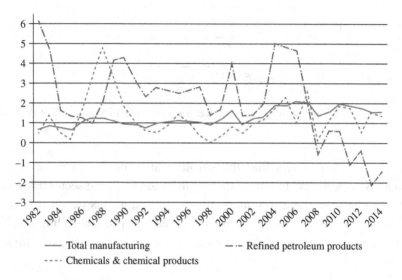

— Total manufacturing　　　　　　　— ·· Refined petroleum products
---- Chemicals & chemical products

Figure 16.8:　Surplus Ratio for the Manufacturing Sector, Refined Petroleum Products and Chemicals and Chemical Products, 1982–2014

How to attract Firms with higher ASR

We want to attract quality foreign investment from the advanced countries. Thus, we cannot be more expensive than their cities. In Chapter 1, we compare business cost across selected cities. But we need to compute UBC across cities.

Table 16.6 shows the cost of employing a person to work across selected cities. The business cost of employing a person to work in Mumbai is US$ 29.088 per year. The corresponding figures for Shanghai and Singapore are US$ 44,044 and US$ 67,491 respectively. The most expensive city among these cities is London with US$ 118,425. As mentioned in Chapter 1, we have to compare UBC. Hence, we need to find business volume in each city. The proxy for business volume is GDP per capita as shown in Table 16.6. Per capita GDP for Singapore is US$ 66,864 and the business cost is US$ 67,491. Hence, UBC for Singapore is about one. The UBC for Shanghai and Mumbai, are 2.78 and 14.62 respectively. In other words, in order to produce one US$ in per capita GDP, the business cost in Mumbai and Shanghai is 14 times and almost three times the business cost in Singapore respectively. It is no comfort at all for Singapore to be cost competitive to these two Asian cities as our "*W*" is not from these Asian cities.

Table 16.6:   UBC for Selected Countries

City	Average per head live/work accommodation costs June 2015 (US$)	GDP Per Capita for City Dec 2014(US$)	UBC
San Francisco	88,177	72,390	1.22
New York	114,208	69,915	1.63
Los Angeles	53,192	65,082	0.82
London	118,425	57,157	2.07
Sydney	52,994	46,344	1.14
Shanghai	44,043	15,847	2.78
Paris	84,344	57,241	1.47
Mumbai	29,088	1,990	14.62
Hong Kong	116,661	57,244	2.04
Tokyo	71,296	43,664	1.63
Dubai	59,426	24,866	2.39
Singapore	67,491	66,864	1.01

Source: http://www.worldsrichestcountries.com/worlds-richest-cities.html

Singapore "*W*" is from Tokyo, London and the cities from the USA. Fortunately for Singapore, the UBC for London, New York city and Tokyo is 2.01, 1.63 and 1.63, respectively. We can conclude that Singapore is cost competitive to these three cities and we can attract "*W*" from these three cities and there is room to increase in wage costs and non-wage costs. Unfortunately, this is not the complete picture. UBC for Los Angeles, an advanced city from USA is only 0.82. In this regard, Singapore business cost is still too high. Since 2008, Singapore has used the exchange rate policy to control imported inflation and selective credit controls which limit excess borrowing with regard to purchases of houses and cars.[2] As mentioned in Table 1.3 in Chapter 1, the business cost in 2015 is almost 17% lower than the business cost in 2008. We need to do more to lower UBC. In principle, Singapore's UBC has to be lower than those cities where we get our "W".

Overall, education and lifelong learning is key to attract firms with high ASR. But it is easy said than done. We can attract good investment because our ULC and UBC are competitive.[3] But costs in developed countries have decreased and many developing and emerging countries have improved their efficiency of operation and human capital. In other words, it is increasingly difficult for Singapore to keep ULC and UBC competitive at the same time wanting to improve the standard of living by raising wages for all.

Private–Public Partnership, One Belt One Road, Investment (W, X and Z^4)

Investment in private sector is efficient. But there is market failure in private sector investment if the risk is too high, the amount of investment is too big or the nature of the project has a positive externality. On the other hand, public sector has money but public sector entrepreneurship is not as efficient as private sector entrepreneurship in the marketplace. One of the important objectives of private–public partnership (PPP) is to lower the UBC so that many projects can be activated and operate on the sustainable basis. This is the same as One Belt One Road (OBOR) initiative as they involve private–public partnership but

---

[2] Singapore's inflation rate has been negative though deflation eases in August 2016. See http://www.tradingeconomics.com/singapore/inflation-cpi.
[3] See Chapter 1 for statistics on UBC.
[4] See Figure 16.1 for the meaning of W, X and Z.

across national borders. OBOR will lower UBC and increase the volume of trade. Figure 16.9 shows that without PPP, UBC is at UBC^1 and investment is I^1. But with PPP, UBC is lower and many projects are not sustainable and investment will increase. With OBOR, there will be more in-bound and out-bound investment. This implies that W in Figure 16.1 will increase, X will increase and Z will increase too. It is a win–win strategy for all countries.

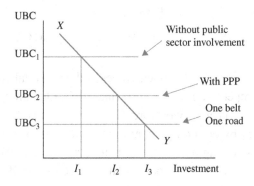

Figure 16.9:   UBC and Investment

Trade Agreements and ULC

Any trade agreement is to reduce transaction costs across countries, implying that ULC will decrease due to formation of a trade agreement for trading partners. Figure 16.10 shows that ULC curve which relates ULC to output level. ULC has a negative slope implying that there are economies of scale as more output leading to lower business cost per unit of output. Hence, the movement from A to B represents economies of scale. Economies of scale are likely to be disappear when output level reaches a threshold level. A trade agreement will lower ULC, shifting UBC curve downward. The movement from A to C represents the free trade agreement effect. What is most important in this diagram is the learning effect which is represented by the movement from C to D. A self-learning workforce will produce learning effect continuously.

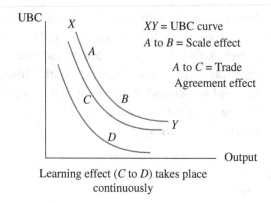

Figure 16.10:   Free Trade Agreements and UBC Curve

In a nutshell, Singapore competitiveness relies on total commitment to maintaining a competitive level of ULC and UBC. Our strengths in having a macro-focused union and a workforce that believes in no free lunch cannot be emulated easily by our competitors. As we have discussed in Chapter 1, Singapore adopts a pragmatic approach to competition. We use PPP to encourage investment and Singapore is supportive of OBOR initiative. We have always been focusing on developing world-class labour markets, which pay dividends in terms of attracting foreign investment of our choice.

Discussion Questions

1. Does Singapore's ASR for the manufacturing sector remain constant over the years?
2. Which countries investment in Singapore's manufacturing have the highest ASR?
3. In Figure 6.3, when the number of cessation of companies is close to the number of formation of companies, discuss how the Singapore government would react with regard to employer's CPF contribution rate.

Reference

Verma, A., Kochan, T. and Lansbury, R. (eds.) (1995). *Employment Relations in the Growing Asian Economies*. Routledge: London.

Index

Printed in the United States
By Bookmasters